BACKSTAGE PASS
TO THE FLIPSIDE:

Talking to the Afterlife

with Jennifer Shaffer

Part Two

by

Richard Martini

Backstage Pass to the Flipside: Talking to the Afterlife with Jennifer Shaffer Part Two by Richard Martini

Homina Publishing PO Box 248 Santa Monica, CA 90406
"Assumption of the Virgin" by Titian [1]

---

[1] Mary being welcomed "back to the flipside." "The Assumption" was painted by Tiziano Vecellio (Titian) My grandfather Valentino Martini is one of his descendants (born in Pelos Di Cadore). https://en.wikipedia.org/wiki/Assumption_of_the_Virgin_(Titian)

CONTENTS

FOREWORD

by Luana Anders and Jennifer Medlyn Shaffer

Jennifer today and Luana circa 1965.

(This Foreword and Introduction are the same in both Book One & Two, as well as the Workbook at the end. Skip to Chapter One unless you'd like to revisit them.)

Forewords are an unusual introduction to the material inside a book. In "Flipside: A Tourist's Guide on How to Navigate the Afterlife" Harvard PhD Gary Schwartz offered to write the foreword, where he said that "self science" was something Einstein had done, and he felt my "journey into the Flipside" should be considered as part of that canon.

In "It's a Wonderful Afterlife volume one" Charles Grodin suggested in his foreword that he didn't quite know what to make of my forays into the afterlife but enjoyed my passion for them. In Volume two, Galen Stoller, a young man who passed away some years ago wrote an eloquent foreword from where he is now, detailing what he wanted to impart about the journey. *"It is a wonderful afterlife,"* he wrote (via a medium), *"but only because "it is wonderful to be alive."*

I suggested my pal and compatriot in this endeavor medium/intuitive Jennifer Shaffer should write the foreword, as she's the conduit for this research. But while we were discussing this, Luana Anders, my friend and inspiration for this journey (who passed in 1996 after our being best friends for 20 years), suggested (through Jennifer) that **she** wanted to write her own foreword to this book.

> *Note: Luana, besides being an actress who appeared in 30 features (including "Easy Rider") also appeared in 300 TV shows. Her film writing credits include "Fire Down Below" and "Limit Up" written with yours truly.) At some point in this book, she suggested I try "automatic writing." I sat in front of the keyboard, put my fingers on the keys and thought; "Type whatever comes to mind." I opened myself up to the possibility I could write something on her behalf:*

"First, let me be clear. Richard is not talking through me. I am talking to him through Jennifer (usually). She does her best to make it easy for him to understand what I'm trying to say, and I'm doing my best to make it easier for him to understand. But it is *leaning in* from both sides.

> (Note: Like the 11:11 example Luana cites later in the book.)

At the moment, Richard is typing this sentence and has put his mind on virtual hold (he claims it's a meditation technique) to allow "me" to take over his typing. Some people call this "automatic writing." **Doesn't mean it's any good. It just means it's automatic.** No brain stem involved.

First I'd would like to point out that chanting "Nam Myoho Renge Kyo"[2] saved my life. I know that Richard used to tease me about it, make fun of it – and I'm grateful for that because it allowed me to laugh about it as well.

> (Note: Luana would do her "daimoku" ("Nam-myoho-renge-kyo" prayer) in the car on the way to an event. She'd chant at lightning speed, decades of practice, which sounds a bit like "*homina homina munya homina.*" I would imitate her and she couldn't help but laugh. Chanting helped her navigate her *fear of parties*. Luana was an incredible listener, and on more than one occasion, I'd leave her for ten minutes at some tony event, come back to find a close friend sobbing, pouring out his/her life to her. She had incredible compassion, even as a listener.)

But it saved my life. I never would have made it as long as I did on the planet without being able to focus on something else so dear to me. **Saving humanity by chanting about it.** If you're not familiar with it, if you're suffering, I recommend it as a form of meditation and healing. You pray for someone else and you are healed. Simple as that.

I suggested that I write the foreword to this book because after all, much of it is about me – and I have little to say in the matter. Believe me, it was as shocking to me as it was to my

---

[2] SGI/NSA Buddhist chant. http://www.sgi.org/about-us/president-ikedas-writings/gongyo-and-daimoku.html

class to have him (Richard) appear as he did – willy nilly – in front of my classroom over here.[3]

He just started speaking out loud as if was completely normal that some ghostly avatar would appear in front of our class and start blathering away about his "research."

But I applaud him for it. *He's got cojones this boy.* I can call him a boy – because I know him better than most. He's endearing... to me and to others. But at his core, he's that little boy that I've known for a long, long time.

It's important work that he is doing, important work that he and Jennifer are doing. To help us communicate with all of you back there on the planet, and to open up people's minds about the ability to do so. It's happened not because of any great cataclysmic event that's in the offing – it's happening because *it's time.* **It's time to shift consciousness, to shift gears to understand the nature of reality.**

It's going to upset some people, but we're on top of that as well. It's going to liberate most people. Help most people. And ultimately turn out to be completely accurate when others figure this process out.

Some may ask "Why now?" Some may ask "Is this a good thing to do to communicate with our elders and loved ones who've gone on?" **Well, we still have things to communicate to you, we still have thoughts, dreams,**

---

[3] It was during my first deep hypnosis session where I found myself standing in her classroom, interrupting it. Everyone turned in shock as I appeared. She looked at me as if to say "WTF?" She looked about 20 years younger than when I knew her – at least 10 years before I met her. She looked embarrassed to see me standing in the class talking – but I continued to speak. (*Flipside*)

feelings and hope for humanity – because we consider ourselves part of your journey as well. You may not think of us that way – but we think of you that way.

So please, allow me to offer this small token of appreciation for the fellow who is typing this sentence. Yes, you are a goofball Richard, you are someone that has vexed and frustrated me during my life, but also during other lifetimes.

But you also taught me how to laugh, how to let go, and how to be more of myself while I was on the planet. I know what my path was about, I know why I had to depart early – eventually you'll come to know these reasons as well. Suffice to say it's okay not to "know everything" or "why everything happens" but it is good to trust in the idea that they do "happen for a reason."

And let's focus on that for a moment – "focus on reason." What is reasoning? Taking the evidence presented in front of us, and trying to figure out what it means and how it can help *me* in my journey. We reason things out because that's what we do with our minds... we also can go "beyond reason" and allow things to happen to us, or for us... and that's how I want you to consider what you're about to read. That this goes "beyond reason." And there's a reason for that as well.

Okay, I'm telling Richard to stop now – and to let our mutual friend Jennifer go over this text and see what "resonates" or rings true for her. After all – it's those "feelings of resonance" when we get a shiver of truth, or when we get a feeling that we're actually learning or talking about something that's beyond our logic and thought, beyond our mind... that we truly are able to learn things... about the nature of reality and about the nature of ourselves. I'm fortunate because

8

Richard can type at the speed of thought – I'm watching him do this as we speak, and I suggest a plethora of ideas and he's able to blast them onto the page.

One more thing about love. **I love you all.** I'm not just saying that as a phrase – but I want you to really feel what I'm saying. I LOVE YOU. I send my heart and soul and unconditional love to you who are reading this sentence. I hope and pray that you receive this love because love is what moves this universe, it is the giant engine of who we are, it's what or who God is, it's what or who *we are*. If you can wrap your mind around love – that's great – if you can't, that's okay too, just open your heart up to the idea of it.

Love yourself. Love your neighbor. Love your enemy. Love the idea of love, of creating love, or spreading love of being loved and giving it in return. That's about all I have to say on the topic except... "See you on the flipside." (To quote a corny phrase too often used by a close friend of both of ours.)

PS: (It's) Just a few days after my birthday – I would have been *xxx* age in your realm – but over here – not such a big deal. Which I prefer. Enjoy the cake.

Written *(as if channeled)* by Luana Anders

Photo of Luana by Tom Pittman circa 1958

Jennifer Shaffer

So, when someone asks me "What does Rich Martini do?" I tell them, **"He can do anything and quickly."** Like he can write a book really fast. Even though in *his* mind it takes *forever*, he can do things that nobody else can do.

I consider him to be, not only a close friend of mine, but a person who has so many great ideas about everything. He knows enough about so many different things to make *this* (what I'm saying about the spirit world) seem tangible. Part of the problem many mediums or intuitives have, is that they have a lot of great ideas, but they can't make them land. Richard makes them land in a great way.

I tell them "**He can take you for a past life adventure like that**" (snaps her fingers). You don't have to lie down or be unconscious for it, it's a state where you are awake, but the information comes through you.

It's just like my work being a medium... I don't remember any of the things that are said to me during my sessions, but I remember feelings associated with it. I feel like I'm in a dream state. And you know how when you wake up from a dream, you think you're going to remember it? But you don't. (Laughs) That's basically my whole day at work.

It's something he can do while you're fully conscious. **He asks questions that nobody else asks, that's why he's such a great interviewer. He gets to the core of things that you didn't even know existed.**

And for people that are afraid of this kind of investigation, Richard has a way of just making them open up; whether they want to or not. He has a great way of bringing forth what's

10

bothering you or hurting you to the surface. I've had situations where I've often looked to him for guidance.

I think he is like a therapist for mediums, and he does it in a way that is non-threatening. You may not remember the things that happened in a previous lifetime, but your energy field does. And by examining what may have happened your energy field slowly but surely starts healing; not just from this lifetime but from all different lifetimes.

In terms of what it is we're doing: I was talking to someone this morning. When I get direct information, sometime I don't say it the way that I hear it, because I don't want to offend them. This woman came through, and said, "Tell my daughter the reason she is a good mother is because I was not a good mother. "

But I was trying to sugar coat for her and her mother came through and said "Stop sugar coating it! Tell her exactly what I'm trying to say! I was NOT a good mother and that's why she IS an incredible mother." The mother was grateful that she lived *her* life so that she could be an example to help her daughter become a better mother. The daughter started crying, saying "You're right."

Speaking the truth doesn't mean you can't be loving or kind; but you must stop sugar coating the truth. When I report what I'm seeing or sensing, I often think "What if I'm wrong?" But when someone says blatantly "Stop sugar coating it. Tell her I was a horrible mother and she's going to understand it" – I have to repeat what I'm hearing. As it turns out, that comment meant more to her than anything. So that's one thing I try to do; it's not my job to prove to anyone that I'm speaking to the afterlife, but it is my job to speak truthfully about what I'm getting.

Rich: In that vein, a film studio friend told me he thought what we were doing had to be either "imaginary" or "coincidence." I was reminded of a story he once told me; he was meeting the new head of the studio and was asked "How many movies do we make a year that fail?" My friend answered, "Statistically, about half." And the new studio head said "Well, let's just not make the ones that fail."

I try to focus on the examples where we get positive results and try to understand how that can occur. For me, it's important to ask, "What is the mechanism that allowed Jennifer to get new information from the Flipside that turned out to be true?" And "how could she casually refer to something that only I could possibly know?" In that sense this investigation helps those on the flipside to better communicate with their loved ones back here.

So in this book there's not going to be any sugar coating. But "Caveat Emptor;" buyer *"be aware:"* If this book is going to disturb you in any way, please, give it back, get a refund. *"These are not the droids you're looking for."* We aren't here to change your paradigm or prove anything to anyone.

But for those of you who do stick around, I want to remind you; *"All roads lead to home."* It doesn't matter what your background is, what your beliefs have been; what you are about to hear is verbatim from people who are "back home" – (the term they use to mean *no longer here.)* We're going to help those folks "back home" to stay in touch, stay connected with those who are *not yet* back home.

But buckle up; it's going to be a bumpy ride.

12

Luana and author on Via Veneto.

When I put this photo on the fridge I said aloud *"Well, that's the essence of our relationship."* (Drinking cappuccinos and eating cookies.)

After she passed, we invited medium James Van Praagh to appear on our mutual friend Charles Grodin's talk show.

Secretly, Charles arranged for me to call in and see if we could "speak" to Luana. On air, James said, "She's saying to tell Richard there's a photograph on his refrigerator that she says is "The essence of your relationship."

It was the first time I realized it was physically possible to still talk to her. Recently, while discussing her foreword and how she helped me write it, she gave Jennifer the image of Tinkerbell, said to her "I sat over his shoulder and whispered it into his ear. He should look at page 13, at the end of that chapter, for verification." (This message was before I'd shown the book to anyone.)

Notice what page the foreword ends.

The following is a continuation of that conversation.

INTRODUCTION

"A FRIEND REQUEST"

Jennifer and Richard in our usual cafe.

It all began with a *"friend request"* on Facebook.

It was from someone I didn't know, had never met. "Hmm. Who's this?" I thought. When I clicked *"accept"* she replied with a clip of holding up her cell phone to a cheering crowd of friends saying, *"Rich Martini accepted my friend request!"*

I thought that was pretty funny and assumed she must have mistaken me for someone else entirely.

Jennifer assured me she was a fan of my books "Flipside" and "It's a Wonderful Afterlife" and told me that during her recent Thanksgiving festivities, the audible version of my books played in her headset while she was doing the dishes. She said she felt as if I was "speaking directly to her."

She told me she was an intuitive/medium and that she worked in nearby Manhattan Beach. "Maybe we can have coffee or lunch sometime," she said.

I told her that I had not focused on mediumship in my research about the flipside for a couple of reasons. 1. People go to mediums, generally, to learn their future. My research shows that the future is not set but there are "likely outcomes." And 2, people tend to see mediums for advice about their love life. *"Will I be with this person in the future?"* Well, if you understand the architecture of the flipside, you've probably already been with them before, likely will be with them again, and even if they run off with someone else, you can address that at a later date with them when "you're back home." And besides, like Jennifer, already happily married.

But then I realized, *wait a second,* I had spoken to a couple of mediums in the past who had claimed to be in contact with a famous individual on the flipside.

I was working on the film "Salt" in Manhattan, and a close friend introduced me to Pattie Canova, a tough smart medium who grew up on the streets of Manhattan. I helped Pattie with some advice about a script she wrote; she said, "Let me do a reading for you as a return favor."

I said, "No, thanks, *you're preaching to the choir."* She insisted. She laid out some playing cards and said "You're working on a film about a pilot. A female pilot. Amelia Earhart?" I looked at my friend as if she had set me up for a laugh. She had not. I had been working on a script about Amelia Earhart for around 20 years at this point.

I thought – "Well, why am I resisting this?" If she can "speak to Amelia" maybe I can clear up some issues about her story. So, I spent two hours interviewing someone who knew more about Amelia than anyone I had ever encountered in my years of research. I pursued this new information and her new leads until I ran into another medium. That was through Dr. Elisa Medhus, a Houston doctor whose son had died, and had "called her on the phone" from the flipside.[4]

Elisa wrote about her son's passing, and what he told her about the flipside and later, with the help of medium Jamie Butler, her son Erik wrote a book about his journey ("My Life After Death"). I began conversing with Dr. Medhus about her method of "interviewing people in the afterlife" with her son's help. I casually said, "You should interview Amelia Earhart sometime." She said, "She's scheduled for an interview on Tuesday." *(What are the odds?)*

I asked to see the questions she was asking the famed aviatrix, mostly culled from Wikipedia and "common knowledge" about her journey. I asked if I could supply the questions and amended hers to reflect what I knew about Amelia.

For example, I had the medium (Jamie Butler) ask "Who was the love of your life, and was it a painter?" Now in this construct – Jamie is sitting in front of the camera and is seeing "Erik Medhus" on the flipside, who brings forth various people to be interviewed. In this case, the medium Jamie said she saw both Amelia and what appeared to be her husband George Putnam standing behind her.

Jamie confirmed to me later that she didn't know anything about Amelia's life, that she doesn't prepare for these interviews, but just reports what she "sees."

The answer Amelia gave to my question was "I think my life has been a good example to young girls everywhere, and I'm

---

[4] ChannelingErik.com

not really interested in changing people's opinions about my journey, but yes, the love of my life was a woman, and she was indeed a painter."

How did I know that? Because I worked on her life for 20 years, I'm credited for research on both Diane Keaton and Hilary Swank's film versions or her story. I knew she had an open marriage, found out through interviews that Dorothy Putnam (George's wife) had walked in on her husband with two other women in his bed (one was Amelia) prior to their divorce. (Their divorce was amicable, mutual, as Dorothy married her boyfriend the following weekend in Vegas.)

Dr. Medhus asked my questions, including what really happened to her after she disappeared (Amelia landed the Electra on Mili atoll, which I already knew and have filmed eyewitnesses about) and learned that indeed she was incarcerated (arrested by the Japanese and taken to their Military Headquarters in Saipan) and how she died of dysentery on Saipan just prior to the Americans arrived in 1944 when they found her plane and her briefcase.[5]

As it turns out, Pattie Canova had told me roughly the same story I was now hearing from Jamie Butler (even though I wasn't present, Dr. Medhus filmed the session and sent me a copy.) And at the end of the interview, "Amelia" said something to Jamie that I did not hear until I transcribed the audio two years after it was made.

Jamie asked, "So how did you die? Were you shot or beheaded?" (At that point, I'd heard both.) Amelia didn't respond for some time, then said "I'm not comfortable

---

[5] Covered extensively at the website EarhartOnSaipan.com

discussing that in this public form, but if the person **who wrote the questions** wants to speak to me privately, I will tell him."

At the time, when I heard it, my skeptical mind thought that was the medium saying, "But if the guy who crafted these questions wants to do a private reading with me, I'll help him." It wasn't until I transcribed it, I realized Amelia was speaking directly to me. *Cause I'm the guy who crafted the questions.*

This all flashed through my head as I was speaking to Jennifer on the phone. I said, "What kind of mediumship do you do?" She said, "Well, I work with law enforcement agencies nationwide to help with missing person cases."

I said, "How'd you like to work on the most famous missing person case in history?" She said, "I'm in, whoever it is."

So, when I went to meet her, I brought my camera, and filmed a three-hour interview with her and Amelia Earhart, George Putnam and whoever else wanted to swing by and put in their two cents. She confirmed precisely what I had learned in 20 years of research, and said the same answers that the other two mediums had told me – I asked roughly the same 20 questions to all three mediums, and all three replied with information that is not known to the public, including new information about what happened to her.

Got that?

It was new information about Amelia from people who could not possibly know the information. Information that confirmed my decades of research, but also new information that I've been able to subsequently research and verify. (Or in the case of "where her plane is," the next time I get to Saipan, I'll dig it up.)

This story for the most part is covered in *"Hacking the Afterlife."* I won't be discussing that part of it here, except that indeed, Miss Earhart shows up in our "group talks" in this book, and still has a thing or two to say about her life story. (So, she will be referenced from time to time.)

What made my interview with Jennifer so amazing, was that while we were discussing "What happened to Amelia's body?" Jennifer said, "She's showing me that when the two soldiers dug up her body, they only found an arm."

Not everyone is aware that two GI's claim they dug up her body on Saipan (Fred Goerner, CBS correspondent wrote about them in his book *"Searching for Amelia"* but it's not common knowledge), and I was startled to hear Amelia say there were "two GI's" – something that Jennifer did not know. But further there was **"new information"** in what she said.

In Goerner's book, there's no mention of what they found. Just that they had been ordered to dig her up, and in the second edition of his book, he interviewed both GI's who confirmed that indeed they had gone out into the jungle and dug up two bodies and were told one of them was Amelia's. But nothing about an arm.

Ten minutes after my filming Jennifer, I got a call from Jim Hayton, an NTSB expert who lives in Seattle. He's been on the forefront (with his friend Dick Spink) of verifying pieces of her Electra that Dick Spink found on Mili Atoll. (They were featured in the History Channel episode about her.) Jim was calling because he had just seen documentation from another researcher that "proved everything I had told him about Amelia." Jim said, "Rich, that story about those two GI's who dug up Amelia's body was in the research, but it says something different; "they only recovered her arm."

I gasped. I had just heard the same obscure detail "from Amelia herself." *What are the odds?* The exact same sentence said ten minutes earlier about these GI's only finding her arm. I've subsequently found an interview with those two GI's (from the Chicago Tribune 1977) where they said they "only recovered an arm and a partial rib cage." Which verifies what Jennifer had told me, corroborates what Jim had told me, and was a "new piece of information" that came to me direct from the flipside.

But again, this introduction isn't about Amelia.

One day I hope to make that film about her, I've reported this information on my website "EarhartOnSaipan.com" and in the book *"Hacking the Afterlife"* – But I'm here to introduce to you, ladies and gentlemen, the one and only Jennifer Shaffer.

Since that first meeting, we've been getting together a couple of times a month. I bring my camera along with me, we have lunch somewhere and I film our chats about the flipside. I may ask her to "bring someone forward" or she may announce "so and so is here." I am not trying to prove that person is "here" – because as you've just heard, she's already proven her accuracy to me on many occasions.

She's the first person to observe that what she sees or hears is subject to interpretation. She may see a metaphor, or hear a turn of a phrase, and then tries to explain what she thinks they mean. Folks on the flipside generally don't "speak" – they show an image, sometimes impart a feeling. So communicating directly to the flipside, to loved ones no longer on the planet, is not a "dial up" kind of process.

It depends how good *they* are at communicating (apparently it takes some learning and getting used to) – if you can imagine a jet plane slowing down to drive alongside of a Volkswagen van and communicating with the passengers while the windows are rolled up... it's an apt metaphor. Or think of a person standing outside the fish tank and tapping on the glass, and we, *the little fish,* come to the edge of the tank and stare at them as they try to speak slowly and loudly to us. It's not an easy task.

But we'll get into all that.

We're going to show how easy it is to speak to people on the flipside and gain new information from them. It won't be information that will harm your own path or journey in any way, but it will be enough verifiable information so that you realize "There's more than meets the eye" with regard to reality.

Jennifer works with law enforcement agencies nationwide to help with cases, including "missing person" events. I've met some of the parents whose lives she's healed with her work. I'm aware of a few cases she's solved using her abilities, and know why they seek her help. She's an excellent reporter of what she feels or senses.

Let's chat about the process for a moment; I liken what we do to stringing up paper cups as we did in our youth. Jennifer is my Dixie cup connection to the afterlife. She's my cellphone to those who no longer on the planet. My friend Howard Schultz (creator of "Extreme Makeover" and other TV shows) did a between life session with Scott De Tamble[6] (it was in the book "Flipside" - "River of Souls.") Scott helped him chat with his mother, who had crossed over. Howard said his mom explained how "talking to her" was equivalent to picking up a cellphone.

She said "You push buttons, don't know how the process works, but when we answer you know it's a loved one on the line. When you think or pray to us, we can hear you – we might not be able to answer you right away but if we can respond to you, we will."

Howard passed away a couple of years after that filmed session. Happy to report that Howard has made a number of appearances at our lunches. He continues to be an active source of comedy from the flipside.

I film and transcribe our sessions; the interviews have been edited for clarity and time and sometimes "to protect someone still on the planet." Although they tend to have very little discretion when telling Jennifer something about their path, neither of us want to embarrass anyone still working their way through their journey. Grief and grieving are key to our development as souls; we must allow that "hearing someone is still accessible" could be disconcerting to some folks.

But by and large, by "opening ourselves up to the possibility" that there is an afterlife is a therapeutic method of healing. I got that turn of phrase from Harry Dean Stanton, after he crossed over, as you'll see in an ensuing chapter. **"Allow for**

---

[6] www.lightbetweenlives.com

the possibility that there is an afterlife" – and that goes a long way to relieving stress for many people.

Finally, a word about *"celebrity."*

As reported in "Flipside" I heard a phrase in Latin during a dream; *"Vanum populatum."* I learned during my between life session (conducted by Jimmy Quast, trained by Michael Newton)[7] that the phrase was said to me by my "higher self" in order to get me to look it up in the dictionary and contemplate it's meaning.

It means *"annihilate vanity."* (My answer; "I live in LA, where do I begin?") But since then, I see vanity, celebrity as icing of the cake of who we are – fame, fashion, money, ego are all extensions of that concept. "What someone looks like, what kind of car they drive, none of that's important..." (I just remembered I wrote that dialog in a scene for *"You Can't Hurry Love"* which the character Eddie Hayes says directly into camera. I was annihilating vanity even when I wasn't aware that it was something I was doing back in the 1980's.)

But when someone "famous" shows up at our classroom, I ascribe that to Luana. As noted, she was in 30 feature films (from Dementia 13, to Easy Rider, to the Godfather) over 300 TV shows, was friends with many icons in her field including Charles Grodin, Paul Simon, Art Garfunkel, Robert Towne and Jack Nicholson.[8] I've had several friends claim that she "appeared" to them in a dream with specific messages for them. (Even from friends who "never met her.") They claim

---

[7] eastonhypnosis.com

[8] LuanaAnders.com

her words of wisdom "helped them" navigate some issue in their lives. *So that's a bit unusual.*

Recently, my wife Sherry said Luana visited her in a dream. Sherry asked her "But how can you be here? You died over 20 years ago." Luana jokingly showed her a toy "rocket ship" as if that was her mode of transport. But then she showed Sherry an image of "11:11." She said. "You're on one side, and I'm on the other side, and we meet at the decimals."

Sherry didn't understand the comment but I feel I do. If you think as 11 as a hallway on this side (like an architect's drawing or blueprint) and the other a hallway on the Flipside – she's saying, "we both need to adjust our frequency in order to meet in the middle where the decimals are."

11:11.

Which is basically what this book is about. Adjusting your frequency so you can communicate directly with your loved ones who are no longer on the planet. Not gone, just not here. To figure out how to gain your own "backstage pass" to the flipside.

This book is not about *celebrity*, not about *talking to celebrities.* As noted, the people who show up are people that I knew, Jennifer knew, or who knew or met Luana. The idea is, if there's a frequency we are familiar with, or Luana is familiar with, they have an easier time of showing up "in our class." It's short hand to ask for someone that we all know to come forward and speak to us – whether it's Bill Paxton or Harry Dean Stanton. They are celebrities to some, but old acquaintances of mine (as we'll learn.)

And finally, a word about mistakes and errata. I noticed recently that somehow my computer would open a copy of my screenplay about Amelia Earhart. I asked Jennifer about it – she said, "Amelia did that, to remind you to stay engaged to a film about her." But back home, my daughter admitted she "clicked on the icon that brought up the script by accident about once a month."

So, there you have it! Proof that the afterlife does not exist! *Amelia was wrong!* It was my daughter accidentally hitting the same button... but then *in my head,* I heard, "Yeah, but who do you think gets her to click on that button?" D'oh! Foiled again by *the voice in my head.*

In that vein; please take this research with as much salt as required. Jennifer *may be* talking to people on the Flipside, we may be talking to *versions of people* on the flipside, we may be *"meddling with the primal forces of nature"* (a quote from the film "Network.")

I wrote music reviews for Variety in the 1990's, a gig offered me by my dear friend, music editor and bandmate Bruce Haring (Variety, Billboard). Bruce and I would sometimes travel together to music festivals and there was always a *meshegas* of obtaining the right pass for the right venue. We had run into our mutual pal Edna Gundersen, the then music critic of USA Today who was wearing a particular colored pass. When the promoters handed over our passes, I noticed they were a "lesser color" than hers. I said, "Excuse me, we'd like the same color pass that Edna has." He scoffed. "You mean an "All Access Backstage Pass?" Sorry. *Edna is Edna.*"

25

Well, we do have access to the backstage, and we're going to grant you, dear reader, an "All access backstage pass" to the flipside.

But first, let's ask the "bouncer" that protects your subconscious from these flights of fancy to take a step back from the velvet rope guarding your mind so we can all go into this Afterlife Club together.

Join us on the other side of the velvet rope, won't you?

*****

Luana is tapping her wrist; class is waiting.

CHAPTER ONE:

EDWARD TAYLOR, ROBERT AND HIS OSCAR NOMINATED DOG HIRA

"It just isn't fair."

Robert Towne, Edward Taylor and Jack Nicholson circa 1960. Photograph courtesy Luana Anders

I met Luana when I was in film school. We were both taking the same screenwriting class, and were assigned by the professor to the same script. After a few hilarious evenings, we started dating, and I eventually moved in with her. At some point she was hanging out with her friend Robert Towne, helping him coach the actor/athletes for the film "Personal Best" and overheard Robert was looking for an assistant.

She mentioned me. They had a stack of resumes from Harvard and Yale grads, but Robert chose his old friend's young film school boyfriend. I went into his office and was assigned to answer the phone in his second office.

One day the phone rang. I answered it, heard Robert ask, "Who is this?" I said, "It's Martini." He asked where everyone was. I said, "I think they're at lunch Robert." Being the days before *being connected everywhere all the time* (about 1979) Robert said, "Get down to my office now!"

I went over to his ornate bungalow next to Clint Eastwood's bungalow assuming I was to be fired. Robert looked me up and down and said, "Can you drive fast?" I thought "Is this some kind of quiz?" I shrugged. He pointed to his Mercedes 500 SL in the parking spot out front. "You think you can drive that car fast?" I said "Yeah, I think so."

He said "Good, because my wife just called from the airport and she's on her way home. I need you to go to my house and get my mistress out of my bed because the phone is off the hook." He dangled his car keys in front of me.

I jumped in his car, raced across the valley into Westwood, bounded up the steps, found his girlfriend in the shower, dragged her out, threw clothes at her. We got in the car and pulled out of the driveway... just as his (soon to be ex) wife pulled in.

Needless to say, my importance at the office rose with that single act. I became the person who was assigned to walk his dog Hira every day. But Hira wasn't *just any dog*. He was a Hungarian Count – he had "papers" listing his heritage from Hungary and was a famous Komondor. They have long white

28

dreadlocks for hair, and Hira was about six feet tall when he stood up. A huge walking shag carpet of a fellow.

Hira was unusual in the sense that I never "walked him." He would look at me; "it's time" and I accompanied him on the grounds of the Warner Brothers lot. For some unknown reason, Hira would make a beeline to the President of the Studio's office, Frank Wells, and leave a giant steaming deposit in front of his door.

One day his secretary called screaming *"I saw you! I know it's you walking the dog over here!"* I would say "I'm so sorry. But I don't walk that dog. He allows me to accompany him around the lot. I have no idea why he chooses your doorstep to do his business." That went on for years.

We made the film *"Personal Best"* and I was the lowest man on the totem pole – my title on the "call sheet" was "Guido the Dog Walker." It was the story of how athletes train for the Olympics, and it focused on two female athletes (Patrice Donnelly and Mariel Hemingway) who happened to fall in love.

But while I was working 18 hours a day on this film about these Olympians, I had been hired to write a script by a Japanese film company – the true story of the first woman to win the LA Marathon, who set a world record in the process. *("Run Miki Run.")*

While writing at night, by day we were filming at the University of Oregon in Eugene and there were 5000 extras who had to be shuffled from one side to the next depending on the camera angles. My duties on set were basically typing up Robert's notes in the exact format that he liked; "Martinus! If I wanted to use three dots at the end of a sentence, I would

have used three! This is how bad movies get made!"
(Martinus would be Latin singular of Martini.)

But when I wasn't walking the dog, I would survey the crowd,
tell jokes with a bullhorn and entertain myself and the old
hippies from Eugene Oregon who worked on the film.

The Assistant Directors would bark at the crowd "Let's get
the long hairs out of the shot. We only want *All American*
looking people in the front row." When they left, I'd seek out
the fellow with one tooth and hair down to his waist and say
"Except for you. We need this All American fella right up
front."

If the AD's fired an extra, I'd say "Woah, hang on. We
established that guy in a shot last week. He's gotta stay here."
I guess word got around the set that if you got fired or
harassed by the Assistant Directors, "See Martini."

Finally, I was notified my script needed to be delivered and I
should fly back to Los Angeles to pick up my check. I went
to the Assistant Director on the film and told him I'd be late
for work the following Monday. He replied "So, I guess
someone else will walk the dog?"

Off to LA I went, picked up my check. I was now officially a
writer. I flew back to the set and arrived a couple of hours
late. When I walked towards the stadium I heard an unusual
sound – 5000 people chanting *"We want Martini. We want
Martini!"* The billboard was flashing "Martini! Martini!"

I entered the stadium and a roar went up from the crowd. I
looked around – *what the hell was going on*? Robert walked
up to me in one of his antique Hawaiian shirts, his face red as

a beet and grabbed me by the lapels. "Who are you and why have you done this to my movie?"

I stammered. *"What did I do?"*

He told me that the Assistant Directors had come to the set, and the extras had refused to listen to any of them. A chant began in the crowd, **"Where is Martini? We only listen to him!"** They must have thought I'd been fired. Robert, who had battled with the producer David Geffen to make the film, thought somehow, Geffen had arranged for me to help stop production of the film – or worse, to help *take the film away from him.*

I blinked. "Robert. I think they're chanting because your AD's have been assholes to the crowd. I was nice to them."

Robert picked up the megaphone and shouted *"You wanted Martini. I brought you Martini!"* The crowd roared. *"No one on this set is allowed to speak to an extra unless he goes through Martini!"* Another wild cheer.

From that point forward, I was "Joe Crowd Control." Bud Smith, the editor (who edited most of William Friedkin's films) later told me "They're the best crowd scenes I've ever seen on film."

A few years after the film wrapped, Robert called me to help run his office. His former secretary had quit, and his dog Hira was on his last legs. I knew Robert's affection for Hira, and said I'd be happy to help in any way I could.

Robert credits Hira with inspiring him to write the Oscar winning film "Chinatown." They were on Catalina together, and Robert was watching Hira smell the flowers on the island, and those smells took Robert back to his youth growing up in nearby San Pedro. He started to think about how Los Angeles had changed over the years, and why. And "Chinatown" was born.

Robert began writing "Greystoke, the Legend of Tarzan" also because of Hira. His sentience inspired Robert's unusual take on the saga. He spent ten years working on the script, and many considered it one of the best ever written. But the studio decided to let Robert direct this "small film" "Personal Best" first, and in order to finish it (due to the Actor's Guild Strike) he had to give up his rights to "Greystoke."

There was an epic lawsuit so when "Greystoke" did get made, Robert refused to have his name on the screenplay and used his "pen name." His pen name being the name of his dog; "Hira P Vizak."

Hira is the only dog ever nominated for an Oscar. It's a shame he didn't win, as it would have been fun to hear him bark at the podium in accepting the award for "Best Screenplay."

But Hira was on his last legs when Robert called me – and I was there for the last day of his life. Robert had two doctors on two different phones – one in each ear, doing everything possible to save Hira's life. One doctor told Robert to give Hira "mouth to snout" (still sounds funny) and Robert got down on his hands and knees and *I'll be damned* if he didn't bring Hira back to life doing just that.

Robert picked up Hira and we raced to his car to take him to the vet. I was in the passenger seat when a cop pulled us over for speeding. I rolled down my window and shouted, "Medical emergency, we need a police escort!" The cop said, "What hospital?" I said, "Wilshire Pet Clinic." Through his speaker, the cop said, **"Pull over asshole, *this isn't Hollywood."***

Robert got out of the car and stood a few inches from this cop's face and in a heightened whisper persuasively used every swear word he'd ever heard. (Robert was responsible for the most F bombs ever written in a film; "The Last Detail.") Suddenly it *was* Hollywood, and with siren blazing, we raced to the clinic.

At the clinic the cop threw me against the wall and said, *"You fucking Hollywood assholes think you own this town!"* and I said, "I'm terribly sorry officer. I can promise it will never ever happen again." At least I'm a polite Hollywood asshole.

When Luana died Robert was directing his *sequel* to "Personal Best" - "Without Limits." He'd asked me to come up and "direct the crowds again" but by this time I'd already directed a few films of my own. I sent him an envelope off all of the love letters he had written Luana in his youth, which I found hidden in her garage. Beautiful, intimate letters.

There was a stack from Jack Nicholson as well, less flowery, but equally filled with *love.* Here she had these two amazing talents in her life, both fell in love with her – she didn't tell anyone, but kept their letters. I sent them to Robert and Jack anonymously – just putting Luana's return address on them.

Later I heard from a pal that Jack couldn't open the envelope for fear of heartbreak – but Robert called in tears. Needless to say, when I told Robert about recently what I've been up to – conversing with his old friend, I offered him a chance to join us if wanted to.

He said, "Well, I'd like to speak to Edward (his best friend, Edward Taylor) and of course Lulu." (His nickname for Luana.) I suggested he might be able to talk to his dog Hira as well. He said "Really?" I said, "No idea, but it's worth a shot."

Edward went to college with Robert, was at Robert's side for many of his scripts. Eddie started writing scripts on his own, ("V.I. Warshawski") and moved to Ireland to take advantage of the liberal tax laws for writers. He died of cancer a couple of years prior to this conversation. I knew him well and was at the memorial service where Robert scattered his ashes in Marina Del Rey harbor.

The following is their edited conversation. My questions are in italics, **Jennifer is in bold,** Robert is in normal font.

*****

Robert is on Skype in Jennifer Shaffer's Manhattan Beach office. I'm standing off to the side with my camera, recording.

Rich: Hi Robert. This is Jennifer. She knows nothing about you.

Jennifer: I only know your name, Robert. Richard told me that today, and that you are in the industry. He also showed me a picture of your friend (Edward Taylor).

Robert: Was I in the picture?

Rich: I have a couple of you and Eddie, and one of Luana. When I got here, Jennifer said "Luana came in earlier and squeezed my hand."

34

J: She squeezed my hand and then took me on a (visual) roller coast ride.

Rich: Perhaps as if to say, "This is going to be roller coaster of an interview?"

RT: How is Lulu?

J: She showed me speeding up – like going all over the place... kind of funny. (She's showing me) **She just grabbed your hand.**

RT: She grabbed my hand? I didn't feel it.

J: She shows me – the way I try to explain this; she'll show me the dimension she's in and then she showed me that she grabbed your hand, as if she missed you. Did you feel her just brush your hair?

RT: No.

J: The other world is right here within this world. She's showing me little things. She's mentioning a birthday in June. Is there a big birthday that's happening in June?

RT: Not that I'm aware of. Lulu's birthday is in May.

Rich: It's tomorrow. This session is our birthday gift to Luana. (It was May 11th).

JS: The first thing she says is "You haven't changed."

RT: (He laughs.) She says I haven't changed?

J: She says that you're a little bit ornery. She pointed to a TV in front of you – is there something on the TV, like a picture? (To Luana: Can you be more clear?) **Do you have a picture that is up somewhere with her in it?**

RT: I have a lot of pics of her, but none that are up right now.

There is one she's showing me. Do you have one with your arm around her? Was it on a movie set?

> (Note: Robert and Luana have been on few movie sets together.)

I just don't have any right now.

She says, "It was a lot of fun." She was really, happy back then. Does that make sense?

I think we were both happy, yes.

She's saying, "That time period went by too fast – in more ways than one." Does your knee bother you?

No.

She's pointing to your knee, top of your knee. I don't know why she's showing me that... okay. She's trying to show me your leg, "She wants you to get out more," she says. You don't go out as much as you used to?

That's right.

She's trying to tell you to go out more.

Rich: Are you still swimming, Robert?

RT: I had this minor operation; I can't go in the water for 4 or 5 days.

J: Okay. She's trying to make a joke about the operation, but I'm not sure what the joke is. She's making a joke, the "The extension I'm sure, is great."

(Note: Okay, an obvious dick joke. Like he had "an extension" done. Which is odd, because Jennifer isn't laughing, Robert isn't laughing, but inside I'm saying "Really? Dick jokes, Lu? That's not going to help Robert believe it's you!" But whatever – I got it.)

Jennifer: Did you write something last year?

Robert: Yeah.

She showed me a project you wrote last year. You haven't shown it to anyone yet?

A couple of people.

She's showing me chapter three - or the third section... could be in three sections.

Rich: Third act maybe?

(Jennifer; to me) **She says, "That was the appropriate time to say that."**

> (Note: She's saying interjecting the term "third act" was appropriate. A screenwriting term. Jennifer does not know that Robert is a screenwriter, but Luana does. At this point in the conversation, I can see that Robert isn't feeling very connected. Sometimes it takes awhile to warm up the connection.)

J: She really likes what you've written. (Robert laughs) **Why are you laughing?**

RT: Thank her. Tell her I miss her very much.

She has that sense of love for you; she knows (you miss her). **She's saying, "There's something messy in the third act."**

Rich: Luana's giving him writing advice? Well, you get it where you can I guess... (Robert laughs.)

She's saying, "You're holding back." Either in the third scene, or the third act... something emotional needs to be revealed.

RT: I don't know.

Jennifer: I'm just getting bits and pieces; some things won't make sense until later... hold on. It's about the ending. She's saying to "Hone in on how you see the ending, it feels like it's spread out." But she's saying to hone in on how you... "be authentic with the ending." Or "Be more "in your face" with the ending."

(Note: Robert is one of the most famous screenwriters and rewrite artists in the industry. He's been paid millions for his craft and has been at it since the 60's. He's credited with rewriting "Bonnie and Clyde," portions of the Godfather, the "Mission Impossible" scripts, many of Tom Cruise's films, aside from his films "The Last Detail" "Personal Best," "Tequila Sunrise" and winning an Oscar for many consider the best script every written; "Chinatown."

He knows Luana primarily as an actress, once told me "On stage, she was the most thrilling actress I have ever seen." He considered her stage work (with Jack Nicholson in the same acting class) as inspirational.

"She was never cast in a role that matched her talent," he's said in the past.

Later in life she took up screenwriting, was working on a script the last day of her life. Jennifer is only relating what she's hearing or seeing, and Luana is phrasing it in such a way so that Robert might realize she is aware of what he's working on.)

Rich: Robert, do you want to ask her any questions about her point of view or what she's doing?

RT: Sure, I'd like to know what it's like for her to observe me.

J: Okay. She's laughing. **Um... she says that "You have so many thoughts constantly going and it's hard for you to shut them off."**

Rich: Is she seeing him in terms of energy or visually?

J: Both. If you were to look into a hologram and see the heat sensors; she showed me the color red, she can see the energy, she goes back and forth (seeing both from her perspective).

RT: Ok.

Rich: Luana, when you see an old friend, are you seeing them as they are now or how they were 20 years ago?

RT: If Lulu said, "It looks as if I haven't changed that much," then it seems to me, she's looking at me now.

J: She is. Time is not linear over there, so when she sees you, she sees your essence throughout all of your journey; when you were younger, etc... in one fell swoop. She likes

to go back in time and have fun with you, when you two were together.

RT: It was fun for me too.

J: Did you guys sing together? It felt like you were singing. She's laughing about it.

RT: It was sort of a joke. We would sing... I can't carry a tune very well, but she would sing with me anyway.

Rich: Did you guys do that in class as an exercise?

RT: That's possible. Jennifer, is this your first time talking with Lulu?

J: No, she shows up a lot.

> (Note: I haven't told Robert much about our conversations other than "I get to talk to Luana often.")

Rich: Sometimes when we're having a conversation with a friend who has crossed over, Jennifer will say "Your friend Luana is here." Apparently, they "show up" whenever they feel that connection.

J: It's the heart strings that are still attached; it's a frequency you can call up at any time. (Pause) **She's showing me that you're not sleeping well, or that you're tense.**

RT: That's true.

J: She showed me that it feels like you're stiff when you're sleeping.

(Robert shrugs) I don't know; I'm asleep.

She says to "Relax more before you go to sleep." She showed me a yoga position, she showed me like a crossing your legs... in lotus position? **She's trying to show you how to "ask her to come and see you."**

(Note: This is clarified later on.)

RT: (smiles) Lulu why don't you come and visit me before I go to sleep?

Rich: Luana, we want to invite some of Robert's other friends that you might be able to bring with you.

She goes, "Oh, they're boring!" She's kidding. She's like "I want to be first." (Jennifer listens) **She says, "I miss you."**

Rich: Can she bring Edward forward?

He just appeared like Kramer used to enter ("Seinfeld"); **slid into the room.**

Rich: How does he look to you?

He looks young. 40's. Hair is kind of like sandy.

RT: That sounds right.

Eddie Taylor and his daughter

41

It feels like he's in good shape, feels strong to me...

Tell us about yourself Eddie, what's going on?

He's actually doing stuff... sounds weird, like working on a space rocket. (Jennifer to Eddie:) Looking at space stuff?

> (Note: It's one of the questions I ask people to answer about their current journey. They often reply with working "back home" with others on physicist type problems. Often in a classroom seeing, often a class in "etheric energy transfer." Sometimes they describe it as an occupation (engineer, etc) sometimes as a student in a class that deals with their topic. I've heard this type of answer before, it doesn't surprise me that someone as intellectual as Edward was is continuing in that vein when he's "back home.")

Rich: Edward is working on these projects by himself or with others?

J: He's working with lots of people in a university environment. He's creating a way to transport people from one place to the next. He showed me a "beam me up Scotty" version (the transporter in Star Trek) – wait... (he says) He says he's learning to matriculate in further dimensions. (Matriculate: be enrolled) **I asked, "To come here?" and it feels like there's block with that...**

> (Note: Again, I'm familiar with this kind of answer, but am aware that Robert is not. Before Edward can go into the description of the kind of work he's doing in "etheric transport," I suggest Robert ask him direct questions.)

Rich: Robert, do you have any questions for Eddie?

42

J: He showing me you guys were out on a boat... he's showing me being by the ocean.

> (Note: *(ding!)* Afterwards I pointed out to Robert that when he scattered Edward's his ashes, it was aboard a boat in Marina Del Rey. Perhaps he was referring to that trip.)

J: It felt like he didn't have any worries, (when he was here) it was about taking care of everybody else... I don't know what he did for a living or his work. Did you guys work together on like three movies?

RT: We did. *(ding!)*

J: It feels like the last one was *the best;* it was the most fun.

RT: I don't remember what the last one really was.

J: It "was *the best*" because he was able to spend more time with you.

> (Note: That could be a pun. I met Edward while working on Robert's film **"Personal Best."** I think it was the last one he worked on with Robert, but that could have been "Tequila Sunrise.")

RT: Well... the last we worked together was in my house on Lucca Drive; he was there. We were actually physically together for about three or four weeks.

J: He said you guys were able to spend time together. You knew each other's "dirty secrets?"

RT: I don't know that means...

(Note: *Oh c'mon*. Yes you do. Doesn't mean they're "dirty" if they're just secrets. Edward knew Robert as well as he knows the back of his hand. *No secrets on the flipside!)*

J: It might be Luana interjecting. He's mentioning your script again. Did he die of cancer?

(Note: Going back through my notes, and transcription, neither Robert nor I mention he's writing a script. Could have been a best guess, but she's using it now.)

RT: Yes.

J: Did he hide it from people that he had cancer?

RT: Yes, he did. *(ding!)* I don't know if he would put it that way – he just didn't go to doctors or anyone for awhile until it was very far advanced.

J: He's saying he didn't tell anyone for awhile, that it happened fast, but he knew it before he was diagnosed.

(Note: I didn't know the answers to these questions, but Robert (and Eddie) did. So this was new information to me as well.)

Rich: Eddie, who was there to greet you when you crossed over?

J: There were hundreds of people to greet him. He had already left his body before he died. I feel like there was a period of time that... I don't know if it was morphine, but he was already outside of his body and watched himself (cross over). **It was kind of like that.**

Rich: So what's it like for you to see Luana and Robert now?

J: It's not bad. It's a lot of memories all at once. From all of us. Not just from Robert but connected to everybody.

*Rich: On the way over here, I was asking Luana a question in my head. I had this thought to ask her "What's it like for you..." I was going to ask what it was like for her to meet up with us for these sessions, and before I could finish the sentence I felt I heard, "**It's like acting, like taking on a role; you prepare yourself for the performance to come.**"*

J: She likes that. She says, "You go ahead, Richard."

RT: Let me ask Edward a question. What was the last thing that you said to me before we never spoke again? I was calling you, you were in the hospital in Ireland.

J: My first impression was him saying "Thank you" and something about getting something done on time.

RT: That sounds like he's referring to a script.

Rich: What was the last thing that Eddie said to him?

RT: It was very specific.

J: When they give me words it's interpretation as well – if I could get everything verbatim, I'd get the lottery numbers... give me a second. Were you waiting to come back or go where he was?

RT: I was getting ready to leave (to go over and be with him in Ireland).

J: Did he say something about him waiting for you?

RT: It's what I wanted, but no.

J: I feel like he was playing off that you didn't need to worry - "that everything is okay" kind of thing.

RT: Edward definitely did not want to leave as near as I can tell.

J: He didn't want to die in this way – he did not want to die in this way. On a subconscious level; he was still fighting consciously.

Rich: Once you crossed over, Eddie, was it a relief?

J: It was mixed, he said "Everything at once." Um... and Luana was there.

RT: Luana was there to greet him?

J: That's what she's saying.

Rich: Can you walk us through that moment? How did she look when she greeted you on the other side?

J: In her 40's.

> (Note: This is the same thing that Harry Dean Stanton said to us about when he crossed over. He said at first, he started to see Luana in his hospital room, and he thought he was hallucinating. But when he did cross over he said he saw her in her 20's, they were on their way to the Monterey Pop festival (with Fred Roos). Fred later confirmed everything that Harry said about the trip, and at his memorial service, the women who were with him when he died also confirmed the details he told me and Jennifer.)

Rich: You recognized her immediately?

J: "Yes."

Rich: Who else did you see when you crossed over?

J: I feel like his mom...

Rich: Eddie had a girlfriend who passed away, a girlfriend who committed suicide, whom I saw once.

> (Note: I was staying at Peter Peyton's apt, which was Edward's old apartment in the Sea Castle Apts in Santa Monica. I awoke and saw this pretty blond with long hair sitting on the edge of the couch I was sleeping on. She was crying and then disappeared. Later I asked Peter who the ghost was, and he said, "It sounds like you're describing Eddie's girlfriend who killed herself in this apartment.")

Rich: How is she doing now?

J: He's seen her. She couldn't... stay... Edward showed me dying of suicide or cancer is pretty tragic (either way) **and he's saying she left a mark at that place you were staying at. It's an energetic pattern** (or her memory) **but she wasn't being held back** (by the experience).

RT: You never saw her before? Did you know what she looked like?

Rich: No, not at all. I described the blond I saw on the couch as I woke up, and Peter said, "That sounds like Eddie's girlfriend who died in this apartment." Years later, when I met Edward's daughter (from this same girl) I recognized her. I told this story to Eddie at some point and he looked at me like I was nuts.

J: He's saying, "You were nuts."

RT: That sounds like Eddie. All right, I'm going to tell you what Eddie said to me. The last thing he said; he said, "It just isn't fair."

J: That's what my dad said. He passed a month ago. He died of pancreatic cancer. He said, "It just isn't fair."

Rich: What does that mean?

J: He's showing me that it was *stolen*; it wasn't fair that his time was taken away from him. I probably wouldn't have said it to you even if I got that (Edward saying "it's not fair") because my father said the same thing! Even if I got that information, I wouldn't have repeated it to you because it's what I heard from my father.

Rich: Let me ask, Edward, what was the theme of your life? What were you supposed to learn?

J: It was... to learn not to (try to) control everything. Not control over people or things, but within himself. It was after he learned he didn't have any control over things; there are things we can't control.

Robert, anything else you want to ask him?

RT: Do you miss being alive?

J: He does.

RT: I miss him being alive.

J: He misses smells, the scents of things. He first showed me dancing with Luana but then said "No, not that..." He showed me feeling things tangibly.

RT: You don't have feelings (over there)?

J: I think he means tactile sensation. We've heard this before; things over there feel different. Nothing over there is hard to the touch, since it's a construct, it's "spongy." That when we are over there, we miss the tactile sensations here, the tastes, smells... a slice of pizza, flowers, those kinds of things of specific things are harder to create energetically.

RT: You mean where he is?

J: Am I asking that correctly, Eddie? Please correct me.

> (Note: Once we discussed this with Luana, what she missed, and she said, "I miss the wind on my face when driving in a convertible.")

J: Okay. He's saying that everything is a construct, like you said, if you were to take a card file of a memory to reconstruct it... (Like smelling a flower). **But he says he is missing everything here (on the planet) "the smell of a car, even gasoline, those strong scents." But the thing that doesn't die is that love. He said "I love you" to you Robert,** (he's making me feel) all **that emotion, in that phone call** (you made to him.)

Edward didn't want to go, like you said... but he didn't want to stay in the condition he was in either. He's saying the same thing that Luana is saying -- that "You shouldn't hold back on the script that you've been writing, at all."

"He wants you take it further, go past the boundaries with that" - if that makes sense. **I'm not here to tell you what to do, I promise.**

49

RT: I understand. I have always felt bad and I just worry I left it too long... I always felt that I could get you back to California and to certain doctors, that it... was the best chance I had of saving your life and I wanted to do that and uh, you know... I didn't get their on time.

J: "It was aggressive," he said.

RT: Oh, I know.

J: (An aside) I don't know. But he said, "It was aggressive, and we had no idea it would happen that fast." He said, "Please don't feel bad or guilty about that... there was nothing you could do."

RT: Obviously not. I wanted to... there were a couple of times in his life... where when he was ill, I helped...

J: I feel like you helped his family; either his daughter... or son?

RT: I've talked to his daughter a couple of of times.

J: That's what he said. He feels like she's "*out there.*"

RT: What do you mean?

J: He showed me that it feels like she has a lot of his characteristics. The positive ones anyway.

RT: That's a good thing.

J: Meaning that she doesn't know "how to *be here*" - she's super busy or not grounded...

RT: She's a wonderful girl.

Rich: Should we see if our friend Hira is available?

50

RT: I don't know how you're going to do that.

(Note: I don't know how we are going to do that either. I just tossed it out there like a hot potato. I know who Hira is, and was, but I also am aware (as reported in my books) that sometimes people claim that they can access a beloved pet that has crossed over. They ask questions and get *answers*. They're telepathic answers, but they're answers either way.

I have often asked people to address whatever or whomever they see during either their past life memories, (trees, pets) during near death events, out of body experiences, under hypnosis, and have them ask direct questions to see if they get a reply. (And they often do!) In this case, I was his dog Hira's assistant – even though Robert paid the checks. During his *"Personal Best"* days, my main gig was walking Hira around the Warner Brothers lot... *and away we go!)*

Rich: Eddie, Luana; you both know who Hira is...

RT: I have a picture of Hira... handy.

J: That's great... that helps me.

(Note: "Hira" is Robert's Komondor (Hungarian Sheep Dog). Robert holds up a giant photograph of his friend for Jennifer to see.)

J: There's Hira! I was looking for a person... awesome. Okay give me a second... Was there something wrong with Hira's chest? He had a hard time breathing when he died.

RT: He had a heart attack. *(ding!)*

J: I was just shown it was heavy right here, he couldn't breathe...

RT: He died in my arms.

J: I'm sorry.

Rich: I was there.

RT: You were there.

J: Luana's holding onto Hira.

RT: She knew him, yeah.

J: She's showing me playing with him. Hold on a second. **Hira is saying "That you have felt him after he passed, like an energy on the bed or next to you." Did you ever feel that next to you?**

RT: Yes. *(Ding!)*

J: He's showing me that you felt that and that was him. Give me a sec. He's showing me by the kitchen area... He's showing me a mouse?

RT: Like a toy?

Rich: Hira was very intelligent, could be a metaphor.

J: He comes across like a person; like someone that you cherished. There's something about 12?

He died at the age of 12. *(Ding!)*

J: He says, "You know it wasn't the way you fed him that caused his illness," he's saying you cannot feel bad about that. He's saying, "It was actually a birth defect when he

was born, something that didn't show up until he was 8 years old." Does that make sense to you? Did you feel bad about the food that was given to him?

RT: Well... yes and no.

> (Note: Some years after "Personal Best" wrapped, Robert asked me to come back and run his office. At the time, chaos reigned because Hira was sick, and a number of doctors came to see him daily. I was told his prostate had "swollen to the size of a melon," making it nearly impossible for him to walk or pee and surgery was out of the question. Robert carried him out each day to do his business. I've never seen or known a bond between two people that was as close as these two.)

J: All he's saying is - "Don't feel bad about that... It's wasted." I felt like you took him everywhere. He says that "You were the best owner in the world... that everyone wanted to come back and be Hira because of how he was treated by you." I almost feel like you put him first, more than everything else, or any human.

RT: At that time in my life I certainly did.

> (Note: It's not possible for Jennifer to know that from looking at a photograph. I was there. I know for a fact that what she is saying is *spot on*. I had no idea if we could talk to Hira, but here she is communicating with him, giving direct information to the man who loved him most.)

J: Hira is saying that he's putting in your head that you should get another dog.

RT: I have a cat that would argue about that.

J: Hira showed me the cat – he showed me the mouse, he showed me he plays with the cat.

RT: He likes my cat?

J: Is your cat lazy?

RT: No.... Well, I mean, they sleep. More than they do anything else.

J: He's saying, "The cat's lazy."

RT: My cat is 20 years old.

Rich: Hira, I want to ask about your relationship with Robert, it was as if you knew each other in a previous life or connected on a higher plane. Did you know each other from before and can you show that to Jennifer?

J: "Yes." He's showing me in England. I felt like he was a horse (during that lifetime.)

> (Note: This isn't the first time I've encountered a pet or an animal in this research. It's the first time I've asked Jennifer to ask direct questions, but in a number of deep hypnosis sessions I've filmed, people have "conversations" with their pet on the flipside, often "seeing them" as a light.
>
> If I was filming a deep hypnosis session with a person and their "pet" I would ask the same question. "Have you ever had a lifetime together in the past?" They can say "No" or "Yes" or "I don't know." Sometimes they say no, sometimes they say "I'm seeing a lifetime where we were together in another fashion

54

(always as animal and human, but a different configuration, as we're about to see.)

Rich: What year comes to mind when you remember having a lifetime with Robert in England?

J: 1627.

Rich: Give Jennifer an image of what Robert looked like in 1627.

J: Male, dark dark hair... he died from war – in a war. Something that... okay.

Rich: If you can – what was Robert's name in 1627?

J: Loesser? Lesserman?

Rich: Was he from a wealthy family? Land owner?

J: Yes.

> (Note: Loesser and Loeser are common names in Northern England and Scotland. Doesn't mean it was him, just means that this name was common enough to find.)[9]

Rich: Did you die when he died in this battle or did you survive?

J: It felt like you (Robert) were wearing armor... on this horse – He's showing me circling you after you were off your horse... something killed him.

---

[9] according to ancestry.com/UK. Williame Lesser was christened in 1689 in Stirling, Scotland, son of Williame and Jeanne. (Later than the memory of 1627, but sometimes you get lucky in a search)

Rich: Let me ask you; what kind of horse were you Hira?

J: He was white.

RT: Hira was a horse in 1627?

Rich: I'm asking if you've both known each other from a lifetime before and he is saying you did. Hira, are you and Robert going to have a lifetime together again?

J: "Yes."

Rich: When Robert checks off the planet 100 years from now, will you be there to greet him?

J: "Absolutely." I can see Hira licking Luana's face.

Rich: Lu, anything you want to say to Robert?

J: She said, "He needs to love again." Whatever that looks like to you. "To not give up. To open your heart."

> (Note: Robert is happily married. His wife is lovely. "Falling in love" is a metaphor; includes falling in love with a topic or story or another dog.)

Rich: Who was that girl we were going to talk to who showed up in your dream Robert? Who died when you were 15?

RT: Ruth Mary Nash.

Rich: Lu, I know you don't know Ruth – but can you bring her forward?

J: She has reddish hair... auburn?

RT: Dark.

J: I feel like she's showing me in her 30's...

RT: Well the girl didn't live past the age of 16.

J: Did she pass away 30 years ago?

RT: More like 60 years ago.

J: Sometimes we try to call people up and others come forward. The person I'm seeing has auburn hair and is in her 30's.

> (Note: Robert may remember his friend at 16, but between lives we appear in our "idealized version of ourselves" so others can recognize us. She may have had a longer life as a 30 year old with dark hair during some other lifetime and is comfortable with that construct. According to these accounts, age is relative when creating an image of ourselves for others to see; Jennifer is just observing what she's seeing. It's entirely possible "Ruth" appears to friends on the flipside as 30 with dark hair, as it is equally possible someone else has appeared instead.)

Rich: What else is coming through from her?

J: Her back feels like it hurts really bad – I don't know if her back was injured. It feels like it was an accident of some sort...

RT: It sounds like you're talking about Ruth... she did have back problems.

J: Did she have problems with her blood? I'm seeing that she might have.

RT: I don't know how she passed away. It may have been some sort of blood disease, I don't know what it was.

Rich: So why did you appear in Robert's mind recently Ruth? What does she want to tell him?

J: It feels like it was to forgive someone... almost feels like that. Are you mad at a family member of hers, or yours, haven't spoken to someone?

RT: Why do you ask?

> (Note: Knowing Robert as well as I do, this answer means "Could be, but I'm not going to reply either way.")

J: I feel like her coming into your consciousness is because it might be a way of dealing with (feelings about) **a family member...**

Rich: Did you have a dream about her or sense her around you, Robert?

J: "A dream," she's saying. You did have a dream about her, didn't you?

RT: It was years ago.

Rich: But she's outside of time – and this is why Robert and I had this initial conversation. He mentioned that she was on his mind, had appeared in recent dreams, and I did some research and found after she moved away from San Pedro, she had gone to school in Novato, CA and had passed way. But she was so popular with the school there is still a scholarship given out in her name all these years later.

J: You guys weren't that close.

RT: No.

Rich: By appearing in his dream, what was she trying to tell Robert? Is it that she's part of his soul group?

(Note: A "soul group" was identified in Michael Newton's work. He wrote in the thousands of cases he examined, people claim to have a group of people they normally incarnate with. He noted they usually contain 3-25 people that we "recognize" during these between life sessions, and that people we "feel a close connection to" are often included.)

J: It's definitely a "soul group" connection and understanding of love. I feel like she's trying to tell you to not hold onto things... I don't know what it is, but I feel like she's saying... to almost, like "forgive and let go" kind of thing. I feel like you would know what she means; I'm just the messenger... Were you angry about, or was it challenging for you about how she passed or who was involved?

RT: I was upset about it; the last time we saw each other she was 15 and I saw her at a friend's house in Palos Verdes and we quarreled. As we did often... and I always felt bad about that.

J: So that's what she's saying... she's saying to "Let that part go." That she's the family member, to let that part go. It's not worth it. The arguing, that's what you guys did.

RT: I just... we fought a lot, we liked each other a lot too. So...

J: I'm getting that... so maybe just forgive that part of what happened.

59

RT: It was my fault too.

J: She's saying, "It was both (of us);" she instigated a lot too.

Rich: Okay, Jennifer has to go, thanks everyone for showing up today... Thanks Robert, Eddie, Hira, Luana... all you guys, we miss you!

J: It was great talking to you Robert, I'm sorry if the content was a little heavy.

RT: I'm glad... let's do it again.

Rich: Robert, I love the idea that your old pals Luana and Eddie are trying to help you with the third act of your script or story. I haven't a clue what that might be and Jennifer doesn't know anything about your work or what that might be.

J: What I do know from that, is that they loved you. What they do tell me to tell you is that they love you.

Rich: Eddie, can you give Robert a one, two, three example, to get a sense of when you're in the room?

RT: That's a good thing to ask.

J: They're showing me you in a lotus position (meditating), **just calm. They're saying, "Then open your heart, and use your heart to think of them." It's like a calling card; they'll be right there. You have the only phone number for them and vice versa; it's a unique frequency. Just think of Luana and the times you had with her and you'll feel her essence.**

Rich: What about Eddie?

J: He just said to "Knock on his door." He's making fun (of the idea) that he doesn't have the "essence" that Luana does. He says, "Think about the four weeks you had with him, those times, and that'll (be the) knock on his door to get him down (next to you)."

RT: All right. I miss them both very much. All of them. Three of the most important people in my life; Hira, Eddie and Lulu.

J: Hira is being well taken care of and no one did it better than you.

RT: We had great times. Jennifer, thank you very much.

J: This was fun for me. It's wonderful to feel your loved ones. In my career, I'm known for other things, I'm known for my crime work and it's a lot more fun doing this... than finding dead bodies.

RT: I'm sure it is.

Afterwards:

I direct Jennifer to IMDB to look up Robert's credits.

J: Oh my god! Holy shit. I cannot believe he wrote "Chinatown!" That is so cool! I'm so glad I don't know anything before I talk to people. Oh my god, he wrote "Shampoo?" Oh my god! (etc for about five *fangirl* filled minutes). That is so cool! Thank you.

Rich: Thank you! You're the skilled surgeon; I'm just the DJ.

(Note: Another day. Robert wanted to continue the conversation. This time over a cell phone speaker)

61

Jennifer: Hi Robert.

RT: Hi.

Rich: We were just talking to Lulu; we were just addressing our class like we do every week.

RT: How is Lulu?

J: Busy. There's too many people coming here... it's getting bigger and bigger.

Rich: Meaning the classroom. When I told Jennifer we were going to talk to you today, Jennifer got an image of Luana putting on padding – you know how a cop puts on Kevlar?

J: Only it was white.

RT: Well why would she do that?

J: I don't know that's a good question.. let's ask her. (Listens) **She said it was as a joke – just a joke. Comedy.**

RT: Is she around right now?

J: Yeah.

RT: I'd like to ask what she's up to?

J: She showed the top of Richard's head.

Rich: My bald spot no doubt. Lu give us an idea of what you do to prepare for this class.

J: She showed me sitting down like at a desk, gathering tons of information about the people who are in the class, about their connections to the class, and how that comes

about. It's almost at random, the extensions of the people who show up there, but it's not random.

RT: Who are these people, are they alive or dead?

Rich: They're all dead.

J: She put the thought in Robert's head yesterday. To call Rich, to ask to speak to his parents.

Rich: What's she's saying Robert, is that the way this came about was that your parents came to Luana, and she helped them put the thought into your head to call me; to suggest we have a conversation with them. Luana could you please invite Robert's mom and dad here?

J: They're here.

Rich: Your dad's first name is Lou, right?

RT: Yep. My mom's name is Helen.

J: His mom has a great smile. (That is accurate). **Give me a second. I'm getting something from one of your parents... it felt like it was the chest area or a lung issue...**

RT: What are you talking about?

J: How they passed.

RT: That would be my mother... She had difficulty breathing, her lungs were affected by cancer.

J: She has a beautiful smile by the way, she's very sweet... It feels like she got a lot done. She was a very happy person.

RT: Yeah, much of the time, she was.

J: She had a very dry sense of humor, I feel like the times she wasn't happy had to do with your dad...

Rich: Does that sound right?

RT: Yeah.

J: Okay, then your dad... I'm getting that he was losing his memory or out of it... and something to do with his colon?

RT: No memory loss – basically he died of congestive heart failure.

J: Okay, hold on... your mother took care of him, correct?

RT: Yeah, she did. He also had a couple of nurses.

J: He went before she did.

RT: Yes.

J: About a year or two?

RT: Yes.

Rich: I'd like to ask question for Helen; were you aware of your two boys eulogy at your funeral?[10]

She showed me the apple tree, as in "The apple doesn't fall far from the tree."

Rich: I was there – Roger and Robert gave the best eulogies I've ever heard.

---

[10] Lou Schwartz passed a few years before his mother Helen. Robert's brother Roger is a screenwriter as well ("The Natural") and the two of them gave the best eulogies I've ever heard.

She says, "Robert didn't hold back." She loved it. There's something of your mother's that you're trying to get back or find?

Yes, a poem.

Who has that now?

> (Note: The cell phone connection suddenly disconnects.)

Rich: That's funny. Isn't that weird?

Not in my world.

> (We get the connection back.)

Rich: Sorry about that... you said a poem? That you wrote or she wrote?

RT: She wrote.

Rich: Let's ask her – Helen where's the poem?

J: Feels like a family member would have it. Someone related to Helen has it... like a boy or a wife or ex might have it... it's in what looks like a file cabinet. I'm also getting something that is framed. It almost feels like an attic or a room that's up high.

RT: I just don't know... I know that I have no recollection of seeing it written down somewhere, I used to know the poem... but unfortunately with the passage of time I've lost most of it.

J: When you get inspired, she's saying you should sit down and you will remember it with bits and pieces. She says she loves hanging out with you.

65

Rich: Let's ask his dad – what's he doing?

J: I got him outside...

Rich: Doing a sport?

J: He's watching something.

RT: What's he watching?

J: Did he ever bet on horses?

RT: Yeah, he did.

J: That's what I'm getting.

Rich: Lou are you going to the track? Is it a real track from your memory or an imaginary track?

J: It's a track that he invented...

Rich: We've heard this – that you can create an environment over there. Who's with you when you go to the track?

J: His dad.

Rich: Your grandfather Robert.

RT: I never knew him.

Rich: So Lou, you go to the track with your dad and do you bet?

J: He showed me the build of the horse – almost like the science behind it.

Rich: He's showing her the complexity of how you do that how you create the horse track and the smells and visuals and have them run.

J: "It's like creating a movie," he said, "only its over on the other side."

Rich: We've heard this often Robert. Someone says, "I'm on a sandy beach" We ask, "How do you do that?" They say, "It's a mathematical construct."

RT: On the track, are there horses that he once knew?

J: Yes.

RT: One of them was very famous.

J: I just got shown it was a horse that they made a movie about. Like "The Black Stallion." I can see it, but I don't know the name of it.

RT: There is a horse that I'm thinking of in particular that I used to hear him talk about it.

J: I felt like it made him a lot (of money).

Rich: Robert you had a newspaper in the film Chinatown – was that the same horse?

RT: Yes.

Rich: I knew that, but Jennifer would never have known that. But there was a film about this horse... like the Black Stallion. I can't think of the name either.

RT: It was a bay horse. I'm thinking about the horse, he was very famous.

Rich: We'll get to it in a minute; let's ask, so when you create that horse at the track Lou, who wins? Is it always the same or different?

J: Oh wow. He's showing me it's not about winning over there on the flipside, it's about winning in the future. He's showing me that for his next life he's compounding the frequencies to understand them, so he could win.

He's practicing for a future lifetime?

J: Like how to pick a lucky horse.

Rich: Lou, anything you want to tell your son?

J: I'm getting that there's a celebration coming up. (Listens.) **He says you don't celebrate the Jewish holidays? What I'm getting is there's supposed to be a celebration in August. Could be a premiere or a film, or a party.**

Rich: But Helen what would you like to say to Robert so that he'll know he's talking to you?

J: "Tell him not to be himself in a movie?" (to me) What is she talking about?

Rich: I think she's saying, "Tell him not to be in his own movie" – meaning allow yourself to "live life" and don't be a character in your mental film, or get stuck with what you're "supposed to do." Live life.

(Jennifer taps her nose as if to say, "that's correct.") **Just be yourself and be your own movie.**

What about his father?

Luana just kissed him on the cheek... and Lou patted her on the butt. (Jennifer aside) Maybe that's why she's wearing the padding. (Luana knew both of Robert's parents.)

I remember having to track your dad down on a golf course and assumed your dad was talking about playing golf

RT: Yes, he was a golfer.

J: At first he showed me him playing golf, but he was more interested in showing me the horse racing.

RT: I'm going to give you the horses' name. Seabiscuit.

J: Seabiscuit! That's the movie I saw.

Rich: Your dad knew Seabiscuit. Wow.

RT: Thank you Jennifer.

J: Thank you Robert. (Afterwards) That was so cool!

Rich: Lou and Helen, you guys remember Luana don't you?

J: Yes, they do – and I'm just seeing this for the first time. Luana is like me... "She's *me* over there." In other words she has my gift of translating the ethers... she's like "I'm the stewardess over here who helps people connect over there; they want to connect but they don't know how."

She's you over there? Cool. Does everyone need a medium over there, like you, in order to do that?

J: They have to learn how to do it. Hold on she's laughing. **She's showing me that she put you in my head – I was doing dishes on Thanksgiving night when I first heard your voice doing the audible for "Flipside." She did that.**

So it's that time of year for grades. Luana, who's the most difficult student in the class?

69

Harry Dean Stanton was the hardest to work with when he was still alive.

Who's the easiest person?

Robin said, "I got an A plus" – David Bowie said, "I showed everyone my death before I died."

Okay, Robin and David both get an A plus. Anyone got a beef about the book so far?

Luana said "Yes, because you're still holding back."

What, are we supposed to run around naked screaming "There is an afterlife! Read all about it?" What do you mean we're holding back?

"Don't hold back in your mind. Or worry about who should publish it."

If you guys can help get it out that would be great. All right class, see you on the flipside.

*****

Robert Towne and me "Personal Best" Photo: Steve Vaughan

CHAPTER TWO:

SYDNEY FROM GROUP

"It's fun over here."

The Maestro in his office

After hearing in our class that we *could* access our loved ones, or people whose energetic frequency we know (via memory, photo or something connected to them) I tried an experiment.

I was driving down San Vicente Boulevard in Brentwood, and was passing Sydney Pollack's old home. I had never been in his home, but I had met him a few times and spoken to him over the phone. As a test, I said his name aloud. "Sydney Pollack." *Almost like announcing him for an Oscar.*

In a split second, I heard his voice saying *"What?"* in my head. I hadn't planned on asking him any questions, as I was just driving by his old home. I decided I'd just ask if he wanted to join our Luana class for a discussion in a couple of days. He said, "***I knew Luana from group.***"

I didn't know what he meant at first, but then as I thought about it, I thought, "*Wait a minute, there was a group therapy session that Luana occasionally attended with Sally.*" Her friend Sally Kellerman was in that "group" and I knew a number of famous people were associated with it, but *I had no idea* if Sydney was. I thought "If that really was his "voice" I'll do research and see if he did meet Luana in "group."" If he did, I would try to interview him in our next class.

After searching for "group" and the psychiatrist's name who ran it, "Milton Wexler," I found that in the introduction to his documentary about the architect Frank Gehry, Sydney revealed that he had met Frank "in group." I knew Luana had met Frank in that same group, as I'd scattered some of her ashes at the reflecting pond at the Guggenheim in Bilbao and had told Frank about it. My questions *are in italics*, Jennifer is in normal font, and answers she's getting **are in bold.**

*****

Rich: Okay class, we have an invited guest. A person that Luana and I met many years ago, I'll tell you his first name is Sydney. What's relevant is that I said his name aloud as I drove by his house and in a few moments, I heard his voice in my ear. He said, "I knew Luana from group."

> (Note: Sydney and his wife used to come by Sally Kellerman and Jonathan Krane's house and I'd cook fajitas. He called me the "Fajita King." I wanted to get my script about Amelia Earhart to him, so I called his office. His secretary asked, "Who's calling?" and I replied, "Tell him it's the Fajita King." He got right

on. Unfortunately he had a similar project about another female pilot, Beryl Markham.

But Sally Kellerman met her husband Jonathan Krane in group, Jonathan met Blake Edwards, started a management company with him, Dudley Moore, Jennifer Jones, Frank Gehry and others were in "group" as well.) [11]

Jennifer: **"Group?"**

Yes. Something I didn't know until he told me from the Flipside. Let's talk about him in general. Sydney, who was there to greet you when you crossed over?

Felt like his sister. Felt like his mom died after he died.

I don't know, but will find out. (His wife did pass after him.)

She was sick for two years before she passed. I'm seeing two daughters and a boy; did the boy pass before him?

Yes, that's right. Does he want to talk about that?

(Note: His son Stephen died in a flying accident in Santa Monica.) [12]

"Yeah." First thing he showed me was a car or vehicle of some kind. He's very sweet. Hold on. Was his son in an accident?

Yes. But it wasn't on the ground.

---

[11] Footnote: http://www.pbs.org/wnet/americanmasters/frank-gehry-filmmaker-interview/612/

[12] https://www.nytimes.com/1993/11/28/us/film-maker-s-son-and-pilot-die-in-crash-of-small-plane.html

A plane? What I was being shown was there was one of the engines didn't work...or the engine did not. Feels like he got blinded by something.

So what are you doing now Sydney? What point did you realize there was an afterlife?

"When he couldn't get back."

He wrote a letter to our mutual pal Phillip Noyce who posted it recently online.

It felt like it was two letters.

Same day I was talking to you, while driving past your house, Phillip posted one of those letters online. It said, "I'm so upset we can't make another movie together." Was Sydney referring to his illness?

It made him very angry. The letter was like 3 weeks before he died? Feels like.

> (Note: Phillip Noyce (*"Clear and Present Danger" "Salt"*) had posted Sydney's letter on Facebook which said in essence "I'm so angry that we don't get to work together again." Phillip directed "The Quiet American" which Sydney produced. As mentioned, Phillip posted the letter the same day I was thinking of Sydney while driving past his home (*are the odds?)* Editing this passage, I reached out to Phillip to ask, "Silly question. How long before he passed did you receive that note from Sydney Pollack?" Phillip replied; ***"3 weeks prior."*)*

Rich: Sydney – let's talk to Luana first so you can get a sense of what we're doing here. Please, take a seat. And welcome to class.

Jennifer: Luana said, **"It's about time."** Books are flying (around the class), the class is shouting.

Hang on, I have to change the camera battery. (During the battery change, she said "Michael Newton just threw a book against the wall.")

Who needs to speak to us first?

Morton.

What does he want to say?

(Michael had a private message for the head of the Newton Institute. I passed it along to him.)

...He also said, **"You need to know that you will be changing the way that this method is done. His method (of hypnosis)."**

So Michael threw a book to get Jennifer's attention? Class – can we just raise our hands please?

My dad said, **"Thanks for talking to your mom (Jennifer's) for Valentine's day."** (He had specific gifts he recommended.)

Are you talking directly to your wife, Jim?

"Yes."

Is she hearing you?

"No."

75

In her dreams?

"Yeah. That's the most fun."

I'm going to bounce around the class. Bill Paxton, anything?

He came in earlier. Has to do with the guy who did the film "*Avatar*." He says, "I feel like he's going to do another movie that has to do with the afterlife."

After "Avatar" two and three?

Feels like it's something separate.

Jennifer and I were talking to you a year ago Billy, around Valentine's day. You said, "The anniversary is coming up" I realized later, you meant your passing. That was correct. You also said that your family was considering suing the hospital. Anything you want to say about that?

"They should."

Well, they just filed the suit.

He's showing me they decided to do that back in January.

According to the suit, they're saying the doctor who did the surgery wasn't really the right guy to do that kind of surgery. What happened? Did you get a second opinion?

I asked him, "Was it a panic attack?" He said "No, I needed it (the surgery)." Why does it feel he had one surgery for something else?

I think he went in for heart pain – but from what I understand, he had scar tissue from heart problems when he was a kid, but his surgeon wasn't on call after the surgery, etc. My question was why didn't you get a second opinion or another doctor?

He didn't have time, it felt like. He's saying something like "My heart was at fault too." But I think the doctor wasn't... (the) doctor was having issues too.

I'm just asking if there's anything you want me to add about this case... from your perspective.

> (Note: As mentioned in "Hacking the Afterlife" there was a court case in Seattle where a confessed killer said during the sentencing phase "I had a dream where the victims came and forgave me. I wish I could take it back, but I just wanted to tell the family that they're okay, they came to tell me they were." The jury, hearing his remorse, did give him life instead of the death penalty.)

Um, he basically gave them permission from over there.

That would also help the grieving process, I'd guess.

Yes, knowing that he didn't die in pain.

Harry Dean Stanton, are you still in class?

"Ha-ha..! Yes."

Anything you want to tell us?

"It's fun over here." He (Harry Dean Stanton) showed himself surrounded by women, like in the show "Big Love." He's playing his guitar.

I talk about you often Harry Dean, people ask me for proof you still exist and I tell your story about entering the afterlife via the Monterey Pop Festival. Thank you. Let's return to our new student Sydney Pollack. Sydney, can you see now what we're doing? We're just having conversations.

He feels like he's getting it, but that he's chained to the (student's) **desk. He wants to talk about his son,** hold on. **He said, "His son wasn't there at first when he first crossed over... at the time that he died, someone else (had) died..."** relatively the same time." **Something like that.**

You gotta explain that one to Jennifer, Sydney.

Somebody else had died before Sydney and that's who his son was with.

So when your son came to see you someone else was with him?

"Yes." But he wasn't there right away.

Okay, thanks for clarifying. Let's talk about your career.

Felt like it was "All over the place."

Your background was as an actor, you served in the military, where you became friends with Robert Redford who had a big influence on your career.

Oh, that's what he was showing me... Redford in "All the President's Men."

Sydney was a producer, director and actor. He won an Oscar for directing "Out of Africa." Directed "Tootsie." Why did you choose this lifetime Sydney? What were you here to teach or impart to other people?

"To get people to think. At first it felt as if it was to bring joy to people but also to get people to think from a political point of view. It feels like..." Okay, hold on. **"To think of how to pull the boundaries down."**

Political is a good choice of words, he made "Three Days of the Condor, and "The Interpreter" with Sean Penn.

He just showed me like walls coming down.

To give insight into a different perspective?

Hold on... **He was really an adventurer, he showed me... "To say the least" he says. He was so well traveled, he showed me his view of wanting to experience everything.**

Anything you want me to tell (film director, whom he worked with on "Quiet American") Phillip Noyce?

He pulled his chin... everybody wants to talk to Noyce, so it's funny.

What do they want to tell him?

"Don't wait on your next movie."

To do what? Sydney, is that coming from you?

"Yes. He needs to stick with what he initially wanted to do with it."

With what? A project the two of you were working on?

"Like ten years ago."

"Do it, don't wait on it?" Is that it?

"Yes."

Phillip will know what that means?

"Yeah." There's one project they were going to do, but then he passed. It was only in the beginning phases, he showed me, but also again in 2012.

I'll pass it on. You've met our classmate Amelia, haven't you?

"Yes," he knows. He has the biggest grin.

It's a shame we didn't make her story back when I pitched it to you. You would be having a different experience seeing her now.

He says, "He's still trying to get it made."

I was with Phillip the night before 9/11 when he was about to show the finished cut of "The Quiet American." I didn't realize at the time that they were working together.

"You get around," he says.

You want to be part of our group?

"Yes." They're teaching him how to access us and his family.

How do they help you?

Through (people like) **me – showing him the side of my head and the ability to shift focus. To speak to someone and send them thoughts, sound bites, frequency.**

Anything you want me to tell your daughter(s)?

> (Note: Sydney has two daughters (his son passed away) So not sure which one this is for.)

"To not give up on her work." (Jennifer listens.) Okay, I don't know what it means. **-- It feels like she does research or something like that.**

You mean to not give up on the artistic work?

Feels like music... or something like music.

How do you reach out to her, so she knows you're there? (Or them.)

"Late at night."

Does she sense you?

"She does. She does. Yeah." (She gets) **"The chills."**

I asked you about your and Luana's old friend Dr. Milton Wexler. He was the psychiatrist who had "The group." It was popular in the 70's; "group therapy."

They were trying to show me like a therapy group, I didn't know what it was.

"The group" included Blake Edwards, Dudley Moore, Jennifer Jones, Sydney's wife, Frank Gehry and Luana's best pal Sally Kellerman and her husband Jonathan who produced three of my films. They once got robbed in his office, and the thief didn't realize who these rich famous people were. Some of them gave over their jewels, some hid them. Sally told me recently, the thief said, "If you don't give me all you have, you will all be dead; d-e-d!" She laughed about that later.

He says, "After that, they needed more therapy."

Were you there that night?

"No." He was gone.

Any other messages for your family Sydney? He has two daughters, we talked about his son who passed from the plane crash...

It broke his heart.

I'm sorry, I'm sure it did. I reached out to his daughter recently.

Is she the younger one?

> *(Note: This is accurate) Anything you want me to say to either one?*

"Tell her to breathe." He says she's so worried about things... **Tell her to breathe, something with her ear...** (listens) **One hears him. "Yeah."**

What does she hear you saying?

"Go and don't hold back." She has a feeling; it feels like "don't hold back."

The message is that "You are able to hear him and the message he's trying to tell you is don't hold back." Correct?

"Yes. So when she breathes or takes a moment.. listen." (Jennifer aside) I asked why did you tell her to breathe? He said, **"She's going so fast, that's why she can't hear him."**

So "take her time, perhaps through meditation, open herself up to the possibility of communicating."

"Gain insight."

Any messages to the daughter I reached out to?

He's showing me something with her hand, her pinky... I'm seeing it this way from him... (Pauses) "She needs to write."

I think we talked about that. Do you mean automatic writing? (Asking questions and writing down "whatever you hear.")

"She needs to write."

Is there anything you can say to her that would be a verification that you're talking to us?

"She has to watch her sugar levels."

> *(Note, after reaching out to her and passing along this information, she said this note "couldn't be more true.")*

Rich: How about some memory from her youth?

Jennifer: "She wanted to be a play... when she was young..."

She wanted to be a playwright?

That's what came into my head. **I saw her wanting to be a playwright but wanting to be bossy... so more like being a director.**

Bossy like her dad?

(Jennifer smiles) He says, "**He was *demanding*; not bossy.**"

What were you demanding about?

"Time. Finishing up on time. He was demanding about finishing up on time."

> (Note: Typical director's response. Actually Sydney was pretty famous as a filmmaker for being "on time and under budget." *Ding!)*

So why did you finish up early from this lifetime?

He just showed me smoking. He just sat back, got out a smoke. He's tapping a cigarette like he's taking his time responding.

> (Note: I see this gesture as his reaction to my annoying comment. ("Why'd you leave early?") Not Jennifer's construct; she's never smoked. He "takes out a cigarette, taps it" is often a way of saying "I don't like your question." But I forge ahead anyway.)

What are you smoking by the way?

Looks like a cowboy scene. Red?

Are you smoking Camel straights, Lucky Strikes or Marlboros? (Two are unfiltered, one is not).

I'm getting Marlboro...

You're tapping it because of habit, right?

"Yes."

I mean, I used to smoke, there's no reason to pack or tap a filtered cigarette. People did that with unfiltered cigarettes; he knows that. I'm asking this small detail because it's very specific.

I don't know, I don't smoke.

It's something smokers do – tap their cigarettes or pack. People did it with unfiltered cigarettes to pack the tobacco. Sydney, whenever you were thinking, or being interviewed, you would pull out a cigarette, tap it and smoke? Was that a habit when you were thinking?

"Always."

It's a way of thinking aloud. By the way, are you relaxed talking to us? What's your comfort level?

"90% comfort level."

> (Note: I'm not quite sure why I asked this question, but it popped into my head. I should have followed up on the 10% discomfort he was feeling answering my questions. But it's a bit like "being back home" and suddenly a camera crew shows up at your front door to "ask you questions about your journey."

Rich: Let me ask you - who lights the match?

Jennifer: "It's in your mind."

I know, it's a mental construct. But I'm just curious what is in his mind. Is the light a thing you scrape or a thing you click?

He said, "He's using two rocks." (Jennifer laughs.) **First he showed me someone in** (our) **class lighting it.**

But let me ask, was it lit with a lighter or a match?

"A lighter."

This seems insignificant, I know. But let's look at the lighter. What color is it?

"Red." He's showing me he had like a silver one... he had something professionally made. Like a lighter for cigars.

Okay. Who owns that lighter now?

One of his daughters has it.

Only someone who knows him would be able to verify that. This is why I ask these mundane questions.

He has a great dimple.

Who, Sydney?

Yes.

(That is accurate) You made a great documentary Sydney (about Frank Gehry). Let's have you ask another class member, the fellow who just lit your cigarette, a question. What would you like to ask him?[13]

He asks this other class member, **"Why are there ones who don't get to experience this?"**

Rich: You mean our "class in translation?"

Jennifer: "Yes."

What does the other class member answer?

"Because they don't believe." (Jennifer aside) Wait.. I need to ask. "You mean the other side doesn't believe all the time that they can talk to us?"

You mean some people on the other side don't think they can talk to us or is he talking about people over here on this side?

He's saying... – weird, what I'm feeling is that if you have family here *that don't know* you can talk to other side, their belief system makes it so they can't communicate. They don't believe it, either. And they (on the flipside) **know there's no awareness on either side.**

---

[13] I'm not identifying the class member Jennifer saw light Sydney's cigarette, as his name causes brain freeze. I'm just asking about the construct of "doing the math" to create cigarette and flame.

"Belief" meaning "their loved ones don't believe they can communicate" because they're not listening?

"Yes. Speaking is different than communicating... they always know you can give them signs."

All right, thank you Sydney, you're welcome to sit in anytime. Bye class; see you on the flipside.

*****

This was an experiment in "speaking to someone I met but don't really know." As noted, according to one of his daughters, the information he gave was spot on. According to the film director Phillip Noyce, the letter sent to him was "three weeks prior" to his passing, I did not know he was a "member of group" but researched and found it to be accurate. I find it interesting the question he asked a fellow class member "why doesn't everyone get this kind of exercise in translation?" was unusual... it's the only class of its kind I'm aware of.

Luana in "The Last Detail;" written by Robert Towne, with Randy Quaid, Jack Nicholson, directed by Hal Ashby

CHAPTER THREE

JONATHAN, SALLY & MARLON

"Love is a higher frequency."

Luana's pal Sally Kellerman and her late husband, my pal and producer of three of my films, Jonathan D. Krane and their twins Hannah and Jack

Just after film school, Luana took me to meet her best friend Sally Kellerman. Sally lived in a house up above Coldwater Canyon. She had been nominated for an Oscar for her film "M.A.S.H." and she and Luana had been in acting class together. They remained pals then, and to this day.

Jonathan was a strikingly handsome young lawyer that Sally met in group therapy. He was a successful tax attorney and money manager, who convinced another group member Blake

88

Edwards to start his own production company, Blake Edwards Entertainment.

Jonathan was three years older than me, and it was unusual that Luana and I were 18 years apart, and he and Sally also shared over a decade apart. Jonathan and I became friends, and after USC film school, I was on my way to pitch a film (*"Limit Up"*) to a production company, and I told Jonathan the story I was about to pitch. He said, "I want to buy it."

So my first film deal was with Jonathan, and I became a client of his new company, which managed writers and directors. (Eventually he'd manage Howie Mandel, Paul Feig and John Travolta.) Later, I told Jonathan I was going to direct a short film as a show reel. He suggested he produce it, pay to make it, and we'd split whatever proceeds came from it.

I brought a bunch of my comedy improv friends from the Lembeck Comedy Workshop (Robin Williams was once a member, Steve Harvey and many others) and we made this short film "Video Valentino." Jonathan showed it to Vestron Studios and they agreed to make the feature length version. So in six short months I was directing my first feature film *"You Can't Hurry Love"* which had appearances by Charles Grodin, Christy McNichol, Sally and Jonathan. We made it for a million dollars and it made ten million for Vestron.

Jonathan produced two other films of mine, *"Limit Up"* and *"Point of Betrayal."* He was an eccentric fellow, had a version of Tourette's where he had a tick that he could successfully hide in public, and I'm fond of saying "He'd give me ten ideas in a sentence. Eight would be brilliant and two were shouted at me." I just would ignore the ones I didn't agree with.

89

He had Frank Gehry redesign their home, produced films with Blake Edwards, and a number of John Travolta films, including *"Look Who's Talking"* and *"Face Off."* He was easily the smartest guy in the room whenever he was in a room, but he could be difficult to some folks, and a pain to others. All I know is how he was with me, and it was always as my champion. *Who else has had me make three films?*

Recently, he called to tell me he had raised a film fund for making films, and he wanted me to be part of it. His first film was going to be one he wrote, and asked if I could come and help act out some parts for a reading. We met and his son was in attendance, a handsome young producer in training.

I was shocked when a few weeks later, Jonathan was suddenly felled by a heart attack. A month after, his beautiful daughter suddenly passed – I knew she had been battling addiction for years, but she didn't win that battle.

Needless to say, I was hopeful to reach out to Jonathan at some point in this research. In general I try to just ask *"Who's here?"* when we do a session, but in this case, I thought I'd reach out to someone that I knew on the planet.

*****

Rich: Hello class. Tell me who's here.

Jennifer: They're all here. **I saw a spirit showing me how to focus, putting hands over my ears and moving my head towards them. My dad's here.**

Funny. Jim! What's up?

He's telling me it's my sister's birthday. To tell her happy birthday.

90

Can you see what he's wearing?

Blue shirt, button down shirt. Blue jeans. I can almost smell his cologne. And his boots; cowboy boots.

Jim appears to be about what age?

Older, right before he left.

Rich: Let me ask Jim, how do you manifest clothes?

Jennifer: He took it from my brain – pulled out a memory. (Aside) **Never saw that before.**

So when she sees your shirt, blue jeans – that's a memory she has of that material, or is that your construction?

"Both."

If you could dissolve into light for Jennifer what color would she see?

"Blue."

Is it flat, matte color?

Bright blue like his eyes. It became pink, then went away, then came back.

So it's moving?

I asked, "Did you create the color blue or did I?" He said he did... – but it's also something I've seen on him.

You both have to make an adjustment, to see that color, right?

"Yes." Morton is here.

So Michael, you threw a book against the wall to get our attention recently, and you asked me to contact your institute – I did. Anything you want to add about that?

"Yes." He says, "I want to say not to judge it."

What does that mean? Not to judge his response or what it was I was contacting them about?

"Either."

How enigmatic. Okay, "Don't judge the answer." I wanted to invite our old friend, Jonathan, who was an attorney, film producer... who checked off the planet suddenly.

"Heart attack." I felt his chest. It felt abrupt.

That's correct. (Ding!) And his daughter Hannah a month after from a drug issue... so Jonathan, your wife Sally and I were having lunch a couple of weeks ago.

He was there. This is "Hot Lips," right?

Rich: (Startled) How did you know that?

Jennifer: She just appeared.

> (Note: Sally starred in the film version of "M.A.S.H." creating the role of "Hot Lips Houlihan." *(ding!)*)

Rich: Sally and I had lunch and I asked who was taking care of his estate. Where do their residuals go?

Feels like a son gets those. **He has beautiful eyes.**

Jonathan produced three of my films; the only person on the planet who appreciated my work as a filmmaker.

"And then some... and he's appreciative of what you're doing with Sally."

Well Luana and Sally were best friends.

They danced a lot together, "It's collective," they said.

Anything you want me to tell your son?

"Tell him to slow down. On life."

I think we did mention something to him about too much vaping.

He just showed smoke going in one ear and out the other. Were their children adopted?

Yes, both were. You and I spoke to their daughter when she crossed over after Jonathan. She gave us the name of the drug they would find in her system (she was in recovery, it was an accident) and she told us when she sends butterflies in the direction of her mom, brother or step sister Claire, that's her way of saying "I'm still here." Why did you ask about being adopted?

It's just something to keep an eye on; some people carry that "excessive" gene that comes from their birth parents.

Okay. He's probably aware of that. Luana, what's going on?

"Herding cats to get here." She shows me like putting a lasso out there.

Who's the most reluctant to show up?

Billy. Actually he's one of the first, he was kidding around.

Billy, I got an email from your pal the actor the other day and I sent him your note.

He said, "It was perfect."

I sent him a clip of our conversations, he said it it was painful and powerful to watch.

Wow. Billy said, "We believe in you."

You're the only ones. Listen guys, how are we going to make this class or dialog part of the common language? We need your help to make this into something valuable for the planet.

Luana put her finger in front of her mouth... hold on.

She's shushing me? What else is new?

(To Luana: Thank you.) **She showed me language, the whole language thing, she showed me we're all collectively doing what we can to make sure that this comes about in various ways. The more that gets out... it's like, 'If you see it, if you hear it enough times, it's getting out a lot more. People are talking about it... belief still gets in the way or lack of belief, but they're working on it."**

You've said, "the best communicator to heaven is the heart." So how do we talk to the heart?

They just showed me *my* heart...

How do you open the pathway with your mind to open the heart?

(Jennifer asks, "Show me again, please?") **"You let go of the how."**

"Let go of the how?"

94

"It's like having a cell service, you know you're connected to the internet, so you're not worried about it."

So just "dial."

"Envision the person you want to talk to and just dial."

> (Note: In "Flipside" I interviewed lifelong pal Howard Schultz, prolific producer of TV shows like "Extreme Makeover" and others. He did a three hour between life session with Scott De Tamble. An avowed skeptic, Howard went to some amazing places (including a lifetime during the Holocaust that ended in Dachau.) The chapter is called "River of Souls."
>
> But at one point during his sessions, as noted earlier, he was speaking to his mother who had passed away. She said to him "*Howard,* it's like your cell phone. You pick it up and push buttons and your loved one answers. You have no idea how that happens.
>
> Reaching out to us in the afterlife is the same – you *just think of us* and if we aren't busy we'll get back to you. We hear you when you think of us, it's just not easy to reply." Howard passed away a few years after that interview, and has appeared often in our class.)

How about addressing larger concepts? Like the environment or world peace?

"Send out the change you want to see, through your heart energy, and then visualize it being changed."

You're saying, "Don't focus on the how?"

"No." They just showed me someone taking your hand.

So you could say "Could my spirit guide help access this energy and put it in the right place?"

"Yes. That's it."

Could you use Jesus or some avatar that you believe in to assist, or would that water it down?

"No, use it. It's very powerful, that frequency has a bigger bandwidth. Choose an avatar that you know that you think will be able to help."

You're trying to affect the change, using an avatar is a way of opening your heart to affect that change?

"Yes."

Whether it's Beethoven or Aunt Betty; doesn't matter?

What is interesting is that I saw that by doing that, you're sending the energy up to that avatar; they're basically helping to get it to where it needs to go.

Because people call on Jesus or other avatars for help all the time.

"Yes." (Touches her nose.) **"Love is a higher frequency."**

If you are going to make a wish or prayer, attach love to it? Let love be the vehicle that rides this prayer into the universe?

"Right. Don't attach it but feel it."

I'm just asking, if love has a higher frequency, if tuning into love allows you to have greater access...

They're trying to get you away from *terminology*. I know you have to explain it, but it's quicker to just envision it. Then you'll start getting pictures that will come into your mind, and you can dive in further deeper with those.

And allow whoever the icon is to be the icon. Jesus the gardener, or Krishna the avatar, or Buddha, Tara.

"Right."

Who wants to speak up over there from class?

Billy Paxton wanted to say something. **"Tell Rich to not worry how to get this work out... these books out... everyone's interested in it."**

I was going through what Harry Dean told us the other day. It was awesome.

Harry Dean said, "I win."

Harry, I think you've opened up their minds a bit.

He showed me they had to open up... showing me how we are opening up our minds, here in this restaurant.

Yeah.

It's like trying to get other people's awareness that don't believe in this; it's like trying to blow out a candle that won't blow out.

Ha. Funny. You mean it's going to take a lot more time for people to realize that they can get through somebody?

They said, "No, it's possible. They feel better when they open up."

Like Harry said, it was a waste of energy to argue about the afterlife; if you allow yourself to believe in the possibility, it saves time.

They're all laughing about that one.

It occurs to me some of the people we've talked to in the past are reluctant to speak. Harry Dean knew Brando for example. When we spoke to Harry he was effusive, when we chatted with Marlon, he didn't have much to say.

> (Note: In a previous session, we had a brief exchange.)

"He didn't talk in life!"

But I wonder if that is because of his reflecting upon things that he did in life that were troublesome.

"Yes."

So he's not ready yet to come and joke around with us?

"No."

Can we help those people?

"Yeah, but he would never do that here (on the planet), **so they won't do it back there** (on the flipside). **So whatever his idea of fun or entertainment would be;** (it's) **what he wants to do."**

Like hanging out with his pal Wally Cox.

"Yeah."

> (Note: Luana knew one of Brando's close friends, Sam Gilman, who I met a few times. Character actor

98

who appeared in Marlon's films, Sam would report he was hanging out with Marlon and Wally Cox (the character actor "Mr. Peepers" and "Underdog.") Brando was quoted as saying "If Wally had been a woman, I would have married him and we would have lived happily ever after" admitting Wally was "the love of his life." They met as preteens in Chicago.)[14]

Rich: Well, let's see if Marlon can answer a couple of questions for us. Marlon, I have some of your ashes in my house. I've also seen his will and was aware there were some issues with it.[15]

He has a daughter right? I'm seeing three kids. (Note: There are 9 out of wedlock, 12 in total, including an adoptee) **There's a child nobody knows about that should get something. I feel like there's someone who deserves...** (Laughs) **I just asked him "Was it a child from a woman you slept with?" And he showed me thousands.**

How old does he look to you?

He's very handsome. He says, "In his Copacabana days." about 55...

Age 55? Or 1955...

---

[14] http://articles.latimes.com/2004/oct/17/entertainment/ca-brando17
In light of Brando's bisexuality, Wally married three times. What's interesting in light of this research is how little sexuality has to do with reports of unconditional love.
[15] https://nypost.com/2004/08/26/brandos-estate-proves-heir-splitting/

The year (1955).

> (Note: Jennifer doesn't know what "Copacabana" refers to, I thought it was a film until I researched it. 1955 was the heyday of the Copacabana club in NYC where Sinatra performed, and Brando held court.) [16]

Oddly enough, I've seen your will, Marlon. Someone left a copy under a chair in the home next to yours and I have a friend who has a copy that was mailed after your passing. It's clear it wasn't your signature on it, it was signed two weeks prior to your passing when you were in hospital suffering from emphysema. The single Notary who witnessed it, wrote on the will that they didn't see you sign it. I heard later the will was contested but the statute of limitations had run out. Is that something you're interested in people pursuing?

He says, **"He had two love children... and there were two ex-wives** (that were) **contesting the will."**

So Marlon, do you care about your island?

He's showing me a pair of shiny shoes. He says he, "Cared a lot about shoes."

I'll take that as a "no." Who are you hanging out with? Is Wally Cox hanging out with you?

He showed me... (Jennifer asks, "Why are you showing me Steve Martin?") He's saying, **"That for his next role in life he wants to be a comedian."**

> (Note: This is a common refrain. When we get back home with our loved ones, we reportedly work out

---

[16] https://en.wikipedia.org/wiki/Copacabana_(nightclub)

who or what we're going to be the next time around. They claim it's up to us if we want to come back as well as what role we're going to play, with guidance from our guides and loved ones, or soul mates.)

You were best friends with the comedian Wally Cox, and you often said you wanted to trade places with him. Are you guys hanging out?

(Jennifer giggles.) I love hearing Marlon's voice, sorry. Um... **They were very close. Did Wally die of a heart attack?**

Yes, at age 49. (Ding!) Well, people have said they thought they were so close, they were lovers. Sally Kellerman told me she had a massive crush on Marlon, then one night, he came into La Poubelle where she worked as a waitress, and he took her home. No one believed it happened. Is it true they didn't sleep together?

He just made a **"tiny gesture." Like "a little bit."**

Meaning you chased her around all night, or she chased you?

He's laughing.

Anybody else want to come forward?

Your mom.

My mother Anthy. Are you playing the piano over there?

    (Note: Mom was a concert pianist.)

Mmhm... She's playing piano for your uncle there.

    (Note: Earlier in this conversation, my cousin Mary Vey had come through, who had just passed. We talked about her handsome dad, my uncle "Rig" who

101

purchased a concert grand piano for my mom to play at their estate in Ohio. Their home had 40 foot tall ceilings, and hearing her play on a summer's eve was a bit like being in Carnegie Hall.)

Mom tell me about playing the piano over there. How do you create that?

"It's the frequency, through mathematical equations. It's not nearly as fun to play here (as it is over there back on earth)**, but you can do it by thinking of a frequency."**

By doing so, can you create a piano? All 88 keys?

"Yes."

Let me ask, what piano do you choose to create? Is it a concert grand or a spinet? Is it short or long?

First I saw an etheric image of a piano with lots of layers, and then I got shown an antique piano.

Is the piano you are playing a piano that you knew during your lifetime?

"Yes. Her first piano... the one she knew as a child."

There was a famous Cuban piano teacher who taught you how to play in college. Have you seen him?

"Yes." She's saying, "In her life music was everything." She says, "It affected all of her connections."

And we've heard that music is an amplification system to talk to the flipside, is that right?

"Yes. It's a higher frequency."

Let me ask you an off the wall question. Your father was in the office of Naval Intelligence during World War II. Was your father the source of my investigating Amelia's Earhart's story all these years, even though he passed a month after I was born?[17]

"Yes." There's someone else with your grandfather.

His wife Mimi, I imagine. I've dreamt about visiting them at their home in Chicago – a home I was never in, but when I described the place to my brother, he said "that was their home over Lincoln Park."

He's showing me Amelia.

Okay, that makes sense. I imagine this setting is getting crowded with all these people.

They tell me, **"They're learning over there."**

Learning what?

(Jennifer listens) **"Learning the different waves of energy to go through...** (to navigate) **through different dimensions, to make the energies get through to the energy to manifest here."**

Okay. So you strengthen the energy to make it manifest here?

---

[17] Navy Commander Edward A Hayes. Assistant Secretary of the Navy to Frank Knox 1940-44. During the period when the US found Earhart's plane on Saipan, he was in "CinqPaq" the naval headquarters in the Pacific with Admiral Nimitz, who famously told investigator Fred Goerner "You're on the right track with regard to Earhart being on Saipan. Keep looking."

They're showing me that by coming together with a group, like family members -- they are able to sustain the connection way longer than they normally would.

So the group helps amplify the signal?

Yes. It's like a cellphone tower.

It's like when my friend Iris did a deep hypnosis session and saw herself between lives in a classroom that was learning how to lift giant objects, like slabs of rock. There were 28 people in class and she said "This is a class in learning to share energy as a group. I can lift the rock myself, just thinking about it, but we're teaching how all 28 need to work together to lift he rock." She said, "It's not a class in how to lift rocks, but how to get the group to lift the rock together."

"Yes, the collective is always stronger than the individual."

So when we pray, and ask for guidance, we should ask everyone to show up?

"Yes."

Hmm. (Joking) What's an app I can use to do that?

They showed me ancestry.com to find names. That's how I connect – I need to get their name to get a hold of the person.

It makes sense; a person's name is a place holder of their energy; if you're searching for someone you need a name.

Having the name makes me feel more secure as well.

Like we asked Morton, "Should we say the name of the person we want to speak with aloud?" He said, "It doesn't matter."

You can think of colors as well. Like, "What's the first color you associate with that person?" And when you get that color, you draw upon that color and bring it in to you.

What about this thing of people believing they can manifest wealth through intention or prayer?

That means you have to give it away in order for it to be replaced. The more positive energy you give away, the more it returns to you.

I'm including the idea that you may have a spiritual path that may not include gaining wealth in this lifetime, so it it would be worthless to try to attract money if it's not part of the path that you signed up for.

My dad Jim showed up. He's showing me how these things aren't brought to us through intent – we may have signed up to learn different lessons. Where you put your intentions, it results in things that come to you.

Once you start to redefine what money or wealth is – wealth may come in terms of health or some other way... Once you redefine what wealth really is - then whatever comes to you should come to you.

They're giving you standing ovation for that observation.

Rich: Like I asked your dad, Jim, about how people manifest "making a drink" with friends over there. They have to agree on the bar as well as the bartender.

Jennifer: They made a joke... "It's like a "party line" (over here) **A frequency** (signal) **goes out like "It's a party!"**

A 976 party line on the flipside. I think it's funny to hear about people manifesting objects, homes, classes, even cigars.

They don't need to.

But they do because it's fun. Am I right that some people smoke all the time over there?

"Yes."

But it's unusual to see. Ghosts smoking.

They know the frequency of it.

Even if they died of lung cancer they can continue smoking, having fun with the manifestation of it.

"Yeah."

I was thinking that by examining this stuff as we do, we can change our future by examining the past.

Morton just said, "It works."

We alter our past when we examine previous lives. Not "changing the fabric of time" but by seeing we chose those lifetimes to learn lessons, we then alter our memory of having suffered in a previous lifetime. It's not suffering if its a lesson we chose to learn; it's learning. By changing our "past" be accessing it, understanding it, we change our present and our future.

"Yes." I just got the chills. Wow.

106

If you can observe your lifetime in the past, whatever it was, and see that it was part of your blueprint, creating who you are - you can see why it was completely necessary to go through whatever it is we've gone through.

"And see the love."

By seeing the love that existed in that lifetime, you've now altered that past. So this research alters your past, it affects your present and can change your future.

"It alters your frequency. It makes it lighter."

So you're not carrying that stress. Sorry guys, there's the bell. We've got to go, see you next time you on the flipside.

*****

Luana and Vicente Price (*Pit and the Pendulum*; Photo courtesy Roger Corman)

CHAPTER FOUR:

STEPHEN HAWKING, GARRY SHANDLING, CHRISTOPHER HITCHENS

"Black holes and the infinite" and the ultimate atheist afterlife party.

Photo: Nasa

As noted, Jennifer and I generally don't reach out to people we don't know. However, in editing this book, I notice that each time we've asked Luana for someone to "show up", Jennifer says something along the lines of - "she just yanked him in here."

In light of that, I was thinking about Stephen Hawking's recent passing. But not from the aspect of "Gee, I wonder if he's out of his wheelchair?" I know that he's out of his wheelchair, as the thousands of cases I've examined, the 45 between life sessions I've filmed, and the countless testimonials that Jennifer has given me in her sessions attest to knowing that "*Stephen's okay. He's fine. He's just adjusting.*"

This following conversation occurred about a month after his passing. I decided to include some other famous atheists – just to see if it was possible. Prior to this conversation I "asked for" (said their names aloud) of a number of people that I wanted to see if we could chat with.

****

Rich: Okay, we decided to see if we could do something unusual. We're going to interview someone neither Jennifer or I know, or have ever met, and are not aware that any of our group members know.

Jennifer: I did ask them if we could do this. I got (we will be) **"shooting to his frequency." That was the visual that was given to me.**

Shooting to his frequency? Whose?

Stephen Hawking.

(Ding! I had yet to mention his name.) We know it's easier to communicate with people we know. But we are going to try an experiment.

I know nothing about him other than...

He had a "Brief history of time." (Name of his book)

And he had that disease... what was it? Lou Gehrig's disease?

I think that's correct.[18] But we're not going to try to speak about his career or the stuff that is common knowledge, but we want to ask him about his journey or path. That is, if we can access it. Class? Who's here?

That was interesting, Luana brought forward Stephen, but he is standing. He is very handsome.

About how old is he?

"About 29," he said.

Is he wearing glasses?

No glasses. He just looks healthy, vibrant, that's what I'm being shown. I'm asking, "Is he 29 or 19?" They said, "he's 29." I asked if this was when he had the disease...

> (Note: I also listened later to Dr. Elisa Medhus interviewing Hawking via a medium at ChannelingErik.com She also said the same physical things here; that he looked 29, no glasses, etc.)

As we know, from our research, we appear as we'd like to appear on the flipside.

I'm being told he did have it when he was 29...

But let's talk about your path and journey - first of all welcome to our class, Stephen.

(Jennifer smiles) **He finds this fascinating.**

---

[18] "Stephen Hawking had a rare early-onset slow-progressing form of motor neuron disease (also known as amyotrophic lateral sclerosis, "ALS", or Lou Gehrig's disease), that gradually paralyzed him over the decades" Wikipedia

From your point of view, who do you see in our class? Just us or others?

He just showed me the tops of our heads; an aerial view.

Can you see any of the members of our class?

"It's frequencies, it belted out to like..." I asked him, "How many would you say?" **He said, "In all dimensions."** I asked, "One hundred?" **He said "No, hundreds of thousands of people."** I asked, "In this dimension?" **He said, "In all dimensions."**

What's that answer in response to?

(The question) **"If he can see our class."**

Are there other galaxies and dimensions that he can access or that access him?

"Both."

Have you talked to anyone back here since you checked off the planet?

"Yes." His wife.

> (Note: Stephen married Jane Wilde, 1965, divorced 1995. They had three children, Robert, Lucy and Timothy.)

I think he was married three times... which wife did you reach out to?

"First wife." He's laughing; **"I wasn't the easiest person to get along with."**

111

I know, you did have difficulty, but you spent a lot of time together. You were very close, you had kids together.

"Three."

I think that's right. (It is. Ding!) Who was there to greet you when you crossed over or what was the process of crossing over?

He says, "I didn't believe there was a cross over." I asked, "Did you believe in the afterlife?" and he said **"No, I believed in the universe." He's being literal. Showing me that he didn't "cross" anything.**

I'm aware that he was famous for being an atheist and didn't believe in an afterlife. But can you tell us, what was the process? Did you see anyone from the other side before you died?

He did see people before he died. He said he saw his caregiver. (She) looked kind of like a nanny, she took care of him when he was first sick... felt like, a long time ago, as a young man. She greeted him with a smile.

Did you realize you were in the afterlife or did you think you were in a dream?

"I didn't feel like I was in the afterlife." He says he was realizing he was not understanding where he was... or what he was coming to. It was a "dream within a dream." Luana just showed me the example of the car as a reference.

> (Note: In Harry Dean Stanton's story in Book One, he claimed that Luana showed up prior to his death, which he thought was a hallucination. Then when he

found himself in a car with her, he thought he had "fallen into a dream" of their trip to the Monterey Pop festival in 1967. At some point in the journey, they suddenly had a flat tire, and as he was fixing the tire, he said "Wait a second, we didn't have a flat tire during this trip. So this isn't a dream." And the driver replied, "I know." Harry said Luana had given him a "soft landing" by making it appear as if he was in a dream, but then made him realize it wasn't a dream.)

Rich: Right, so then what happened?

Jennifer: "I was met with such *love*."

By friends and family; people you knew or didn't know?

By both; people he knew or recognized from the past and family members.

Was it that feeling of love that made you realize you were in another place?

Jennifer touches her nose as if to say, "right on the money." (Aside) I only get that in our classroom discussions with Luana.

Once you realized where you were and that the laws of the physics of this place were different, what did you think? Or what have you been doing in terms of your adventure since then?

(Jennifer laughs.) **He says "I'm taking a break from not having to do anything. I was so focused. I was so focused on the universal existence. I didn't think there would be a continuance in the way we view it."**

You're saying there is (an afterlife) or there is not?

"I did not think there was a continuance. Of how people viewed the universe. Or god."

In terms of the concept of God; have you had the experience of "opening your heart to everyone and all things?" Is that the unconditional love that we've heard about?

"Yes." (Jennifer aside) **I asked him, "Did you call it (that experience) God?" He said "No."**

> (Note: in the discussion of "God" it becomes a brain freeze moment or a religious moment to discuss "God" for most people. In this research I've consistently heard that God is not an object or a person, but a mechanism or a medium, the way consciousness appears to function. The response I reported in "It's a Wonderful Afterlife" to *"What or who is God?"* was "God is beyond the capacity of the human brain to comprehend. It's just not physically possible, **but you can experience God by opening your heart to everyone and all things."** By taking this answer literally – that God is an *experience* of unconditional love rather than an object, I find its easier to refer to "God" as an "experience" to avoid full religious brain freeze.)

But for the purpose of our understanding that word that we use (to refer to God) - am I correct in saying God is not a physical object?

I asked him, "Is God a physical person?" and he said "No." He said, "It's the frequency of the heart."

114

Let me ask you about consciousness; please correct me if I'm wrong. My theory is that consciousness is not an object but a medium or mechanism to understand what is going on.

Funny, he just showed *me*... and then he showed me *my heart*... and he showed the frequency of my heart, how it acts like a boomerang.

So, consciousness is not an object but it's a like a frequency?

"Yes." That's why he showed me my heart. (As an example of consciousness being the "frequency of the heart.")

We talked about this before, that ricochet or boomerang effect, of sending out love, and feeling a wave that comes from the heart; we send it out and the frequency comes back to us like an echo... But maybe he doesn't want to talk about this topic, we may not have enough time.

"It is time."

It is time?

"Yes. It's so esoteric that many people won't get the concept..." and he just showed me the word *"terminology"* and just showed me the word going "poof." (Meaning *don't focus on the terminology*.)

Since you've been back there, have you visited a black hole?

"Yes."

What was your impression?

"Infinite."

What's the function of a black hole? A portal to another universe or realm?

115

"Neither." (Jennifer pronounced the word as "nigh-ther" rather than the way she normally says "nee-ther.") **"It's a way that people from all dimensions get to communicate without any static."**

Well, that would be a portal, wouldn't it? For people to communicate through?

"Terminology." He just showed the word again (and waves her hands as if it was being blasted away.)

All right, let's bounce around a bit. Stephen, did you know or ever meet Christopher Hitchens?

> (Note: Jennifer has no idea who this is.)

"Yes."

Can you bring him forth for us, so we can have a conversation with Christopher?

He said, "No. Because that means I would believe in the afterlife."

Hahaha. Very funny.

> (Note: After Christopher Hitchens passed, the New Yorker ran a cartoon of a man on a psychiatrist couch saying, "I had a dream last night Christopher Hitchens came from the afterlife to tell *there is no after life*."
>
> This is an opportune moment to remind the reader that no one has claimed during any of these reports that any religion is accurate or correct about the afterlife, or even about a god or an existence of God.

In fact, every report is contradictory to the dogma expressed **by religion, every philosophy**. These reports are not saying anyone, including atheists are wrong or should "believe in God" – no one has been able to define God or consciousness accurately. "All roads lead to home."

During these interviews, we've often heard atheists express they wished they hadn't "wasted time to argue about it." From Wikipedia's entry on Hitchens: "As an anti-theist he regarded the concept of a god or supreme being as a totalitarian belief that impedes individual freedom. He argued that free expression and scientific discovery should replace religion as a means of informing ethics and defining codes of conduct for human civilization. The dictum "What can be asserted without evidence can be dismissed without evidence" has become known as Hitchens's razor." Wikipedia)[19]

I want to ask Christopher about his friend who jumped off the Golden Gate Bridge? Is he aware of that?

(Note: This is a detail not known by the public in general, just one of those odd things I happen to know via someone who knew this person in Palo Alto where Hitchens once lived.)

"Yes, they're all together."

Who greeted you as you crossed over?

I want to say a daughter.

---

[19] https://en.wikipedia.org/wiki/Christopher_Hitchens

What was the mechanism for you? At what point did you realize that you were in the afterlife?

It was seeing that daughter – I don't know if she was born, she may have been a miscarriage, but she was someone that he saw that he knew that felt very familiar.

(Note: Hitchens had three children, a son and two daughters still living. His mother committed suicide when she was 50. Sometimes, people claim to encounter a child who didn't make the journey (Harry Dean Stanton seeing a "child" in his hospital room, and telling us a week prior that this was his child from a miscarriage), sometimes we're greeted by the conscious energy of person's "higher self" including people who are still alive on the planet – but roughly two thirds of their energy is always *"back home."* (I.e., "I'm seeing my mother, during my near death experience, but she's still alive.")

I try not to judge whatever comes through but report it verbatim. Hitchens does **not** have a daughter who died before him, *("Great! Now I can return this damned book!")* however, Jennifer heard him refer to "his daughter." If I (or Jennifer) had "looked him up" prior to inviting him, we would have known that detail.)[20]

---

[20] "He took pains to emphasize that he had not revised his position on atheism, articulated in his best-selling 2007 book, "God Is Not Great: How Religion Poisons Everything," although he did express amused appreciation at the hope, among some concerned Christians, that he might undergo a late-life conversion."

Rich: Since you've been back there, what kind of things have you been observing? I know it doesn't seem like very long time for you. (He passed in December of 2011 at 62 of a brain tumor)

Jennifer: "Things popping up..." He showed me things... (uses her hands) **like people popping "up."**

Oh, so you've observed people coming from here to there? Have you greeted anyone? They must be startled to see you.

"Yes." Did he have a grandson that died?

Don't know. I have a friend who told me about the suicide of Christopher's friend. Can you tell us anything about that path or journey with that person?

> (Note: A close friend told me about this friend in Palo Alto; it doesn't appear to be public knowledge. I gave my friend a copy of "Flipside" to pass along to the family of this friend of Christopher's. I searched Christopher's life story to see if he had a grandson who passed, as I did, I heard *"godson"* and on a hunch tried that search. Turns out he had a godchild in Zimbabwe, though don't know if it was a boy or girl or if they're still on the planet.) [21]

---

https://www.nytimes.com/2011/12/16/arts/christopher-hitchens-is-dead-at-62-obituary.html

[21] "I'm fairly globalized: My father was Anglo-Celtic; my first wife is Greek; my second wife's family came from Odessa or thereabouts, and I have a godchild in Zimbabwe..."
https://forward.com/culture/148147/the-part-jewish-question-double-the-pleasure-or-t/

Jennifer: They're comparing notes. He put on boxing gloves.

Rich: Who are you boxing with?

His friend who jumped.

You guys like to box over there? Is your friend okay?

"He's way better." He just gave me a rainbow – I don't know know what that means, but perhaps his friend had trouble with sexual issues.

Christopher, what's it like to box or be hit on the flipside? What's that feel like?

He's showing me it's a frequency; if you think of two dials, and one you turn up for pressure, and the other you turn up for feeling. Like you turn it all the way up for the most feeling, and then you feel it... It gives you the sensations (of boxing.)[22]

> (Note: It's likely the last thing many would associate with this famous journalist; boxing. However, according to his autobiography, Hitchens reluctantly boxed in a school at "Mount House School" but remembered it all his life, writing in 2010; **"I had my socks knocked off me in the ring, but why do I remember it after half a century?"**)

Rich: You feel it on your head? On your body?

---

[22] Hitchens reluctantly boxed in a school tournament at "Mount House School." ("Hitch-22 A Memoir" by Christopher Hitchens. Hachette Book Group. 2010.)

Jennifer: "It's a great way to practice, if you turn it all the way down you can do the motions but you don't feel it, but if you turn it all the way up the action becomes more profound." He's trying to show me how to increase the power...

Like amplifying?

"Yes."

That's unusual. Thanks for that. I just wanted to gather a few atheists together to talk about the afterlife. Allow me to introduce you all to Harry Dean Stanton, a fellow atheist who is part of our class.[23]

They know Harry Dean. They loved "Big Love."[24] And your buddy Billy came through and said, "Of course they did."

Stephen what would you like us to impart to your fans or friends who miss and love you, or even people who don't believe in the afterlife? What would you like us to tell them?

Tell them *not to*. (Jennifer aside: "Not to what?") **"Tell them not to fight how we live and die. Eternity exists if you believe it exists."** I asked him, **"What about atheists?"** and he said, he's showing me... He said, **"Atheists get black holes as their heaven."**

Ha. Very funny. So back to black holes for a second.

"It's terminology," he keeps saying.

---

[23] For his last days, Carol Blue wrote about them eloquently
[24] Began airing in 2006 on HBO

I understand, but as you mentioned, its function is a portal or some kind of a communication hub, so people can communicate, so that means... therefore...

"That there is a bigger existence. Yes."

Anti-matter goes through a black hole, is that correct?

"Yes."

> (Note: We asked this question to Julian Baird after I heard it was a key question from physicist Michio Kaku. *"Why is there more matter than anti matter in the universe?"* which was answered in Julian's chapter.)

Rich: People in other realms have their own experience relating to black holes?

Jennifer: "Yes. They feel the frequencies from all of it." I asked, "Are you famous elsewhere or here?" He said, **"I am in the hearts that know me."**

Let's ask you about your journey and path – before you came to the planet did you know that you were going to have ALS and chose this life anyway so that you could focus on the stuff you learned?

"Yes." He's like **"I just didn't know how difficult it would be."** He's saying it was hard on other people, his first wife. He's still in love with his first wife. **"Very strongly,"** he says.

The thing you want us to impart to your friends and fans is to not fear death?

He said **"Don't fear anything. And allow the multiverse to come through you."**

How do we do that?

He just showed me a cutout of a person – that you can hold up, so it's a bunch of people but the same person (a paper doll chain). **He's showing that as an example of all of our past lives. "You and your past lives, everyone lined up – they exist in all of those dimensions with one heart."**

Being able to access all of yourself, to access your other lifetimes in order to access other realms? Cool. So, Stephen, you chose this lifetime, correct?

"Yes."

Why did you choose this difficult lifetime?

(Jennifer smiles.) **He's funny. He said, "Because they had toilets." He said having conveniences meant he wouldn't die as a child. He said it allowed him to have enough longevity to make people think and believe in the stars relative to their own beliefs.**

A few weeks ago, just before you passed, you published a paper about multiverse. Do we live in a multiverse?[25]

"Yes."

How do you feel about that paper now? "Just terminology?"

"It was my last attempt to not to be face to face with... or to come to grips with what was going to happen."

---

[25] Stephen Hawking submitted a final paper days before his death." USA Today. https://www.usatoday.com/story/tech/nation-now/2018/03/19/stephen-hawking-submitted-final-paper-days-before-his-death-and-could-lead-discover-parallel-univers/437237002/

A last attempt of not coming to terms with... one last way of putting off...

"Yes, not coming to terms with an afterlife."

Did you have a near death experience in your life?

"Twice."

> (Note: It wasn't something I was aware of, just popped into my head. During a bout with pneumonia, he reported that he had a "near death experience.")[26]

Rich: During your NDE, did you consciously experience anything other than your body, did you fly around?

Jennifer: He says he "Thought it was a dream at the time, something he didn't understand. Later, he tried to map it, make like a grid, tried to make it tangible – and it came as something to do with the stars."

Since you've been back there, have you been able to visit with any of your heroes or examine any of your lifetimes?

Apollo? **He showed me a Greek god of some sort.**

What's his name? Is this a person?

He then showed me a Trojan. Like "Tommy Trojan" at USC.

> (Note: Listening to Dr. Medhus' interview with Hawking, via Veronica Drake. **With her, he recalled a lifetime as a Roman prelate.** A number of other details are similar. He claimed that he had been wrong

---

[26] https://www.theguardian.com/science/2014/jul/07/stephen-hawking-near-death-pneumonia-1980s)

about the content of black holes, and used the term portal to describe their function. He also said that the big bang was not a singular event, or that there was a specific God per se. But he did talk about consciousness being the "same thing as God" in his interview with Dr. Medhus. It's the same thing Jennifer and I have been hearing from various people – that "God" is the "connection that is between all people, and for a more specific term to use the word "love" or "Unconditional love.")

Did you live in that era of Troy and the Trojan wars? (Taking a wild guess, knowing USC's mascot is a fighting Trojan).

"Yes."

So in a sense, you have been able to reconnect with old friends?

They didn't like him then. He showed me war.

Then didn't like him? Why?

"He was a warrior, not caring about life."

Were you a good at war, a good warrior?

"Yes, very decorated."

What country were you in, Greece?

He's showing me Germany.

What era was this? A long time ago or more recently? Or have you had many warrior lifetimes?

I've had many but am remembering one in particular - I'm getting 1602 but it's negative. Like BCE.

125

(Note: In the interview with Dr. Medhus, he also remembered being a soldier in that era.)

I understand. Before the common era – the Bronze Age.... Who were you fighting against?

"Everybody." (Jennifer makes a frown) **He showed me women and children dying.**

(Note: It's common in people reporting previous lives, they lived the "polar opposite" of another lifetime at another time. Michael Crichton revealed in his autobiography "Travels" that he remembered a lifetime as a Gladiator; a detail I think influenced his later film "Westworld.")[27]

(Jennifer frowns). **Now I'm not going to like him.** (She listens) **Oh!** (As a reply) **He just showed me the era when I was in Salem dunking women thought to be witches.**

(Note: Jennifer is making a point and the person she's speaking to "projects" or "pulls" from her memory an image that can be used as a metaphor to understand what she's seeing. In this case, Jennifer remembered (as reported in *"Hacking the Afterlife"*) a life where she tortured "witches" back in the Salem era. He's reminding her, so she would not misjudge Hawking's memory of a life as a brutal warrior.)

---

[27] The term "Germanic" referred to the tribal groups and alliances that lived in (Northern Europe.) The Nordic Bronze Age is a period of Scandinavian prehistory from c. 1700–500 BC... (Wikipedia) Troy was under siege in 1250 BC. (Brittanica.com)

In your between lives realm, who's your guide? A man or a woman or neither? Can we meet your guide?

He first showed me Jesus, then I saw Buddha; he said it was "That same frequency."

You're saying your guides or your members of your council have that avatar frequency? How many people are on your council?

He said "Three, but (they're) **on a higher level."**

You're saying like a "council's council?"

"Yes." Wow, that's the first time I've seen that.

> Note: It's in a few cases I've reported; people claim to have had access to, or seen "higher councils." Every person has a guide, and a council that helps them evaluate how they did during their lifetime. But I've heard that council members also have their own councils and counselors. Kind of super intelligent, wise souls. He's had so many unusual lifetimes to say the least, so makes sense to me.

"He's saying that you invited five people today?"

*That is correct. (Ding! Before our meeting, I often say aloud the name of the person I'm asking to show up. In this case in my car, I said five names.) I was thinking of what atheists I might invite, I thought of my old professor Julian Baird who we've talked to before, Harry Dean Stanton, perhaps Christopher Hitchens and Stephen. Wait, there's one more. Oh, by the way, how about **Ricky Gervais?** He's a famous atheist. Christopher, did you meet Ricky?*

127

"Yes." He has.

He's a terrific humorist, like yourself Christopher. Any message from you for that famous atheist?

He says **"Tell him to keep it up. It makes people search within for what their beliefs really are. It's keeping them "in the question," even the ones that are angry.**

Even the ones that are upset, that's a good thing?

"It only means he's popular."

What do you want me to tell Ricky?

"That he's *easy access.*"

Christopher, your message to Ricky Gervais is... "Keep it up" and "You're easy access?" Sounds like sex references.

"To not back down. It's not about jokes; it's about the frequency." He says, "Ricky, you can't love cats and not believe in the afterlife. If you love cats, then you must know that they see things that are not there." So he must know there's *something up* beyond cats. Without hesitation, without reservation, Ricky is like a pitchfork – (Jennifer aside: "No pun intended, he's showing me a pitchfork") **- and Ricky challenges people in the best way without them resorting to war."**

> (Note: Ricky Gervais is an important animal rights activist; posts about it often. As to "atheism;" no one in this research (people under hypnosis, or speaking from the flipside) claims any form of man-made religion is "accurate." They often say many are "wrong," use it to "have power over others" but they

offer "all spirituality leads to the same truth" (about "unconditional love" being the normal state of being on the flipside.) That's not my opinion, theory or belief; it's just what they consistently say.)

Stephen, there are people suffering with Lou Gehrig's disease, ALS, they're suffering and their loved ones are suffering... what can we say to them?

He said "It's just a costume. They'll get a new one."

(Note: In his interview with Dr. Medhus, he said it was a "wiring of the brain issue." That if we understood how to rewire the brain, we would be able to help those suffering from it.)

Are they conscious of what's happening around them?

"They are not, but their higher selves are. They're (people with ALS are) **more infused with their higher selves than we are."** (Laughs) **"But Ricky Gervais is not aware of his higher self."** He shows me **"just a teeny bit, just enough; like a kitty treat worth of awareness."**

*I remember the fifth person I requested; **Garry Shandling**. He was a Buddhist, but didn't believe in an afterlife per se.*

I see him. I love his voice.

They just did a film about his life on HBO.

He said it *suucked* how he died. (Jennifer aside:) I don't know how he died.

He called his doctor, said he was having chest pains and the doctor told him to lay down for awhile, call him later if it continued.

"That was a joke," he said.

Who greeted you on your crossing over?

"His *sister*."

> (Note: Neither Jennifer or I were aware that Garry
> lost his brother early in life, and he spent a good deal
> of time in therapy about that loss. After this
> interview, I watched the film, and then came back to
> transcribe this transcript, startled to see this answer. I
> thought *"Why didn't he say his brother?"* As we'll
> see in an ensuing chapter, he changes that answer.)

*Rich: Anything you want to say to your girlfriend who sued
you after you kicked her off the show?*

**Jennifer: He showed me her before you said that. He said.
"She dumped me!" and the group is all laughing... He says
he was mad that she didn't love him.**

*Your pal Judd Apatow made a documentary about you. ("Zen
Diaries of Garry Shandling")*

He says, "He channeled it."

Is that a joke? What do you want to tell Judd?

He gave me a smile emoji.

Any advice for Judd?

"Tell him to stop rethinking the beginning." "Allow."

> (Note: I met Judd and Leslie Mann in my friend's
> Cafe in Santa Monica *"Real Food Daily."* I told him
> about my film "Cannes Man;" he told me to "send it
> over." I thought he'd love the self-deprecating humor.

130

Based on the scene in "The Disaster Artist" where we see how much he likes being interrupted while eating, *I doubt it*.)

Anything you want to tell Jerry Seinfeld?

"To shut up."

Ha. He did an episode of "Comedians in Cars getting Coffee" with you, and you both spoke touchingly about the meaning of your life.

"Jerry didn't get it."

When you crossed over, were you surprised?

"No."

What have you been doing since then?

"Playing golf."

With who?

"With all my atheist friends who didn't believe in the afterlife."

Haha. Okay. What's your handicap?

He showed me "negative 4." Then Stephen Hawking interrupted to show his handicap; "a wheelchair." They're all laughing.

What is the golf course that you are envisioning yourself playing on?

These boys are doing a lot of puns. **He showed me "golfing on water."**

Do you go out and play 36 holes?

"Two holes." He's telling me they go off and play two holes... *very far apart.* **He showed me like you tee off in the U.S., but then you have to cross continents to get to the first hole.**

Like the tee is in California and the hole is in Tibet? That's hilarious. When you're creating this construct, are you actually on a place on earth where you golfed or is it just in your mind?

"Both."

So you might be playing literally on a course in Scotland while others are playing. Gives new meaning to "playing through."

"You take the information from what you have here and infuse it with you have there."

By the way, Garry, have you met our teacher Luana before?

He showed me that brief moment when you spoke with him at the restaurant - I think everyone gets connected when our energies connect.

Did you meet any of these other guys around you? Stephen, Christopher?

"No."

Well class, this is Garry Shandling. He's very funny.

"I guess I am." Oh, Robin Williams just waved his hand.

Oh, of course, you know Robin.

He was one of the friends that met him as he came into the other side.

When he crossed over? I read that Brenner had a joke he wanted to be buried with dollar bills...

"In his pants," he tells me.

Right, so he'd have cash to hand out for tips. "Ya never know." All right anything else you want to tell your friends and fans?

He showed me Julia Louis Dreyfus... the actress? (She chuckles.) He said, **"Tell her he should have listened to her."**

She'll know what that means? Stephen, what else can we tell your friends?

"Tell them to hone in on who they are, and how they are."

In terms of past lives?

"Yes. That will give them the infinite."

Stephen, do you like our concept "You can change the future by changing your past?" Should be a name of a chapter.

He's saying it's "easier access." He's showing me that if... – "If you are someone who has a handicap, then it's easier to access your higher self and this other realm."

Okay, we'll call your chapter "Easier access."

He said he wants it called "Black holes and the Infinite."

Will do. Question I have; can we access your mind later on so that you can help us solve problems back on earth? Not theoretical ones, but ones that deal with water, earth and pollution?

He says, "You can access my consciousness but not my thoughts."

He's very precise. Okay, I just mean, can we talk to you and ask questions we don't know the answers to?

"Yes."

Like "How do we turn salt water to fresh water cheaply?"

He showed me that Tesla had done it in 1938. I feel like Tesla knew how to do that.

I'm familiar with Tesla's life, wrote a script about him. I'm not aware of any invention like that, but of course with all the patents he had, it's possible.

He's showing me somebody's already done that.

That would be an interesting way to access your mind, if at some point you could help us draw what's in the patent.

"Yes."

Perhaps we could do a session with a scientist, someone familiar with that language, or have a physicist do a session, take out a pen, and Jennifer can tell him what to draw.

> (Note: Just like Jennifer did in *"Hacking the Afterlife"* when she drew me a map of Saipan, based on hearing it from Amelia Earhart's point of view, when I had just returned from visiting her jail cell on the island. The map was eerily accurate, as I had just

driven the roads, and knew precisely what she was indicating on the map.)

"Yeah." He showed me a language that he would use.

Is that too mundane ask you to help us do something like that?

He said, "Yes; it's like teaching first grade compared to what he's doing now. But fascinating."

During one of my between life sessions, I saw myself in a classroom on the flipside, and the teacher had drawings on a blackboard and was trying to explain to me how crystals come into being – he showed me symbols and I realized that one symbol was "intense pressure over time." Symbols that I don't understand but a physicist might. In terms of memory... Where does memory reside? Outside of the body? We know it's not only in the brain, where do past life memories exist?

"They exist in your heart frequency."

Does everyone have a unique heart frequency?

"Yes, everyone."

I've heard the description before,[28] of geometric shapes or fractals that contain all of our memories that travel with us.

"That's the frequency in and of itself; it is like the chip that contains memories."

And those memories of previous lifetimes?

---

[28] In transcripts from "Flipside," "It's a Wonderful Afterlife Vols 1 and 2"

"Those memories are held in the electromagnetic field of yourself and is held in (the frequency of) our soul... at least that's our best interpretation."

I'm asking if it's possible to access that information.

"Through your mind."

Under deep hypnosis?

"Belief." And he's laughing about the whole belief thing, by the way.

Question is; how do we access those memories, those fractals, geometric shapes?

"Sitting still. By being still."

Through meditation?

I asked him if he was "being still" while he was in his wheelchair, and he said "No, because his mind was going constantly."

Being still allows access to memories of previous lifetimes, which allows us to access our loved ones on the flipside as well. Further it helps us to change our past by revisiting it as a lesson, or a class that we've had – and by doing so that changes our future. But Jennifer and I are doing it in another way aren't we?

"Yes. Active stillness equals belief. If you believe you don't have to have your mind go crazy trying to debunk it."

You had a number of warnings for the planet about robots, artificial intelligence, etc while you were alive... but now that you can access the other side, any thoughts on those?

136

He showed me robots in movies; **"The fear of artificial intelligence is related to the fear of black holes, of God, and the idea that robots could take over."**

Does he now believe we have no reason to fear?

He just showed me Ricky Gervais – because he just did that same thing to you...

What, make me crazy?

He's saying we allow ourselves to be controlled by AI, by electronics, and we need to detach from them.

He no longer fears that we'll be controlled by these things?

"Absolutely 100% correct," he says.

Anything else you want to tell us?

"You have one more question in your notes."

"Aliens..." he said he was worried about us being visited by aliens because Columbus proved that explorers don't always have the best intent.

He says, "We're all aliens, it's just a construct."

> (Note: In my books people under deep hypnosis claim the process of incarnation is that we are fully conscious individuals who choose to come to the planet, and we do so via the permission and connection to the human animal that we "helped evolve" over millennia.
>
> They claim we only bring "about a third" of that conscious energy to any lifetime, that we don't do that

137

in connection with other animals on the planet, as the animals here have their own "journey and realms."

This short answer contains basically the essence of what people under deep hypnosis claim consistently about the journey. (I've filmed 45 sessions, done 5 myself and have examined thousands of others. **"We are all aliens, it's just a construct"** echoes what I've learned over the past ten years of filming people under hypnosis.)

Not that "aliens" means something strange, scary or different, but that our "conscious energy" comes here from "back home" and we choose to incarnate here to learn or teach lessons, until we're done and then we "return back home." (As reported)

In essence, his "answer" wraps the nature of reality into one sentence, one equation. When we realize "we are all aliens" (or are all *immigrants*) it pushes the onus onto us to realize that we chose to be here, that we must share the planet equally.)

Anything for your pal Richard Branson? The owner of Virgin Galactic promised to take Stephen for a space ride.

"Tell him to dream big. Because it's not a dream."

Okay, thank you Stephen.

Luana kissed your forehead. Do you have an anniversary coming up?

Sherry and I were married on April fool's eve ten years ago.

You've never told me that. **Luana said, "Happy anniversary."**

*No, I have not told you about our anniversary. **(ding!)** But thanks class for proving once again our pals still do exist!*

*****

Some years ago I became friends with Dr. Elisa Medhus, a Houston doctor whose son Erik had taken his life, but who had shown up to continue to converse with her. Just days after he shot himself, her phone rang from an anonymous caller ID. She answered the phone and heard her son's voice say "Mom, it's Erik. I'm okay."

She was not a believer in the afterlife, so this threw her for a loop. Then a medium from Atlanta, Jamie Butler called and basically said "Your son showed up in my living room and wanted me to reach out to you." Since then Elisa has done a number of interviews with a number of different mediums and her son.

In fact it was one interview that made me reach out to her; when I was listening to an interview I heard three different people speaking on the audio; one was the person being interviewed, one appeared to be a friend of Erik's and the other appeared to be Erik whispering.

I shared this with her, and we have shared other interviews. It was her interview with Amelia Earhart and Jamie Butler that I reproduced in my book *"Hacking the Afterlife."* Recently I got an email from Dr. Medhus with a new example of EVP (voices that can be heard from the Flipside.) In this case it was the end of an interview she conducted with a medium and none other than Stephen Hawking.

139

He appeared to be about 29, healthy, happy and telling alternate information about his opinion on black holes and what they represent. In her interview he called black holes "portals," explains they are points where energy can be exchanged. He also spoke of why he felt he was in a wheelchair, that the "frequency of his brain waves" was involved, and that a possible cure would lie in learning how to understand that process.

But at the end of this interview, one can clearly hear Dr. Medhus' son. Elisa says, "Goodbye Stephen, thank you, goodbye Erik, I love you." And as the medium starts to reply, **a voice can clearly be heard saying "I love you mom."**

When you've had experiences conversing with the Flipside that makes one an *experiencer* – not a *believer.* It's okay to believe, not believe, but at some point, actually hearing a voice that could not have been put onto a tape is one way to *"hear for yourself."* Or simply, "Yeah, we don't die; we do live on. Just one more example of verifiable proof."[29]

Yours truly with the pitchfork guy

---

[29] ChannelingErik.com Interview with Stephen Hawking

CHAPTER FIVE:

JENNIFER AND LUANA

"Blueprints"

Luana and furry friend

As I've reported, this research came about from my relationship to the actress and my twenty year companion and pal Luana Anders. She got sick from breast cancer, and at some point, she was unable to walk. I used to go over to her house, carry her out into the car and drive around with her – *like the old days.* We'd stop and get a cappuccino and laugh about the news of the day.

I was in the midst of doing a sound mix in Burbank on the film "Cannes Man" after she passed. It's a scene in the beginning, we're in the middle of a funeral, the Minister has asked for a moment of silence. A cell phone rings loudly and an actor in the back row looks at his phone. He looks to the woman next to him, "It's my agent" then whispers into the phone "I'm a funeral. We're having a moment of silence for

Sy Lerner." Luana's voice can be heard saying "Aw, screw him, he's dead! I just got a part for you in a new movie!")

Even though Luana was paralyzed at the time, I wanted to make sure she was in whatever film I was doing; she joked about literally "phoning in her part." But as I was mixing the soundtrack, her voice went through me like an arrow. As I drove away from the session I had to pull over and sob like I have never sobbed before or since.

You just don't know how connected you are to some people. Some are lucky enough to experience it in a lifetime. In our case, I did have a past life memory of being a friend of hers, a coworker thousands of years ago. I claimed it was in Sumeria (a place I was unfamiliar with) and that we worked together as Priests in a temple. Under deep hypnosis, I said we were in charge of helping people understand the light and the dark, and I saw us performing rituals with candles, incense... and a lot of laughter. (As reported in "It's a Wonderful Afterlife.")

I've done 5 between life sessions and each time I've had the experience of seeing her. Being next to her, looking at her, sometimes laughing with her. I'm at a disadvantage because the times I've experienced this I was in a hypnosis state – not that I wasn't aware of what was going on, but I was aware that I felt inadequate, not very bright, and just hanging onto her toga so to speak, as she navigated these events with me.

I've heard consistently from people across the spectrum; not just Jennifer, but people who knew her, who grew up with her that she had a "mystical quality about her." Someone contacted me out of the blue to tell me they were roommates with her after high school in Hollywood, and that she would cast spells on people or things. I asked for an example and she

142

said, "She had the Simon and Garfunkel album and told me should be wind up dating both men."

Which is hilarious, because she did. I spent many evenings with Paul Simon and Charles Grodin and Luana – and never once did she or anyone come close to mentioning that she dated both Paul and Artie. And further, when Artie told me he dated her, I asked if he had told Paul Simon about it – and he said "No, I didn't bother to tell him" with a smile.

Then when she passed, I've mentioned how I found love letters to her from Jack Nicholson and Robert Towne. There were about 20 from Jack – talking about missing her as she was doing a film and he was till in class. Robert's were filled with the poetry that he lives and breathes. As mentioned, I read one or two paragraphs, shook my head in quiet disbelief, and sent them on to these boys... her boys, so they could hold onto them and her.

I'm startled that I'm talking about someone who passed 20 years ago, whom I met 40 years ago, as if she was standing next to me at this very moment. *What can I say?* It's an unusual path we've had together, obviously "for a reason." I think the reason is this book. Or at least a version of this book that includes helping people to communicate with their loved ones on the flipside.

*****

Rich: Okay, we got a class and they're waiting...

Jennifer: Luana is laughing about the story you were just telling me.

I was telling you how a few nights before she passed, I went to this Hollywood party and all the hoi polloi were there – and

everyone who came in had a trophy date... Botox, implants...
and suddenly I had this vision of all them - old and crippled
and near death. It was like Luana was showing me how they
would all end up.

She says, "She was mad that you went to that party..."
The party you were talking about you went to when
Luana was sick? She says you needed an escape.

It's not easy watching a loved one die, hard to be the one
being watched when they're dying. I had this insight, but felt
it came from her; all these beautiful people suddenly became
old, skeletal as we all become, I saw the vanity disappear and
it gave me a different perspective. But did I create that image
or did you create it Lu?

She did. **I had to ask her again... she was already "back**
home" it feels like, most of her was up above. Luana has
such a beautiful scent.

What's that scent like?

Jasmine and spice.

Okay Lu, I want to ask some tough but interesting questions...
many are worried their lives are written like a script, it's
already been written and we've discussed this before. That
free will makes life more of an improvisational exercise.

I'm getting (that each life has) **an underlying theme...**
"Yours is the camera." She showed me all these people
popping up with that... she showed me a convertible on a
street... all the connections that the street where she grew
up on had.

Is she talking about her street in Studio City or Mar Vista?

144

She's showing me a street and ... all the people that are connected to that street, and how much fun she had, and "How you helped her get out of her funk."

That's true. She was a little bit of a hermit when I met her.

Right. She showed me being curled up like a ball in a tub...

So when you're choosing a lifetime, or choosing to go on stage and play a role... how much of that role do you work out in advance, or is it more like an improv?

She just went like this – (shaking out drawings) **like you have plans for a house in front of you.**

The blueprints?

"Yes." She showed me blueprints.

Blueprints? That's a good pun. Jack Nicholson's nickname for her was "Blu." So before you come on stage, before you come here to be born you pull up your blueprints? They inform what you're doing to do and sometimes you make changes along the way, because someone comes and says, "I need you to participate in this emergency event" and someone comes in and changes the blueprint, is that correct?

"Yes." She showed me how you have a stack of blueprints, a lot of them – they're translucent, so when they're on top of each other you can see the architecture below.

Like the plastic pages of a medical book?

"You build up your translucent papers, one on top of the other, that's how you get to the pearly gates."

Are the various blueprint pages lifetimes?

145

"Yes, so when they go over each other, that's when you feel the intersections... like a feeling of Deja vu. Because there's this one place that you have to get rid of because you want to change the wall, but once you lay them on top of each other, you can see why there's a difficulty."

A crossroads from a previous lifetime?

"No."

We can ask my dad the architect to come forward and help us with this analogy – he did a lot of blueprints.

He said, "It's not." Luana showed me people being dropped into the blue prints, like raindrops ... aaah and wherever you land, you have to make it work.

Some screw up, don't they?

"Yeah."

Lu, who screwed up in your life?

"You."

Very funny.

It's funny when I get shown *you* in my minds eye...

Anyone else you can point to?

She said "Her..." – hold on. (to Luana: Say it again?) She says, "I did not allow myself to love or know that everything would be okay." She loved more based out of fear of being alone. She showed me her childhood was being abandoned?

(Note: It's not something I've shared with Jennifer or many. But Luana's parents split up with she was a baby, and her mother put her into foster care so she could run a dress shop in Mar Vista. She didn't move back in with her mother for years, until she was remarried. And then they fought most of the time until Luana ran away at the age of 16 to work in Hollywood. We've mentioned it previously in the book, but at this point, I had not.)

Yes. Very much so.

I don't know, but I don't want to misinterpret what I'm getting... I don't know anything about her childhood, but she showed me she was almost like adopted, that feeling of being adopted, and the blueprints for her – she showed me your heart – when she met you she recognized the frequency of home and she didn't want to leave it... and she wished she would have recognized it earlier?

How could she have?

Her finger came to her lips to shush you... (Jennifer laughs.) (To Luana) **For fuck's sake!** Um. Go back to that? Back to the blueprints please. (Pause) **She said, "She didn't make the right decisions but you were a right decision and that led to her opening her heart." You said to her that "Everything's going to be okay, who cares?"**

> (Note: This is accurate. She cared so deeply about acting, about her art, that she would tie herself into knots over the work, or over some piece of writing she was working on. If anything, I showed her that you can laugh at stress, or mock those that were so self important that they made everyone else sick with

147

stress. She taught me to care more about the details. But I helped her to laugh about them as well.)

Jennifer: "You wanted her to be free within the relationship, to not worry about you, or not worry about anyone else." She never experienced that before.

Rich: That's accurate. Lu, when you were looking at the blueprints before coming here – you knew you were going to be abandoned, you knew it was going to be difficult for you?

"Location." She focused on the location.

Did that make you a better actor?

Jennifer taps her finger on her nose.

> (Note: Among her pals, Luana's acting skills were legendary. Oscar winning writer Robert Towne claimed she was the best actress he saw on stage. Anthony Hopkins mentioned it after one class we took together with Francis Coppola at Zoetrope studios (Luana was in the first film Francis directed, "Dementia 13" and worked with him on "One From the Heart.") Others felt the same, including her pal Jack Nicholson. He was a loyal pal, he cast her in a number of his films; at her funeral there were two sets of flowers that were monster floral arrangements. One was from Jack, the other from her first boyfriend Dennis Hopper. When Jack accepted the Oscar for "As Good As It Gets" he mentioned her last in his acceptance speech.)

Now I want to ask you about your council Luana. How many people are in your council?

"There are four in here. They're wiping the dust off themselves..."

Men or women?

"They're androgynous."

Looking left to right, let's go to your spokesperson; is that person male or female? Take a hold of their hands in your mind's eye. Who is this?

"My guide." (Jennifer's)

Oh? Is this guide in both councils? Jennifer's and Luana's?

"Yes."

Okay, that's interesting. Can we talk to you directly?

"Yes." She just told me she gave you the idea to ask this question.

So are you a member of many councils?

"Yes."

How many?

"Infinite."

So that's what connects all of us? Jennifer and Luana to me?

"People are assigned to certain frequencies, if you've felt abandoned, or hurt, the frequency that Luana and I shared; I felt lost and abandoned by my religion – the frequency of abandonment."

That's the frequency that connected us? Abandonment?

149

I can't make this up. (Jennifer listens) **"We shared a frequency of not belonging."**

I need a council member neither one of us know. Male or female.

"Male."

How tall?

"16 feet tall. He's an angel."

Okay. What's his usual occupation? What does he normally do when he's not hanging out on Luana's council? How did he earn his position on her council?

Wow, I felt like a screech, like a record scratch. I said, "Did you mean you (work to) **stop us?" He said "No, he stops us from stopping ourselves."**

*Like the opposite of a grim reaper. A grim **opener**. Is he sad? Happy? What's he look like?*

He's like a big enormous light. Like blueish. It changes... he showed me initially traveling... hang on, again he helps us not stop ourselves. "I help people from being afraid about traveling or astral traveling."

Someone who helps people not to stop. What's this angel's name, something we can refer to him by?

His name is... "Michael."

Okay. Mike the Angel.

Happy birthday," he said (to you). **By the way I'm still feeling heavy from experiencing the love that Luana had for you.**

Ok. And who is our fourth member of the council?

An African American... woman. "She represents "Justice" on her council. It's a frequency again... it's interesting how they manifest... the frequencies are similar; feeling abandoned, feeling the need for justice, how that takes over your life in so many ways. When it's the frequency of justice, it's about making things right for how they got bad. **I just got shown all of Luana's lifetimes... all the different papers atop of each other.... like they're blueprints.**

So... do we have other class members who want to say hello?

My dad. He went like this, hand sign of "I love you" but he's like **"You (still) don't believe it."**

How's everyone doing?

"Everything's going to be okay." I got an image of Harry Dean hitting your head.

What do you want to say Harry?

(Jennifer listens.) **He says, "He wants you to talk to that woman you met at his memorial service."**

You mean the wife of the film director?

"Yes."

What do you want me to say to her?

"He wants you to ask you for information that she's learned since your conversation. He says there's (been) a lot of confirmation."

151

I'll reach out to Ed Begley Jr, he organized the service. (I did, and no reply from Ed. I may have spooked him.) Anything else?

Your mom.

Anthy, what's up?

She's showing me when you go into a Buddhist temple, the sound of monks chanting? I just felt this huge like overwhelming noise of that... Oooh...

I have a cd of that I made with the Nechung monks. "Traditional Chants of Tibet" with the Nechung Monks.[30]

I think that monk sound is healing... I was shown all the clients I've had who had kids who died or killed themselves, they all came in at once. I deal with death on a daily basis... I mean, I don't deal with it but I'm a conduit – they showed me all the feelings of grief all at once... And I started crying... it really touched my heart.

So how can we help people deal with grief?

I'm seeing her create a cloud... there's a cloud of grief, show her how she can generate a golden light of love that goes against that cloud... and through the cloud. (Jennifer closes her eyes) **I'm hearing, "1 just need to call upon Mr. Angel and he lifts the frequency up."**

Well, we had a different adventure today! Thanks class. Catch on the flipside!

*****

---

[30] "Traditional Chants of Tibet" with the Nechung Monks. 2004

CHAPTER SIX:

BROTHERS FROM ANOTHER PLANET

"Put it out in raw form."

Mars. Look familiar? (Photo: NASA)

I was having lunch with a couple of my oldest friends in LA, and they were giving me the raised eyebrows about this research. I just have to get used to it – part of the reason is that they've known me for decades as a funny, goofy film guy. But they relate to this research as if it either belongs in Mad Magazine or from a pulpit somewhere. *No one wants to talk about death until they have to.*

I understand that. But when you conclude that death is an illusion – not from a philosophical religious point of view – but a literal, *"Hey! This thing that we're doing here on the planet is a stage play! There's nothing to fear because "everyone gets out alive!"* It's hard to not repeat it to your

153

friends, but equally hard to have your friends not run from the room.

Charles Grodin for example, one of the most loyal friends I've ever known, literally would bolt from the room the moment someone asked me, "So what are you up to these days?" *Not everyone want to hear or talk about the thing they fear the most.* I don't blame him – but there are so many of his friends that I'm talking to, it's hard not to share what I'm hearing.

That being said, one of my friends, Tim, asked me to "communicate with a mutual acquaintance" by way of a test. I asked this fellow the same questions I ask everyone about their journey, who met him, when he crossed over etc, but I found myself more interested in speaking to someone my friend and I both knew but who was no longer on the planet; his mom. So after the "test" I "skipped ahead."

Rich: Luana, I thought it might be valuable for our mutual friend Tim to hear something from his mom who crossed last year. Luana, I'm not sure if you ever met Tim's mom.

Jennifer: **"Briefly in passing,"** she says.

Could we access Tim's mom?

"Yes." She has a message for Tim.

He's an actor, is doing something else now as well.

Real estate? That's what she's showing me.

That's correct.

You didn't tell me that, did you?

154

*No, I did not, deliberately. **(ding!)** My question is "How are you, Tim's mom?"*

She's doing a lot of cooking.

> (Note: "Cooking" is the image that Jennifer got. Could mean she's reminding someone of that act, could be that's what she's "doing on the flipside." When asked "How does one cook?" People respond; "It's mathematics." Meaning, they create the "construct" of cooking, as they remember it.)

Jennifer: I know that sounds generic, but that's what she's showing me. **I'm getting from her that her son is doing much better with real estate than the acting.**

Rich: Tim's a great actor, but yes, he's doing well with real estate too. He was also a coach...

Some sport with a ball... soccer... no, softball?

That's correct.

His mother says, **"Tell him to not work so much." He should be writing more.**

Writing what?

About his life. She says a script.

He wrote a play about his life, performed it in New York.

Jennifer taps her nose.

Okay, I'll pass it along. (Am sure he won't believe me, even reading this, but am keeping this in, because sometimes we want to "prove to ourselves" about speaking to the flipside. Since I knew his mom, I knew it would be an easier

155

*connection, and as noted, it's pretty frickin' accurate.) It's
funny, in our last class, we talked about your guide's
"wings." He said his name was Michael, but to avoid any
connotation of that famous Archangel, I'm calling him Mike
the Angel. I asked him about the composition of his wings and
you said, "It's composed of light."*

"Layers and layers of light... frequencies."

*But what's odd is that I know I filmed the conversation about
his wings, but it's disappeared from the tape. I can't find it.*

We'll ask about it again.

*I remember him saying he's 16 feet tall. But perhaps he
doesn't want us to talk about his wings?*

**He's pointing out that, "It's more comfortable for him to
appear with wings... and also for the people he appears to;
that's (in) their comfort zone." He doesn't want to take
that away from them. (Pause) But you can talk about it.**

*I think I understand. Wings are a mental construct and as a
metaphor they represents something greater than we can
imagine... but they aren't related to religion or hierarchy, but
related to something else.*

(Jennifer taps her nose.) **For light speed.**

For moving and flying?

"Yes."

*People talk about non-reincarnating entities. I've heard
people use that term to describe so called "angels."*

He showed me like (being able to move to) **other galaxies.**

156

Do you incarnate on other planets?

He said "No." He showed me the different galaxies and said, "What we do is bring in the energies from all the different realms..." - he showed me a number planets – "...from the constellations." He brings that energy because if you believe it then you'll feel it.

We were talking about grief being a frequency or a sound. What does that mean?

I saw a ricochet.

Do we generate that or are we tapping into it?

We generate it and also are tapping into it.

Like a water wave that goes out and comes back?

"Yes." They just showed me that we send (the feeling) **out, then it comes back and it gets bigger and bigger, that's the ricochet effect.** I was thinking it just ricochets, (like a bullet) but they're showing me it bounces back, comes back to us (like a loop). **"What you put out comes back tenfold."** It's something I deal with in my work, I deal with a lot of grief on a daily basis. I am fortunate in my work to help people, but I deal with a lot of grief and sadness.

So one way of mitigating the wall of grief it to set it aside when speaking to people on the other side. To acknowledge the grief, "Hello grief" and then set it aside like a suitcase. "I know where you are; I know how to tap into you but I'm going to put it down next to me while I examine something or talk to my loved one."

(Jennifer taps her nose.) **"Detach."** They're showing me that by knowing your own grief... (aside) Like, I know what my grief is... **"By knowing your own grief, you know the frequency of it."** **Like I associate grief with my dad's passing...** (Pause) **Oh, when I said that, my dad said, "No!** *Happiness!***"** He's saying, **"You should associate grief with happiness; the memory of your loved one** (him) **comes with happiness,** *not sadness.***"**

So if you associate grief with happy memories; or nostalgia, then you can alter that experience of sadness?

Instead of associating my dad with grief, he's like... showing me how to flip it.

Turn grief into nostalgia; that's a concept that contains both sadness and happiness.

It's like you said, "Put grief in a suitcase. I know you're there. I know you exist." Last year, after my dad's passing, I was one sick doctor. People came to see me to help them with their grief, it was like going to a doctor with a snotty nose when you're trying to get better. It really took me forever to get into my office, as it was challenging – but the more I do this work, the stronger I get.

I suggest people take out a photo of their loved one, meditate on it, and think of your loved one in present tense.

They just said, **"Don't use meditation as the word."** **I just heard a collective voice.**

Ha. I get it; people associate meditation with yoga, and yoga with exercise and no one wants to have to work for it. I'm suggesting to try to set aside the emotions of the memory, so when you address this person on the flipside, you do it without the emotional baggage; so you can hear them.

Baggage. That's funny. "Set the baggage aside."

A question for Mike the Angel; can you appear on anyone's council?

"Yes." He says he can be a part of anybody's council. He's showing me the frequency; your heart can access him at the same time. That frequency... can connect to an "angel with wings."

He told us he has different responsibilities on different councils.

He's referring to the higher consciousnesses.

Okay, he before that his main role was to help people "not stop." He's embodies the courage to go forward.

"To go inside."

You help drive people to the inside?

"It's a healing vehicle. It's a..."

Merkabah?

"Yes." That's what I saw.

> (Note: Merkabah is a word used in new age circles, I had never heard it before it came up in a hypnosis session. A term used in ancient religions, including Judaism, refers to a literal "vehicle of enlightenment." Not sure why it popped into my head.)

159

Jennifer: I asked him (Mike the Angel) "Do you really exist?" I can't help myself but to ask. He said **"No, I don't exist without a belief in your heart."** That's what makes him what he is and makes him be able to match your frequency. To that end, he just showed me Santa and the Tooth Fairy.

Rich: Woah, hold on there cowboy. What you're saying is when someone sees you, during a near death event, or during a between life hypnosis sessions, they might say, "I'm seeing this angel..." But do they have to believe in you in order to see you?

Jennifer: "They're connecting to their higher selves, they're seeing themselves at a higher vibration. That is why they can see me."

*Rich: Okay, but you're making this argument that you don't exist unless we **believe** in you. Which is kind of weird to be making, don't you think?*

He says he exists, but "You have to believe in him, for him to appear."

So, let's say I have a near death experience...

I'm getting that you've had two. Once when you were little, when you weren't breathing, the next was in a car... like through a hallucinogen, something drug related.

(Note: In high school, I was stupid enough to accept a pill from a stranger at a party who called it "Angel Dust." (*IRONY?*) Turned out it was PCP, a horse tranquilizer. I had no idea – but was driving the car with all my friends in it, and suddenly saw *two* of everything. I was smart enough to pull over and say "I

160

can't drive. Someone else has to." I was sick out the window. Thankfully, my pal *(guardian angel?)* Mark Caplis washed the car, dropped me at my home, and I spent the night under a tree in the front yard. Now that I'm recalling it – I am aware that *someone* visited me during that event. Maybe a guide or angel. But I had forgotten this event until she mentioned it.)

But if I don't recognize you, but see you as this sixteen foot tall dude with wings; you're saying I wouldn't know who you were because I'm not tuned in?

"You would recognize me because of all your past lives. Because you've run into me in some form or other during them." He's saying that "You would recognize his energy." He's showing me a fresco.

Have you ever shown up on this planet? Have you ever incarnated here? (Fresco? Funny, I think I know the one he means; it's from Pompeii, and is in The Met in NYC.)

"No."

Have you incarnated on any planet?

"Yes, but not here." He just *shot* me to a different planet – even when he's showing me, I get this enormous being. I can feel being next to him in my mind, feeling his feathers, knowing his feathers are a frequency but I can feel them.

(Note: When someone says they've "incarnated on another planet" or "in another realm" it's also in the research. Michael Newton claimed when he wrote "Journey of Souls" in 1994, 10% of his clients had "offworld experience." Meaning they'd had lifetimes elsewhere, not on *this* planet. In the interview with

161

Pete Smith, current President of the Newton Institute he says that number has risen to 30%.[31] Meaning Newton Institute hypnotherapists worldwide report that roughly one out of three people that come to see them claim they've had "offworld" experience. When asked "why did you choose to incarnate here?" they answer with variations of "I wanted to be here when the shift in consciousness occurred.")

Rich: What's it feel like when you're with Mike the Angel?

I feel (as if) **there's something that's both comfort and peace rolled into one.**

Like unconditional love?

"Yeah."

All right class. We talked to our angel friend, talked to Luana, we talked to Tim's mom, we talked to Billy...

Bill says, "But I was here first."

What's he want to say?

"Thank you." (Jennifer listens) **For reaching out to his family. They did read your blog post about Bill.[32]**

Did they believe it?

It resonated. They didn't want to believe it, there was resistance there. **He says "No, the resistance was grief."**

---

[31] His interview in in my book "It's a Wonderful Afterlife."
[32] http://richmartini.blogspot.com/2018/03/in-memoriam-interview-with-bill-paxton.html

They have so much grief... but um... you did help on some level.

I understand it's very stressful that kind of loss, you were their everything.

And then some... and he showed me "and a bucket of coal and a bucket of rocks, too." That's a perfect thing to share with others... that will help them even more.

It will help people here or over there (on the Flipside)?

"Both." That's funny. **He said "Rich, you're like a good hooker. Work both sides of the room."**

Very funny. I noted in the post; "The only reason we're doing this is because Bill insists we put it out in a raw form."

"Within reason. But there's no boundaries," he said, "because by not having boundaries you can't limit their thinking."

Well, as an actor and filmmaker you had no boundaries.

"Better than you."

Ha. I agree with that. I finally saw your golf movie "Greatest Game Ever Played."[33]

He made a face; **"Well, it's about time."**

I didn't get invited to a screening the way you were invited to a screening of "Cannes Man."

"You were out of town," he said.

---

[33] https://www.imdb.com/title/tt0388980/?ref_=nm_flmg_act_33

Hell yes. I am out to lunch.

"Off the planet."

It was well done. Shia LaBeouf was good.

The footage you've put together about talking to him on the Flipside was raw, he (Bill) **liked seeing it – he said, "now you have your** (own) **Bill Paxton movie."**

I put together a rough cut of our chatting with him and showed it to a few people. But just as many who saw your golf movie, buddy.

He just made an X at you. Luana said "Happy birthday." I forgot to mention that to you last time we talked.

Luana's birthday is coming up.

Is it May 12th?

Why do I even bother responding? (Laughs) (ding!)

She showed me my daughter. Hers' is May 12th as well.

Cool. Anyone else?

Prince. (reacts to a sound) **That was a loud guitar.**

Tell her what chord that is.

He said, "G." I don't know what G is.

I do.

He said like **"up."** *Not H minor...* I don't know music... but up to next one. I don't know what that means.

"A minor?"

164

"Yes."

Next?

"Then C, E, then down..."

G, Am, C, E or E minor?

"E minor."

And then back to G. Cool. Oddly enough I was playing something like this on the piano yesterday.

She taps her nose.

You're inspiring musicians?

He says, "You have that frequency," and he showed me purple just coming in.

Thanks Prince. Next time we'll ask you for lyrics.

> (Note: Go ahead musicians; play it. Sounds a bit
> Prince-like when you do.)

By the way, speaking of musicians, Craig Cole is a guy who played saxophone in our band, he died while I was in Tibet.

He had a stroke?

Could be. He was ill.

Oh, he had diabetes, something that made his coloring felt off, a kidney disease, his coloring was way off had to do with his blood sugars, may have had blood cancer.

That's true. (ding!) I know my wife saw him in Hollywood prior to his passing and she said he was really pale.

165

His heart just stopped. You had a dream about him.

I did. How do you do that Craig?

He said, "It's an awareness."

Craig, I don't know if you've met Luana before.

A year ago. As a result of one of your books.

Are you playing music with anyone?

Hendrix.

Are you playing with Zappa?

I don't know who that is. **He says "Yes, when he crossed over it was him who came to get him when he got out."** (Aside) **Did this Zappa fellow die before him?**

Yes. So he pulled you out into the flipside?

"Yes." He went *"foom"* like, "come with us!" and they went straight into a concert. He pulled him out, put him straight onto stage, there were thousands of people. And then, when he saw his mom in the front row, he knew he wasn't alive. He said "Wait – my mom shouldn't be here." Remember the car ride when Harry Dean realized he was in the afterlife? That was his "car ride."

Craig used to play with Frank Zappa that would make sense he would be the one pulling him on stage.

I don't know who that is. **Craig says, "Your book is going to be on fire." He showed me flames. He says he didn't believe it when he died, it took him going out there and noticing something different during the event on stage.**

Thanks Craig, hope the class gets a chance to hear your monster talent on sax. Catch you on the flipside!

*****

I was in Tibet when I got an email from pal and bandmate Bruce Haring. Bruce brought together a gaggle of music critics, some ringers like Craig Cole who played with Zappa, and we started playing gigs around town as "Imminent Disaster."

In an internet cafe in Tibet, I got Bruce's email entitled "Craig Cole"; I *knew* before opening it he'd died. I wrote his name on a Tibetan prayer flag at the foot of Mt. Kailash; am happy to report Craig's flag is flying high over that sacred mountain in Tibet. A Buddhist, he chanted Nam Myoho Renge Kyo as Luana did; he's welcome to join her class.[34]

The prayer flag with names of loved ones, including Craig Cole, outside Mt. Kailash

---

[34] Craig Cole in Imminent Disaster. https://youtu.be/mBenjE9BL4c

CHAPTER SEVEN:

CONSCIOUSNESS

"Unearthly answers"

With Jennifer and Hypnotherapist Scott De Tamble

Sometimes our lunches are "talking directly to people on the flipside." Sometimes we just talk about whatever they decide to bring up, but sometimes it leads to conversations that we have, that neither one of us would have had elsewhere.

Jennifer generally doesn't remember anything we talk about in person. Sometimes her subconscious does, will recall something that we talked about when she was under hypnosis doing a session with Scott De Tamble, or I'll reference something that we both heard from someone who is no longer on the planet. But in general, "it's like having a dream."

The important part of our conversations is that we don't edit each other – or judge what we talk about. (And yes, these sessions have been edited and transcribed, and put together to make sense. But for the most part, everything that was said here, was recorded on film.)

But occasionally we converse about things that I too have forgotten we've talked about, and am fairly startled to see that I've filmed us talking about things that I'm not consciously aware we spoke of.

Some would argue that we are both "putting each other into a state of hypnosis," but I'm editing out our conversations with waiters, bus servers, or other chit chat we do during our weekly conversations. You're getting as close to the essence as I can muster.

The point of this preamble it to say, "*anyone can do it.*" I encourage people out there who know mediums, who have the ability to sense or see or experience altered conscious states, whether it's an out of body event, a near death event, or just holding a joint and staring at the evening sky while watching satellites pass by – *ask questions you don't know the answers to.* Ask your guides for help and guidance. Note when you get that help and guidance and don't forget to thank them.

Since none of this research is attached to any religious thought or beliefs, and none of it is tied to any formal concept of what we should or should not talk about in these sessions, we both hope that these "conversations with the flipside" will encourage others to open themselves up to the possibility that we can do this kind of research. Why not? We only have the planet to save.

*****

Rich: I was thinking about monks who could shift their consciousness into animals, people who claim they remember their lifetime as an animal. My suggestion is that they remember a single event... but not the entire birth, life, death of an animal, the way people do during past life regression.

Jennifer: Maybe they could shift their consciousness into an animal briefly, like they do in Native American tribes, are tapping into that day when they found their "spirit animal" and shifted their consciousness into that animal.

If two thirds of our consciousness is always "back home" (as suggested by the research) our conscious energy has plenty to go around. Also there are these esoteric Tibetan practices ("Six Yogas of Naropa") where monks claim they shift their consciousness into an animal that has died; they're able to reanimate the animal, get them to get up, walk, fly around.

Like the film "Avatar." I was asking my dad how he was seeing us on the flipside and he showed me this bubble like vision. Like being inside a submarine and looking out to people floating past, and he was watching us. It's the same thing; it's not to see what we're doing, they see our thoughts in what we do.

What?

I asked my dad "Do you focus on going to our thoughts to focus on us?" He said, "It's both."

Bill Paxton told us "The eyes are the windows of the soul," as he was describing the way to "talk to us;" the ability to shift consciousness to behind our eyes.

I asked my dad "So what do you want to talk about? Something new up there? Bill wants to say something.

170

Okay, so class, we're now in session. Luana, we're going to ask you to help moderate this discussion.

She already was.

One of your students named Bill has politely raised his hand and said he wants to share. What does he want to share?

So funny, he's like "Pick me, oh pick me!" at his desk...

Bill, what do you want to say?

He showed me the article you wrote on your blog about him.[35]

What did I get wrong?

"Everything! But nothing." Jennifer laughs. Um... interesting... He said... he goes **"You didn't get anything right because you downplayed it."**

What does that mean?

He's showing me the guy in Thailand.

Your actor friend, Donal Logue. We had three questions he wanted you to figure it out.

Billy said he wants our book to be just about himself.

Ha. I didn't want to include Donal's name in the article because I didn't want people to bug him.

Bill is saying "Just don't hold back on how this process is." He just showed me you interviewing Jim Cameron.

---

[35] https://richmartini.blogspot.com/2018/03/in-memoriam-interview-with-bill-paxton.html

I've been made aware that Jim is a formidable interviewee.

Bill's laughing.

What's wonderful about Luana and her ability to connect with us, is that she's like my private Joan of Arc. I understand her connection to me, her ability to continue it. And no matter who comes at me from what angle, it's like she's got the vibranium shield up for me. Teaching and helping.

And chanting. She just showed me monks... everyone helping.

We're just trying to understand the nature of reality.

When you said "The nature of reality" I got an image of unreality – the *perception*... of reality. But with precision.

Being more precise?

Of what it is that *really exists*. Which is from the heart. Everything else is just a stage, everything else is just props.

Bill, you were talking about the precision of creating a mathematical sequence of being on a white beach. (When I asked, "What are you doing with your time?" and he replied with an image of a white beach, and I asked about how that gets constructed.) You said it was a math equation – so all the props are equations as well?

"Yes." I'm seeing Einstein.

The idea is that every object is a construct; even the coffee cup I'm holding is just atoms.

"Collectively agreeing to hold that space."

Hold on... **They just showed me something interesting about karma; if you've done things in your lifetime that were bad, or have situations that remind you of something you did in the past, hurt people, that's the frequency of karma. Like an echo** (of that previous event.)

And Deja vu as well I imagine. Karma as in "Not baggage?"

You'll feel anxious around a certain person because maybe you hurt them in a previous life; your subconscious goes batshit crazy because it knows what happened.

We choose lifetimes to examine forms of energy or karma?

Exactly. You try to be free of that... because the good also has bad situations... It's a frequency within the heart, is what they're showing me, what you're trying to do is cure yourself in all dimensions and at all times. Billy is showing me the post that you wrote on your blog.

You're in the ethers, in people's minds and online buddy.

"Always," he said.

I think it's important to know Bill can communicate with anyone who knows his frequency.

"That's the point."

Will people be upset we're "taking advantage of people no longer on the planet?"

"No." He's saying, "But allow the process however it comes." They're showing me an image of you - when you say, "Don't judge it" to me... "try not to judge the answer."

You mean me telling people to "just report, don't judge."

It keeps you out of attachment and it gets you ... (To Luana: "Show that to me again?" Jennifer rolls her eyes). What I'm being shown is that by allowing people... (She stops again, listens) or getting away from the attachment of what you're saying...

(Me, admonishing the class) Hey class, let her talk! Stop interrupting her!

That's what they're always telling you! They are encouraging you ... to make it more raw, so this is more of a documentary. We're not asking people to believe in it – that should be in the title "It's not our job to make you believe anything."

Bill wants his name on the cover? Bill Paxton Speaks?

"Unearthly answers."

How are these unearthly answers going to help the planet?

"Even with friction it raises the vibration." They showed me the vibration being raised – eventually the skeptics will come in – recording like you have been ... making me the guinea pig. Then more people can talk to people on the other side when they don't think they can.

How is talking to people on the other side going to help people here?

"They'll understand that they have help on the other side."

Why do they need to understand that?

174

"So they can start believing in what they're being given."

(Playing devil's advocate.) But what's the value in that?

"Trusting their own ... a confidence of trust."

But from the skeptic's point of view... so let's say they're like one of our classmates, Julian Baird, who said in my interview with him while he was still on the planet, "I don't want to know what's going to happen after I'm not here."

"This isn't telling them what's going to happen. It's telling them how to coexist and detach." They're showing me a Buddha.

This is going to help process what really is happening, that would be inclusive of knowing your attachment to things that aren't of the heart is a waste of time, and help people to focus on those things of the heart?

They're (things that prevent us from doing so) **just props.**

But it's important to say stay attached to things of the heart, is that correct? To not detach yourself from everything?

"Yes. But if you love drugs it's not a good thing."

Funny. But people think they're being told happiness comes from being detached. That "non attachment" includes family members and they literally go off and live in a cave... but from what I've heard, the point of being on the planet, of being alive, is not live in a cave. You chose to be here for a reason, you chose the people around you so you could help them. Hold onto the stuff that's of the heart, but the rest is Vanum Populatum, vanity, and let all that go.

175

(Note: The words "Vanum Populatum" came to me in a dream. I heard it, didn't know what it meant, but wrote it down. Suspected it was Latin. A week later I looked it up and it means "annihilate vanity." My joke became "Who wants me to annihilate vanity? I live in LA. Where do I begin?"

But six months later, I began this documentary into the flipside, and got a chance to do a between life session with a Michael Newton trained hypnotherapist. (Jimmy Quast of Easton Hypnosis). And we got to a point where I was talking to my council and I had him ask "What's the meaning of Vanum Populatum?"

My guide laughed and said, "Ask Rich, he knows the answer." I realized my guide was referring to my temporary self (otherwise he would have said "You know the answer) and that I had given myself the puzzle in Latin knowing I would search for its meaning. **"Everything that's not of the heart is vanity, and wherever you see vanity, annihilate it. It prevents people from seeing their true selves."**)

Anyone want to come forward?

My dad.

Jim! What's up?

"Hi Rich."

So what do you do during the day?

"Teaches," he says.

176

How many people are in your class?

He showed me a ton of people...

We were talking about the idea of helping people change their future by changing their past. I wanted to ask how is this work going to help the planet?

"Raising the awareness. They don't have to believe in it..." they showed me something interesting**... how atoms get stronger.**

They get elevated?

"It's not belief; it's faith."

But once you use religious words like "faith" or "belief," brains freeze. It affects our ability to hear. So Jim what are teaching? How many in your class?

He said, "One." I'm confused... **He said, "I'm teaching myself how I can talk through you (Jennifer)."**

What are you teaching yourself?

"To be more of an effective communicator."

How do you do that?

"By watching the class we have, it raises the awareness of what we can do."

Anyone else want to weigh in on that?

Tom Petty answered "Yes." He said "Yes. It does (raise awareness)." **He feels that he can help other musicians, learning how to infuse his energy with other musicians and help them to learn.**

Are you whispering in their ear, how do you ride that wave into their consciousness from over there?

"By being around them and being with them in their dream state. The more that you're in with their dream state, the more they can be here, bring it (the energy) **through."**

Are you showing them how to play or how to adjust their frequency?

He showed me mathematics, how to adjust the frequency, but in layman terms; "How to play."

Okay class, thanks for coming forward all of you...

Billy still wants his name on the book – he's joking.

"Bill Paxton and other weirdos from the flipside?"

He says, "Don't hold back." That's his title – "No Holding Back." He's saying, "Go for it."

Okay class, thank you Jennifer. Catch you all on the flipside.

*****

Bill Paxton and his mentor Harry Dean Stanton

CHAPTER EIGHT:

JOHN, GEORGE, JIMI

"Blue Suede Shoes"

Author with Basil "Joe" Jagger and his son Mick

As mentioned, we normally don't try to "chat" with anyone we don't know. But based on some of the previous sessions, I just thought "What the hell? Why not try?" As we'll hear in this report, there are some things that are true, some things that could be true, and some things that could be someone on the flipside screwing with us.

Wait, what?

As I try to note in all of these sessions, I'm asking questions and Jennifer gets an image or a sensation or a sentence that she then translates into an answer. She may be mistranslating what she's seeing (a possibility), the person on the flipside may be sending a photograph to impart how they want to answer the question (also possible) or they may be tailoring the answer to their audience (again, possible.)

179

In terms of tailoring an answer, I suggest thinking of three people in a room with one medium. One is the daughter of the person on the flipside, one is the spouse and the third is their business partner. In each case, a person asks a question – let's say *"How or what are you doing?"*

The daughter might get an answer steeped in love or a sweet memory, the spouse might get a different more descriptive answer that includes "flying around to the places we used to visit" and the business partner might get an off color joke.

It could be an answer based on how they "used to feel" or an answer that describes their "memory of how things occurred" – which like *any memory* is subject to all kinds of influences – or they may just be screwing around giving alternate answers at a given moment because they're bored with the questions.

I don't have any doubt that Jennifer is "seeing" or hearing something from spirit – and that it's in a direct reply to my questions – but there are any number of variations that can come into play, including people not knowing the answer but who give one anyway, giving an answer one day and a different one the next, or not liking the question and give an answer that is contrary to what happened.

But that doesn't stop me from asking. What I'm trying to focus on here is that it is possible to converse with anyone we knew or loved. It takes some time and practice and sometimes asking the same question over and over again in different settings, but as you can see; we do get answers.

It's when they repeat their answers over multiple sessions or expand upon them we can gain insight into what their experience might be like "back home." With that in mind, I present you with the chapter where I just "shot arrows into the sky to see where they landed."

*****

Rich: Hi class, how are we doing? Who's here?

Jennifer: A lot. Really interesting.... **Keith Richards is still alive, correct? It's someone Keith Richards knows.**

Yes. People joke about Keith being still on the planet when so many like him are not. We're going to invite a bunch of friends today.

Well, Paul McCartney showed up in my head. I know he's still alive...

Paul, Keith... hmm. Who else?

John Lennon.

I invited him.

You did? That's so awesome. You didn't tell me that.

No, I did not. This morning I thought, "Hmm, I wonder if it's possible..." and then asked him to join us today.

Luana showed me Keith Richards, and I was like "I know they're all alive" but then I saw Paul and John Lennon.

John, this is Luana, have you guys met before?

"Up there, back stage."

I'm going to ask you some questions John, please don't take anything the wrong way. Are you aware of this class? Has anyone briefed you as to what we're doing?

181

He wasn't aware of the class, but "Yes, he's been briefed."

Who briefed you?

(Jennifer asks) Who was it? (Pause). So weird. He said, **"His wife."**

Which one?

I don't know.

Let's ask him. Are you in touch with your first wife, Cynthia?

Jennifer taps her nose with her finger (to signify "that's it.")

I want to ask you both some questions. Both John and Cynthia. I'm friends with your son, Julian, who appeared in one of my films. Anything you want to say to him?

"Tell him to stop dragging his feet."

About what?

I don't know – **Is he supposed to get married?** (Jennifer: I'm just asking him myself... I'm sorry, I'm still shocked by seeing John Lennon.)

Well, we're going to talk to him as a soul, not as a famous person.

(Jennifer laughs) **I know, but you've got to give me a little time to adjust.**

Can I ask Cynthia a direct question, John?

Did she die three years after him? Or three years ago?

I think it was three years ago.

(Note: That's correct. Cynthia Powell Lennon passed away from cancer in 2015)[36]

Did she have cancer? It seems like it was up in this area (waves around her chest and throat). **I'm hearing a thick, raspy voice. She's very funny.**

(Note: Her voice might not have been raspy at all. But that's what Jennifer is "hearing.")

Who was there to greet you, Cynthia?

Her mom. (Jennifer crosses her fingers.) Hold on. That may have been a joke. *Yes.* **It was a joke; they weren't close.**

Is that when you realized you crossed over?

"Yes, I realized I must be in hell," she said. (Jennifer laughs.)

So did John come to greet you as well?

"Yes. Two days prior."

What did John look like to you when he showed up and what was your feeling when he showed up?

(Jennifer looks into the distance) Oh, that's so cool. **She showed me a memory, it almost feels like high school. I don't know if they knew each other in school?**

They did.

---

[36] https://www.telegraph.co.uk/news/obituaries/11509668/Cynthia-Lennon-obituary.html

It was a memory in front of this brownstone, he was smoking, she had this like... her hair was... (Jennifer lifts her hands up).

Like in the 1950's?

I'm getting... 1956?

> (Note: The official record is they met in art school in September 1957).

Kind of when they first met?

"John was way too skinny," she says.

Was he wearing a leather jacket? Mr. Skiffle?

He was "just John." She's showing me that they wrote together... feels like... back then... "It's a circle," he shows me. They were writing together back then and are writing together now. (Jennifer starts to hum the melody for "I want to hold your hand.")

Was that a song written about the two of you?

No. They're both like fighting, laughing about it... hold on a second, I want to ask.

So John...

"You're bossy," says Cynthia... She wants to talk about her son too, so give me a second. (Pause) They're saying it was like a reverse song, it meant the opposite. That *he* didn't like holding hands, she's teasing him like it was an OCD kind of thing, she's totally teasing him. She's talking about someone named Robert...

That could be her ex, who just crossed over recently.[37]

Felt like it was his heart. A heart attack. Okay, so they both want to tell Julian "To not to wait any longer."

He'll understand what that means?

(Jennifer touches her nose.) **"Yeah."**

You mean in terms of marriage? Or something else?

Feels like it could be a marriage with his work or an actual marriage.

John, who was there to greet you when you crossed over?

This is interesting, first thing I was shown was Jimi Hendrix... was he alive when John died?

No, he died ten years earlier.

I didn't know that.

They were friends. So was Jimi there to greet you John?

"Yeah." I thought he was showing me like a dream he had... like he thought he was in a dream.

It felt like a dream?

Now he's showing me Woodstock.

You crossed over and then you saw Jimi Hendrix?

And Jimi said, "Come up on stage."

---

[37] "Cynthia Lennon... In 1970 married an Italian hotelier, Roberto Bassanini, in 1976 an engineer..." (Telegraph, ibid)

So John did you step on stage with him?

Yes. He's showing me the audience. Hold on a second, I just saw something really funny. **"It was like a welcome home party," he says, – "Then suddenly everybody in the audience became like little aliens...** (Jennifer aside: "Kind of like the tire scene in Harry Dean Stanton's story") **– that was the moment he realized he was in the afterlife, because everyone suddenly appeared as these little robot girls – just a funny visual, and he's like "Whaaaat?" and that was like "Oh. Welcome home."**

What was the song you guys were playing when you crossed over?

He showed me... This doesn't make sense. But I'm seeing shoes. Blue suede shoes?

That makes sense. The Carl Perkins tune.

> (Note: Jimi Hendrix recorded "Blue Suede Shoes" during a show in 1970 in Berkeley, John recorded the song in 1969 with Yoko and the Plastic Ono band.)

They're showing me a back-up band playing, a band that looks like Led Zeppelin, but I know it's not them...

This is a concert you're seeing with other band members?

It feels like 1969.

That makes sense, that was the year of Woodstock.

I didn't know that.

That's why I'm here. So Jimi pulls you on stage, John, you notice the audience is not who you thought they'd be... and then you're feeling was...

"Sudden silence. Crickets..." he was trying to figure out what was going on... because I felt his – he was super high when he was shot...

You mean stoned on grass?

"Yes." He didn't know what was going on, until... yeah... it was when he heard his wife... Yoko. All of sudden he heard her yelling and it kind of interrupted his homecoming party... he could feel her shouting.

Rich: Was this an exit point for you?

Jennifer: (quickly) **"Yes**."

> (Note: "Exit points" are term for how people describe key moments in their lives where they have an opportunity to exit. It shows how things are not preplanned, or that the journey is all mapped in advance. They often refer to these "exit points" as something that comes along, and if they feel they've done what they set out to accomplish or have some compelling reason for "returning home" they do so. It's not a pejorative in any way, nor is it meant to diminish a person's loss to the rest of his or her loved ones. It's just a question he could have answered "no" or "I don't know" to... but in this case, his answer came before I could finish the sentence.)

Since then, you've been doing other stuff, correct? What have you been doing, what are you up to?

He showed me channeling into someone else. A musician. Helping musicians.

Other musicians?

Yes, he showed me (a visual of) **the frequency of music – it being in his veins.**

What does that look like?

It looks like a darkish blue (energy), **a metallic blue, it's just a really deep color of blue.**

That's in your etheric veins?

"In your thread of the soul; that's what you're there for."

I've got a couple of questions for John. You told Julian how you might reach out to him.

He just showed me a balloon, something going up into the sky...

I've read that you told Julian if there is an afterlife, you'd reach out to you via this object...

(She laughs.) **I'm seeing something from a bird... a feather? I'm seeing a pink feather.**

Julian told the story of how his dad had said to him at some point, "If I die, I will try to reach out to you in the form of a feather." When Julian was in Australia on tour, an aboriginal Chief showed up in his hotel and said, "We need your help with getting fresh water to our people." Julian said he'd help in any way he could, and the Chief presented him with a giant ostrich feather. So, Julian created the White Feather Foundation, which helps indigenous people around the world

188

to obtain fresh water, including the Standing Rock tribe in the U.S.

That is so awesome... he was showing me different ways to get to that (image) **and I** (had) **cut it off... he was showing me going up in the sky through an image of a balloon and then a bird...**

How do you reach out to people?

"Through the mind."

The other thing I wanted to ask about was when I was staying at Julian's house and heard a voice wake me up with "Who the fuck are you?" I looked around and saw no one, but then recognized your voice. What was that about? Do you remember this?

Yeah, he does. Hold on. (Pause, listens) **He did that so you would tell the story later.**

Okay, well I mentioned that story in "Flipside" without using your name, but in the book "It's a Wonderful Afterlife" I did use your name. Any problem with my doing that?

(She shakes her head, no.)

> (Note: John's relationship with his first born was complex: "Dad could talk about peace and love out loud to the world but he could never show it to the people who supposedly meant the most to him: his wife and son. How can you talk about peace and love and have a family in bits and pieces - no communication, adultery, divorce? You can't do it,

189

not if you're being true and honest with yourself." [38] I mention this to point out that as frayed as our relationships may be while we're on the planet, once we're off it, those "character parts" appear to drop away. Again, just reporting; *don't shoot the messenger.*)

I asked for some other folks to come by today.

I got Prince, but we see him all the time.

Luana, you know who I asked for. There's someone else that I asked to show up today... who was that?

I got Eric Clapton. But he's alive.

Right... but I'm thinking of someone else that John knows.

But what musician is the one whose son died? Who sings the song "Tears in Heaven?"

Oh wow. I forgot. I did ask Conor Clapton to come forward.

You asked for his son to show up?

Yeah, I did the other night and forgot about it. So let's talk to Conor. How are you?

"Awesome," he says.

How old does he appear to you Jennifer?

I feel like he's 18 now.

---

[38] https://www.telegraph.co.uk/culture/4713954/Dad-was-a-hypocrite.-He-could-talk-about-peace-and-love-to-the-world-but-he-could-never-show-it-to-his-wife-and-son.html

(Note: Eric Clapton's son Conor passed away in in 1991. I mentioned him in "Flipside" "Would you know my name, if I saw you in heaven?" but I try to be as accurate as I can in these transcripts. We don't age the same way over there, but it was 27 years earlier than this conversation.)

Conor, who was there to greet you when you crossed over?

I feel like they had a miscarriage before – because he says his sister was there... She was like three years older. She was there to greet him.

But since then, Conor, what have you been up to?

"Playing music."

Have you reincarnated yet, or are you keeping an eye on your mom or dad?

"I have to wait," he says. He has to wait until they come back first.

Are you aware of that song your dad wrote about you?[39]

"The most beautiful song," he says.

I happened to be in the sound stage when the song was recorded. My friend was producing it and I got to hear it just after it was recorded. I saw your dad's handwritten lyrics on the music stand, and have one of the guitar picks with your dad's name on it from that session.

---

[39] "Tears in Heaven" written by Eric Clapton and Will Jennings.

(Jennifer makes a circle with her hand) **That's crazy! Another story that occurred so you could tell it later.**

That's why I was thinking of you while watching a documentary about your dad. So what do you want to tell your dad? Is it nice over there?

"Yes. I'm fine. I keep an eye on him."

Okay, thanks. I'll try to pass that along to him through a mutual friend. Class, there's someone else I'd like to ask John to bring forward. A band mate of his.

The one with the curly long hair? George.

Yes.

Oh, of course. **"Yes, he's here."**

George, we have a mutual friend. I remember him telling me that he owned a piano once owned by you...[40]

(Jennifer laughs.) **He just showed me the piano not being played because he wouldn't play it.**

That's funny. Luana and I were at Russ' house for dinner, I asked if I could play his piano and my friend said, "I listen to music all day long, I'd really prefer it if you didn't."

> (Note: Russ tells me I have this wrong; he **did not** own one of George's piano, but owned a large stone Buddha statute of George's. Likely, I misheard him when he was talking about the statue, and thought he

---

[40] After talking to Russ about this, he says his piano was not owned by George, but the conversation was as depicted about me "not playing it by request."

was talking about the piano. Either way George's comment holds true, as my friend Russ requested I *not play it*. I.e.; "Do you take requests?" "Sure." "Can you play "Far far away?"")

They're all laughing over there. George said, "He had 3 pianos."

I have a question on behalf of my brother Jeffrey.

He's showing me they went out for drinks.

Could be, he was dating your sister-in-law, Linda.

Okay, I just got that as you were saying it.

George's wife is Olivia, and her sister Linda was my brother's girlfriend, and he says he played softball with Tom Petty and George. He asked me to ask Tom a question.

"It's about time!" Tom just said.

Do you remember when you played softball with my brother Jeffrey?

Did he break a window?

Could be.

"It was something that he did..." Hold on. No one was paying attention though.

Okay, he says he hit a home run.. and nobody saw it? That makes sense.

He's saying, "No one was paying attention but yes, they do remember."

193

George – let me ask, who was there to greet you when you crossed over?

His animals. I'm seeing a bunch of them, including a little dog and a big one... a Great Dane.

> (Note: George had a number of pets, including cats and dogs. I've can't find any reference to him and a Great Dane, but there are a myriad of reasons why she may have seen a dog he didn't own late in life including a dog from earlier in his life.)

Did that seem odd to you that you were greeted by animals? When did you realize that you were in the afterlife?

He already had visitations before he left... from John... from... some comedians?

He was a big fan of Peter Sellers and the boys in Monty Python.

I'm seeing there are two people from Monty Python that he knew really well.

Well, Eric Idle and Michael Palin were close (and he produced their film "Life of Brian"). Not sure about the others.

One of them died before George?

Yes, Graham Chapman (who died in 1989, George financed the Python film "Life of Brian" in 1978 by mortgaging his house to pay for the budget).

Okay, but I'm seeing that he was in the back part of their group though. (Note: That's correct, the "lesser known one"

194

but beloved just the same). **All the memories came up all at once.**

George have you met Luana before?

Feels like in a bathroom... It felt like after a concert... because they were laughing and giggling in this smaller place.

Might have been after one of their Hollywood Bowl concerts in the 60's. She told me she and her pals met them at a post concert party. George wrote a song about a house on Blue Jay Way; "there's a fog upon L.A; up in Blue Jay Way." [41]

John says it coincided with "Lucy In The Sky with Diamonds."

> (Note: Inspired by his son Julian's drawing, "Lucy" was released prior to "Blue Jay Way." "Julian inspired the song with a nursery school drawing he called "Lucy in the sky with diamonds."[42] George lived in the Blue Jay Way house in 67, what's accurate is the two songs "coincided.")

George, are you having conversations with anyone back on the planet?

"Yes." Does he have like 5 kids?

---

[41] "Blue Jay Way" was released in 1967... The song was named after a street in the Hollywood Hills of Los Angeles where Harrison stayed in August 1967. The lyrics document Harrison's wait for music publicist Derek Taylor to find his way to Blue Jay Way through the fog-ridden hills, while Harrison struggled to stay awake after the flight from London to Los Angeles." Wikipedia)
[42] Wikipedia.

I think he has a son, but you're saying he has five people he's talking to that he considers family?

"Yes. Affiliated, associated, people he considers family."

> (Note: When Jennifer reports something, I consider possible interpretations; it could mean he "considers" five other people on the planet to be "like children" or it could be she's misinterpreting what she's seeing. It's not meant to offend anyone, or to claim anything different, but the public record is he has an only son, Dhani, also a musician. If this detail would prevent a person from reading further, I concur; *it's time to get a refund!*)

George, are you playing music over there?

"Yes."

Who are you playing with?

"John." (pause) **"And a bit infused with Prince now."**

What was your experience checking off the planet and running into John?

"Old times." And now they're all laughing at the word "old."

I know you're someone who understood Hindu philosophy...

I'm seeing someone greet him on the other side, like a woman on a white horse. He's showing me walking with someone with a horse on a beach somewhere...

I heard in a documentary that you used to think the manner of your death was important – you talked about the time you were attacked in your home and you had the thought you didn't want to die being traumatized. A crazed fan stabbed you in the throat... and then years later you had throat cancer... was that from..?

"Smoking too much."

Okay. But from the angle you're at now, what do you want to say about spirituality?

"It is limitless. It is a frequency that can never be right or wrong, but that's not the right terminology; whatever you believe in, is right; so how can that be wrong? As long as you aren't hurting someone with your beliefs. Hurting someone causes a ricochet in their soul – you know how you see a sandy beach, and if a bullet hits the sand it's hard and it gets stuck? If you hurt someone you hurt them in time and space and in all their environments."

Anyone that you regret hurting?

(quickly) **"John."**

How'd you hurt John?

He says, "He didn't want him to be their front guy."

I know that John and Paul had a financial deal where they got more royalties...

"That was fuuuucked up," he says.

But now it doesn't matter does it?

"Yes. It does." They're laughing. He's saying, "They want their heirs to get more money so when they reincarnate as

one of their heirs, they will have more money to choose from!"

> (Note: This is both funny and odd. Normally we find people who've crossed over have a kind of "live and let live" impression they like to impart. I've never heard anyone say *"Yeah, if we had more money, then we can reincarnate as one of our heirs and have access to it!"* It's not the way people report the process works but of course, there's room for comedy here, or perhaps for it to actually occur. *Who knows?)*

George were you a musician in a previous lifetime?

He's showing me Beethoven...

Someone from the Beethoven era or Beethoven himself?

A musician from that era... but he says, "He knew Beethoven." He says, "He helped him in some way."

> (Note: If you're going to name drop, why not just claim you were Beethoven? But he shows Jennifer an image of Beethoven, and then says he "Knew him and helped him in that era." This is one of those details I'd have to spend weeks researching, asking questions about the name of this person, and who or what he did. But as you can see from this freewheeling discussion, I just let it slide.)

How about you John, are you aware of any of your previous lifetimes?

He's super funny. **He just said** (very dryly) **"I like to live in the present."**

Yes, I'm sure you do, but did you have any previous lifetimes that you remember?

"Yes, one in Asia."

Oh, did you and Yoko know each other from before?

"Yes, as little kids, as brother and sister and they took care of each other."

> (Note: There are reports that John believed in reincarnation, was quoted as saying "it's just getting out of one car and getting into another." However, when we "recognize" someone in our lifetime that we feel we've known forever, it's possible we did know them before.)

So did you recognize her energy when you met her?

"Yeah."

I figured you guys were likely soul mates on some. In terms of your soul group – are you and George in that same group, or are there people in your soul group that we would know, or are you part of different groups?

Interesting. **He's showing me there are people that are like "extras," you may not know them...** (but they play important roles.)

They're people that you knew that you've incarnated with in the past?

"They all take turns."

> (Note: The term "soul group" comes from Michael Newton. In his research he found that people claimed

they had a group of individuals they "normally incarnated with" for many of their lifetimes. The average is 3-25 people. There are "affiliated groups" – people who would play a role during a lifetime to help that person complete whatever task they'd set out to accomplish. If you meet someone that you feel like you've "known forever" it's likely that you have.)

So when you signed up in this lifetime were you aware the way it would end? Or just that you had an exit point somewhere in the future?

That's interesting. **He says he had "Fears about his life ending soon" for a long time.**

As a kid? Or later in life?

"As a kid; he didn't think he'd make it past 25."

Then later in life, did you have a premonition it was going to be short?

"In his dreams." He says, "He had a hard time sleeping." It feels like the drugs made it hard for him to sleep as well, but it feels like he did, yeah. "A premonition in his dreams."

Your dreams were stressful?

"Yeah."

George, did you have any premonition about your leaving? Why did you check out when you did?

"No," he didn't have a premonition... He said **"He needed to help some people** (before he checked out). **That's why it took him the amount of time it did."**

200

Let me ask you about that. Your son, and your wife – are you helping them?

He's like "Of course!" He's telling me that his wife was the one on the horse.

> (Note: Again, we only bring about a third of our energy to each lifetime, according to this research, so two thirds of our energy is always "back home." This is why some people who've had near death events see or experience loved ones who are still on the planet but see them during their event. It's also the case in a number of deep hypnosis sessions where people see "living members" in their soul group. So for him to be greeted by his wife, who is still very much alive, is normal. Two thirds of her energy – of everyone's energy – is always "back home." So it's reported sometimes that a person who is "still on the planet" greets them when they "return home.")

What about your sister-in-law Linda? My brother asked as he regrets he didn't ask her to marry him.

"If he had, he wouldn't be a missing tooth."

> (Note: As it turns out, my brother had just lost a tooth, a funny reference. A bit harsh perhaps, but also pretty funny all things considered.)

"He wasn't ready."

My brother asked this question as well – "Is there auto racing in the afterlife?" He knew George loved Formula One.

"Yeah." Hold on. (pause) "Yes."

(Note: My brother Jeffry is a racing enthusiast. Former advertising director of Rolling Stone, he's owned over a dozen cars, has raced in at least two "Cannonball Run" cross country races (came in second, 5 minutes behind.) He told me about George's passion for Formula One racing.)

*So there **is** Formula One racing over there?*

"Yes. But it's more like Mach speed... it's like racing space ships."

Going that fast? Have you ever done that?

"It's how I got here today." (Jennifer laughs)

Ha. Okay, what's the one, two, three? How do people race over there? What's the math involved?

"You put the thought in your head..." He just showed me **his mind,** (points to her head). Jennifer listens; *No fucking way!* Sorry! **He said, "Then you assume the feeling that you want, so you put it in your mind what it is that you want to do, then you assume the feeling, of like the wind, the speed, everything that is going on..."**

Why did you say, "No fucking way"?

Because it's the same thing a lot of "new age spiritualists" say: "Assume the feeling you want; you already have it within."

A bit like how we asked Bill Paxton about how he creates a place of rest, the white beach he likes to hang out on. So creating this sensation of racing, are you racing against other people?

202

"All the time."

How do they invite you or do you invite them?

"It's the frequency. It's just like the frequency of this class, you send out a signal that the class or the race is about to begin and everyone who wants to race gets involved. They show you what's happening."

Who's they? Who shows you?

"God." (Jennifer laughs.)

You mean the network? You're talking about God as the network?

Yes, "Google."

> (Note: This reference to the "God Network" is something we've spoken of before. The idea that the internet mirrors somewhat the experience of the afterlife. And the idea of "God" is not about a who – but a "what." That God is the network that connects all of us. We can experience God by "opening our hearts to everyone and all things" – but it's another way of saying "open yourself to the network that connects us all." So in his saying "God tells me there's a race about to happen, it would mean "the network" sends out that same message. Not God as an object, or God as person, but God as a Googling device that is both particle and wave, both medium and mechanism.)

Rich: So, you have the sensation "I think I want to go racing," or you're hearing engines start and you say "I want to go do that..." But does everyone agree on when the green

203

light is going to happen, or are they just racing in their own minds? Is it an agreement to wait for the green light or is that just everyone's own personal version of the race?

Jennifer: He just showed me chariots. (She laughs). **He showed me different time and space, everyone's green light is different.**

Okay, so it's a bit like the race in "Ready Player One" – everyone shows up with their own version of a speedster - if you're a charioteer, that's your experience, but you might be a guy in a car which might be a DeLorean?

"Yes." He just showed me Seinfeld in a DeLorean. (Which he drove around with Patton Oswalt in "Comedians in Cars Getting Coffee") Interesting; **so they race against themselves, in their own time period and the frequency of whoever is fastest...**

How about the guy who gets the laurels? Are you creating that in your own mind that you're winning? Or are you actually the winner?

"Eh... it's a bit of both." He showed me like "trying to make a thought and it's not quite working."

So racing in the afterlife is a bit like Little League for kids; everyone is a winner, no one gets to lose.

"Yes. It's like you're winning the vibrations, bringing the frequency up, even if it's just a version of bringing the energy of horses and converting it to cars..."

I just got a thought put in my head. Can everyone play some music for Jennifer to hear? George would you play a G with a guitar? Can you do that?

204

Hold on. (pause) Is G the same tone or note that monks use when they chant?

Sure, could be. Is he playing one note or a chord on the guitar?

I'm hearing the same note on many instruments, guitars, violins, everyone. It's an orchestra.

Okay John, chime in if you want, Prince, can you chime in?

Wow. **It jumps... the frequency is what I can see... and with so many people it's challenging to listen – I have to really focus to hear them.** The other day I asked, "So why is it when I got to concerts or movie theaters, I see more spirits?" And the answer I got was **"Because it's loud in theaters and concerts, it's easier for them to hear it** (on the flipside), **the sound is loud so they can hear more."**

So folks on the flipside like go to the movies... that's funny. Anyone else want to chime in?

(Note: Jennifer's cell phone rings on cue.)

Very funny. All right so...here's a question. John have you ever met Mick Jagger's dad, Joe?

"Once or twice."

Can you bring him forward?

"Yes."

Hi Joe. Who was there to greet you when you crossed over?

He's showing me three people.

Joe, do you remember meeting me?

205

"Yes." He just patted you on your head. He says you met him at a birthday party.

Yes. That is correct. (ding!) It was his daughter-in-law's birthday party. Jerry Hall. How's she doing by the way?

> (Note: I met Jerry through Phillip Noyce's wife Jan Sharp, and Jerry Hall invited me to her birthday party in San Francisco where I met Mick's dad; he had an uncanny resemblance to the great comedian Stan Laurel.)

Jennifer: What's going on with her?

If he knows. She's married to a wealthy fella.

He says, "You should try and reach out to her."

Joe, you probably have better access than I do.

Is Jerry's mom over there too?

Yes, Marjorie, I met her in Austin. (ding!) Original "daughter of the Republic of Texas" she had five daughters, raised cattle. She passed about 5 years ago. She's a sweetheart.

She loved you! She's telling me, "She loved you." She's very loud, by he way.

That's funny. Texas mama. I told her I was thinking about adapting Jerry's autobiography into a film. Her mom tried to talk me out of that.

She says, "You have to try to reach out to her." Tell Jerry "There's more information that she needs, there's something coming to a close; she needs information."

Hard to reach out to her these days. Any suggestion how?

I got twitter... and the message "Just try."

Joe? Any message for your son Mick Jagger?

"Don't forget to dot your i's and cross your t's... and mind your P's and Q's."[43]

Well, he did major in finance in college so maybe it refers to that. Hope he knows what it means. John, anything else?

He just kissed you on the forehead.

> (Note: I don't feel anything, but when Jennifer says someone "patted me on the head," or "tapped me on the shoulder," it's the visual that pops into her mind. Like showing a picture of a red shaped heart would be a way of sending a "message of love.")

Anything you want me to tell Julian on your behalf?

"He needs to look further out... – he gets caught up in... he needs to reach further out... to reach for them."

You mean to reach for his parents on the flipside?

"Yes. Tell him to write. To write and listen."

Like the Morton method?

> (Note: We've heard this before. "Say the name of your loved one. Ask them questions. When you hear a

---

[43] Oxford dictionary says P's and Q's is "old english;" P is a sailor's pea coat and Q is queue, a pigtail. "1602: Now thou art in thy Pee and Kue, thou hast such a villainous broad backe..." https://blog.oxforddictionaries.com/2012/01/09/origin-to-mind-your-ps-and-qs/

reply before you can form the question, you've made a connection.")

"Yes."

Okay, I'll let him know. Any last words from our class? George anything you want to tell us?

"Love."

Robin, anything you want to tell George? You gave us the concept of "Love love."

> (Note: When writing "Hacking the Afterlife" we asked Robin for a quote for the book; his reply "love love." Love *the idea* of love, the gift of love.)

"Yeah."

How about you, John?

"No more guns." That's what he was trying to say back then.

Conor? Anything you want to say?

"Tell my dad to not give up. And to keep writing music. He stopped for a little while, feels like."

Anyone else?

David Bowie showed up. He said **"I forgot to mention. I'm having a ball."**

Anything you want to say?

"Live life to the fullest extent."

Tom Petty?

"Not to dream small. We can help you if you dream big."

George – your comment "Love" is related to what... love as an action? Love as a verb? A noun? Or ...?

"Love is all."

Thank you. How about you Robin?

Robin says, "He said it first!"

Very funny. Thank you. Speaking of our peanut gallery, Garry Shandling spoke to us last week, I didn't realize you were such good friends with Tom Petty.

Garry says, "I love Tom. We go way back."

Garry you were hilarious last week... Jennifer doesn't know because I haven't shown her the transcript yet.

I have no idea (what we said).

At one point you said you were golfing. I asked if you played 36 holes, you said "No, two. They're just very far apart." So class, we just want to remind everyone the reason we're doing this is to help people on the planet... or as Michael Newton can tell you...

Morton.

Morton will tell you...

He's taking notes up there... trying to help people over there help people communicate to their loved ones over here. I just got shown that frequency again, like the car example in Harry Dean Stanton's crossing over... **To show that everyone who wants to talk, can; it's a frequency. He's showing me people over there who are hurting, who**

209

want to talk, who want to help the planet be better, who want to help invent things to help the planet...

Michael, how are you showing them to communicate? Do they adjust their frequency slower? Faster?

He's showing me a grid. (Laughs.) Oh, that's funny. He's saying **"*We know we're no longer on the planet,* it's much harder for people here to communicate with people back there because people don't believe they can be talked to. People claim they're trying so hard to get a hold of us, that we are the ones who can't hear them... but *it's the other way around.* You can't hear us. So, there's a whole big school trying to help. (On the Flipside) They know where they're at, we're the ones who don't. Tell Scott De Tamble that Michael is keeping an eye on him and his daughter.**

I will. George and John, we have a mutual friend June who appears on the film and book "Flipside;" she's having some health issues.

It feels like she has to let go. Not let go of herself, but whatever it is that she's holding onto (that's negative); **to let go.**

Oh, hang on, I had a question for Hugh Hefner...

They're all laughing, "That is going to take awhile."

But one quick question for Hugh from my brother Jeffrey.

> (Note: Back in the early 60's, older brother was the "Playboy Rep" at his college, my dad was an early member of the Chicago Key Club. My brother has kept memorabilia from Hef, including autographed

copies of the first issue, etc. He was and remains a big fan of Hef.)

My brother asked, "Do you regret..."

(quickly) **He said, "No."**

I was going to ask, not regret, but "Do you miss having as much fun as you had over here on the planet or is it more fun over there?"

Hm. He says, "It's not as much fun physically," they're all laughing about that – "but way more fun mentally."

Thanks. See you on the flipside, class!

****

I'm sure this chapter is filled with inaccuracies and points of contention. After all, these folks have had their lives written about for decades. I didn't know any of them closely – and I point out the "brushing shoulders" aspect of how it might be that they are accessible.

Again – not trying to wave the celebrity flag here. All I can report is our attempt at trying to "talk to people we don't know" and see what comes through.

Memory is a tricky thing – while there is no delete key in the mind (everything is recorded) there are selective filters that allow us to access only certain bits and pieces, and sometimes rewritten to satisfy some specific reason. So even a report that comes directly from someone "back home" might be colored or painted with "How they'd like to remember that event" rather than "What really happened."

"We know *we're* no longer on the planet, it's much harder for people here to communicate with people back there because people don't believe they can be talked to. People claim they're trying so hard to get a hold of us, that we are the ones who can't hear them... but it's the other way around. You can't hear us."

Easily one of the most important sentences in this book. Russ Titelman, my friend who took this photograph of George, produced this song for him.

Photo Copyright Russ Titelman 2018, All Rights Reserved.

"Your love is forever,
I feel it and my heart knows
That we share it together....
The guiding light in all your love shines on
The only lover worth it all
Your love is forever."

George Harrison

CHAPTER NINE:

BUDDHA & JESUS WALK INTO A BAR

"Open your heart to reach higher"

A statue of Buddha in Tibet said to be sculpted when Buddha was alive. Barkor, Lhasa.

This conversation occurred prior to our class being formalized. However it's one of our most unusual conversations and is certain to *offend nearly everyone*.

As you've seen, I ask whatever pops into my head. That's a good thing. I'm trying to not filter what Jennifer sees, says or experiences. As you've seen she says whatever pops into her

213

mind and tries to translate it for me and the camera. Sometimes she says things she doesn't remember saying.

In *"Hacking the Afterlife"* there's an interview with "Jesus" – and as I point out in that book, three different mediums "talk to Jesus" with interview questions to understand more clearly who the heck the fellow is. The story so far is that he's an avatar "like other avatars" (his words) and that he brought "more of his conscious energy" than most (again his words) and the reason people feel "unconditional love" around him is that his energy is "closer to source."

Again, *his words.* Anyone in their right mind would discount these words, but as you can see, it's boring to be in our right mind. *We're outside of our minds at the moment, and this chapter will take us further afield.* It's a normal day in Southern California, Jennifer and I are in our noisy restaurant, and I just let the questions take us where they can.

*****

Rich: We were chatting and Prince appeared. I just turned the camera on; so our question for Prince is "What do you regret?"

Jennifer: Um. Robin just came in and tapped him on the shoulder – as if to say, **"I can answer that."** (to me) Do you want me to explain what I see first?

Sure.

I'm hearing Robin shouting "Ooh! Pick me, pick me!" He and Prince both want to talk.

Boys! Settle.

214

Prince says, **"He regrets not caring as much about the other side (the flipside). He's regretting not caring for the other side."**

What does he mean by that?

"He regrets paying more attention on how he was *feeling* **while being on over here, and not connected to the afterlife - if he had, he wouldn't have tried to escape being on the planet."**

He wishes he spent more time connect to people on the other side?

"No. In a way... he says he wishes he would have cared for the other side, he would have tried more to understand what it's like for the transition..." wait... No. **He's correcting me. He's showing me what it's like to go from here to there, he wishes he'd know the fluidity of it, how "we-are-all-one" it is on both sides – he kept it so separate. "He wished he would have thought** *heaven* **was here on the planet, versus escaping it via drugs. He regrets not being more in his body, he wishes he was** *more in his body* **(when here)."**

What does Robin regret?

Robin tapped me on the back, and I'm like **"Okay buddy."** I'm asking, "What do you regret?" (Listens) Aw. **He just showed me his wife.**

What do you regret about her?

"Not playing more of a passionate part with her." He was passionate in his work and his roles, but he wasn't passionate with her... and wishes he'd been that with her.

Wishes he'd given her the same kind of passion he had for his work?

"Yes." It was very sweet.

What do you miss about being here, Robin?

He's laughing. (Jennifer listens.) **He showed me the smells of food, he misses the authentic smells of food.**

What was his favorite?

Something like, beef stroganoff, like pasta with meat...

Who made that for you? A restaurant?

At home; his wife did. At least, I think his wife made it, or they had someone who made it. It was something he ate on his first date with her.

What was the dish called?

I can't get it right. It looks like red sauce with meat in it.

Spaghetti Bolognese?

No, something like stroganoff. Then he showed me an old picture of a California girl, her butt in a bathing suit... he said **"He misses butts..."**

Say what?

He showed me their fannies.

That's funny. That's a quote for the book. "Robin Williams misses butts."

"A whole lot of 'em."

What about you Prince? What do you miss?

First thing he said was a joke – **"I miss being in my head."**
He's showing me how exhausting that was.

You miss that adventure?

**"The music. The music over there... The music here is
infinite... But it's different."** (Jennifer aside) I have a
question for him – I asked if he's working over there on
creating who he'll be in his next life. "Do you make your life
up there so you can get it down here?"

Is he working on his next life or just chilling?

"Both." I really think that's it – from what he's giving me is
that up there you create the life that you want here. **"You
actually create it, then try to be it."**

*But still, you have to pick your parents, the right genetics, the
sociological background; you can pick the theater, the
character, but you still gotta satisfy the role – you still gotta
play Shakespeare while you're having a cappuccino, no?
Prince, I was wondering why you showed up in our
conversation, and I realize we do have a mutual friend.*

"Yes, we do." Luana just appeared. I know that's not her
you're referring to. But he says he likes hanging out with
Luana, says **"He's learning from her."**

*I'm referring to our friend was at his house many times to
interview him – just wondered if she was our connection.*

He said **"Yes, but not in the way that you think."**

*My question for the day; "What do you guys regret or miss?"
Or anything what would you like to impart to people?*

"Tell everyone to reach higher."

How do you do that?

Jennifer: I'm asking. **Prince showed me the heart, "You have to open your heart to reach higher." So, like, when you're upset, your heart is closed up it's ... it's like having your ankles locked – Prince showed me that... his ankles being shackled.**

Prince did have bad ankles.

> (Note: In our first interview with him (reprinted in *"Hacking the Afterlife"*) he was asked, "How'd you die? He replied, "Dancing killed me." When asked to explain, he gave Jennifer an image of jumping off a piano (something he often did) in his high heeled shoes – which eventually injured his ankles and hip, which led to him taking pain medication which led to his death. However, he added that "if you don't jump you'll never get anywhere in life.")

Jennifer: He showed me jumping off a piano. **He said, "You can't jump when you're shackled. Open your heart;"** he shows me literally getting higher. Being pulled up. **He says, "The three keys... are love... kindness... and accountability."**

Rich: Luana can you come forward? What do you regret?

She says "Oh, now, I'm number three in your list of who to talk to!?" She's laughing. She regrets "Not kicking the hairdresser's ass."

218

(Note: As noted earlier, she dated a hairdresser Richard Alcala, who the film "Shampoo" was partially about.)

So what do you miss, Luana?

"Salt air. I like being by the sea. Traveling and seeing different cultures, going through airports, the hot air." She wishes she could write, where it feels like it would help other people (back) **here.**

> (Note: Her SGI form of Buddhism was very altruistic. She chose a life as an actress so she could help people heal from seeing themselves depicted on screen, and she's expressing the desire to come back and write to do the same kind of thing. I knew her well enough to be able to see that thematic connection.)

I still have some of your short stories and original drafts of screenplays, as we met in a screenwriting class.

"It's like "very amateur," she says.

But there is that one script you wrote about your journey with Jack Nicholson and your friends, and Fred Roos and I have been trying to make that for years.

She gave me the chills. Is that about some kind of brat pack I'm seeing?

> (Note: Luana's acting class with Jeff Corey had Jack Nicholson, Sally Kellerman, Fred Roos, Robert Towne, Roger Corman, Richard Chamberlain and others.)

219

Yes, Luana was there; she wrote a script I've been trying to get it made... Part of my question is...

She showed me Paramount.

She was a bike messenger at MGM with Jack in the early days. So do I continue to pursue trying to make your film that or is this a fools' errand?

It's like, "You have to give it to others and let them run with it. Be a part of it that way." She's saying, "That would make it work."

Okay.

> (Note: Oddly enough, Fred Roos and I had come to the same conclusion, and had given it to some directors to consider. We'll see.)

Hold on. Luana regrets, **"Not having more animals."**

I knew of few of them, your dog "Boise," cats Robert, Mr. Bailey and Maggie" – who watched you was you flew around the room...[44]

I see her with a horse – I know she didn't have one in this life... maybe from a previous life.

Any other lifetime you want to show Jennifer?

That was abrupt – she showed me horses and animals and a medicine woman being stabbed in the heart.

---

[44] When Luana passed, both of her cats watched an invisible energy move around the room. Both heads moved in unison, eyes wide. It went on for about ten minutes, then all the clocks in her home stopped at the same time; 4 pm.

What year was this?

Feels like the 1600s... northern Europe. Norwegian, Scotland... up there.

> (Note: My first 4 books are about people remembering past lives under deep hypnosis, so I'm used to asking brief simple questions and seeing where we go, then following up on that path.)

In the Viking era? Women had a lot of power.

She did have a lot of power but from being a medicine woman... she was a triple threat.

Who stabbed you?

"Her husband." He said, "She betrayed him. He just wanted to get rid of her."

Who was that? Was that the hairdresser?

I just got goose bumps. That feels right.

> (Note: I'm aware of how "created" this sounds, but if you've been doing this for awhile, you just "ask questions" and see what you get. Later I can research how accurate or inaccurate these "past life memories" are. But in this case, I was curious to ask her "Who greeted you when you crossed over from a previous lifetime?" In my experience, when someone talks about being "stabbed by a lover" in a previous lifetime, it's often the same person who has been a thorn in their side in this lifetime.)

When you departed after that stabbing, who was there to greet you?

221

She showed me... it's going to sound funny, **but she showed me Buddha on one side and Jesus on the other.**

It's whatever she shows you. "Try not to judge." Let's take a look at Jesus. What does he look like?

> (Note: When someone claims to see an avatar, I try to avoid the "brain freeze" that goes with addressing them as someone beyond conversing with. I try to allow that it could be true, that they may be imagining it's true, or indeed, *it is true.*
>
> As noted, I've had a number of "conversations" with people remembering a lifetime with him (as reported in "Hacking the Afterlife") Not only via Jennifer but a dozen other people, not limited to mediums.
>
> If he "shows up" during a conversation, I try to ask everyday questions, as if it could have been Uncle Pete. In this case, Luana is saying the two people who "escorted her back home" from this previous lifetime were those two fellows; Buddha and Jesus. I've never heard anything of the sort before, but instead of dismissing it, I forge ahead. When Jennifer says "the green eyed version" it's because sometimes he appears with brown eyes with gold flecks in them, or even the traditional "Mormon" blue eyed version.)

Jennifer: She's showing me a green-eyed version of Jesus.

Rich: What's he wearing?

(Jennifer laughs.) I'm seeing jeans and a button-down shirt... light blue.

Long or short hair?

Pulled back.

Can we ask him a couple of questions? How do you know this fellow, Luana?

"From way before."

Did you know him on the planet or off planet?

"Both."

When did you know him on planet?

"Before he died..."

In India or Jerusalem?

She knew him in Jerusalem, but she died young (before his departure.)

> (Note: No reason to go into his whole story here – it's in *"Hacking the Afterlife."* Numerous accounts from people who claim that they knew him, that he survived the crucifixion, that he was married to Mary Magdalene, that she was a preacher in her own right, that he traveled with his family afterwards back to India where he lived out his days. Not my opinion, belief or theory – just what people consistently report in these accounts.)

What is Jesus up to these days?

"He's *very busy*." She showed him being like a shield over the planet. Protecting the planet.

Like a shield of compassion? Is that accurate?

"Yes." What I mentioned earlier; "accountability, kindness and love." That's what the shield is composed of.

So he greeted you Luana, after that lifetime? You mentioned Buddha. Can you give Jennifer an image of how he looks over there? Or how does he present himself over there?

As a bird. I see a white dove.

Okay, as a dove; that can represent consciousness. The whole "holy trinity" thing; father, son, holy spirit as a white dove thing... that represents consciousness... is that accurate?

"Yes."

So can we talk to this bird of consciousness?

He showed up as an owl.

Fine. Stand next to Jennifer, I'm going to ask you some questions.

He showed me numbers. Like in scriptures... Sanskrit.

Okay, for the purpose of our conversation, Sid... can I call you Sid, short for Siddhartha?

"Okay." They all think it's funny; they're laughing.

Can you focus on your lifetime here as Siddhartha? Put that in your mind? Why are you emanating as an owl?

"Wisdom. A symbol of wisdom."

Let's talk about that – your experience under the bodhi tree when you saw people on the flipside, you passed that information on, you eventually shared it with the planet.

"Yes." He showed me an energy force field that went *boom*.

True, like a shock wave that affected the planet. However, you argued that there is no self, that who we are as people is not finite, because it's always changing. Did you find anything contrary to that when he checked off the planet?

"It's interpretation; yes."

But that's a key point – people consider you...

"A guru..."

Beyond guru. An enlightened person... who is infallible.

He's showing me a bicycle wheel going around... and how the spokes sometimes break off, sometimes they're wrong or they don't function properly, but the wheel continues around.

Okay, that's a good example for Buddhists. The wheel. Things can be wrong or inaccurate in the dogma, but it keeps on turning.

"It's a bad thing, because it limited the message."

Watered down the message?

"Fine, Rich, watered down the message."

> (Note: Nothing quite like being chastised by an avatar.)

Do you mind us interviewing you? Talking to you?

"More than happy to show up." He's showing me Robert Thurman. "He did a number on you mentally." I don't know what that means.

Professor Thurman opened up my eyes to your sutras, your teachings.

"Yet it made you more confused."

> (Note: After Luana's passing, Charles Grodin invited me to come and work on his talk show on CNBC. I spent a year doing "man in the street" interviews for him, and on the plane to NYC, read an article about Robert Thurman. He told a story about how he had gone to see the reincarnation of his former teacher, and how the 5 year old had ridden over on his trike to Bob and said "Thurman, you so disappointed me when you left the monkhood." He was shocked to see that the 5 year old was looking at him the same way his old teacher had. I thought "Wow, this man must have insight into the flipside," so I asked if I could audit his class. He told me it was for Doctoral students only, I insisted. Thurman said, "How familiar are you with Hegel and Kant?" and I said, "They play for the 49ers?"
>
> Bob allowed me to audit his class which led to our trips to India and Tibet together. He's easily the most learned scholar in Tibetan philosophy I've ever met, and contributed a chapter "The Death of Death" to "It's a Wonderful Afterlife." If you ever get the chance to hear him speak in public, do so; his public talks are epic and legendary, and his books are filled with diamonds.)

Actually, (my class with Thurman) gave me tools to figure out what you were saying to your followers.

> (Note: Thurman's in depth instruction was key to giving me a method of figuring out the subtle complexities of Buddhist philosophy. It's profound. I found that the Buddhist inspection of the nature of reality is peerless. It's the afterlife concepts where I've found contrary arguments.)

Jennifer: I'm sorry; it's my interpretation (of what he's saying)... **He's showing me you *were awakened*, but after that, you saw a lot of things that were contrary to what you had learned, and you were confused by seeing the truth. "It freaked you out."**

Yes, that's correct.

> (Note: Once I fell into the research, I realized Buddhism's description of the afterlife wasn't the same as I was hearing from folks under deep hypnosis. (I.e., we are "conscious" back home and not wisps of smoke or "clear light.") It made me think perhaps Buddha's "between life" experience of visiting the flipside (during his three days in equipoise under the bodhi tree) may have been misinterpreted. He said he feared that might be the case, as he didn't talk about it for two weeks thinking "no one would understand what he was talking about." But ultimately he decided to share what he'd learned, and people have expounded upon it for centuries.)

Jennifer: **He's showing me that he was imparting *metaphor*, like showing us the owl - everything he tried to relay was**

more in symbols or metaphor. That's why he showed me an owl.

Rich: Because it's not just one thing in terms of understanding, it's the five hundred things?

"Five hundred thousand things."

So you tailored your message to your audience?

"Yes. To different countries, to different audiences."

I have a question for you... since being here, have you reincarnated?

"Parts of him has, many times, in many different... lives."

(Note: "Jesus" was asked the same question during a session between Dr. Elisa Medhus, her son Erik and medium Jamie Butler. (It's a session where you can HEAR voices respond on the audio – Dr. Medhus didn't hear it, initially, but I pointed it out to her.)

In this session, "Jesus" said he's reincarnated since being here on the planet and reported a lifetime in Florida in 1964 where he was born as a child without use of his limbs, confined to ICU. Dr. Medhus knew the name of the affliction (*Osteogenesis Imperfecta*) and he claimed he had done so to help the parents and medical staff to "learn lessons in unconditional love."

Buddhism teaches, generally, that once Buddha was "enlightened" he no longer had to be part of the "Wheel of Life" – the idea that we are forced to reincarnate in different life forms until we achieve perfection. This isn't in the research, by the way – as noted, people claim that we all choose our next lifetime albeit with the help and guidance of our loved ones.

The dialectical question I'm asking – and apologies to Buddhists everywhere who may find this heretical - was given to me by Robert Thurman while we were on Mt. Kailash. Bob said the best debate question was to consider "If Buddha considered himself a Bodhisattva.")

Rich: The argument goes like this; and I heard it from Bob Thurman when we were in Tibet: "If you're a bodhisattva, part of the "Bodhisattva vow" is to continually reincarnate until the planet is liberated. So why haven't you incarnated fully as yourself to do that?"

Jennifer: **"People aren't ready for that to happen or to have someone like Jesus return..." Just not ready for a "second coming."**

Perhaps this research is a version of the second coming. By investigating what really happened way back when – by retelling the story of who you were or who Jesus was or is – it allows both of you to "return" in a form that is part of intellectual curiosity. Question to either one of you - why don't you guys flip a coin and let the winner – or loser – return?

They're laughing.

So let's ask them our question of the day, "What do you regret?" So Sid? What do you regret?

He regrets "not getting along with his father."

(Note: Jennifer is not a Buddhist, nor knows the story behind Siddhartha's life and journey. But in a nutshell he was born into wealth, his father shielded him from any kind of pain and misery, banishing lepers and sick or old people from their city state. And one day, it's reported that Siddhartha traveled outside the city gates and saw people suffering who were sick, old or dying. And he set off to figure out why that was.

"Why were people suffering?" he asked. He left his father in the lurch, not reuniting with him for years, until he was a preacher followed by thousands. That's the basic story of his journey.

While he was under the Bodhi tree for three days, he came to the realization of why we suffer as human beings, and reported it in his 86,000 sutras, or teachings about the nature of reality. I fully realize how "heretical" these questions are to people who are devout – but I try be an equal opportunity heretic – I ask the same questions to everyone, of any avatar we run across in our investigation. As I say – if it offends the dear reader, I apologize. But for Jennifer to note his relationship with his father, would be in line with what the record is about their relationship.)

Rich: I know you reunited with your father later in life. What do you miss about being on the planet?

Jennifer: **"Being a kid."**

Jesus? Same question. What do you regret?

"Dying on the cross." Then he laughed.

230

But you've told us that you didn't die on the cross, is that correct?

He's joking with you. "Don't get your panties in a wad, Rich."

"Dying is easy. Comedy is hard." Very funny JC.

"He regrets that the Romans did not understand what he was about."

> (Note: Although I've interviewed a number of people, or read accounts of people who claim to have known or met Jesus, who claim they "were in awe of him," and that he "radiated love" - obviously there were those who did not; Roman soldiers for example.)

What do you miss about being here?

(Jennifer pauses, hesitates.) I'm just going to say it... he showed me Mary Magdalene's body. That's what came to mind.

He was human after all. It's allowed.

> (Note: I suspect if people are *still reading* up until now, they're *not going to be offended* by this comment. If they are; apologies; Jennifer is reporting what she's hearing or seeing, I'm transcribing what I'm filming. *Don't shoot the messengers.)*

"And children. I'm seeing children. He misses children."

Having them or being around them?

"Being around them." He showed me as an example Michael Jackson. Michael surrounded himself with children, for the most part, and says that it was taken the wrong way... and because of it...

Hang on. Is Michael Jackson available? Can we talk to him?

"Okay."

Michael – same question. But first, "How are you?"

"I'm fine. Fantastic."

We're interviewing people in this unusual way. Class, if you all could make him feel welcome. Today we're asking, "What do you regret?"

He just made a joke, everyone's laughing. He said, "I regret giving kids "Jesus juice." (Jennifer aside) That's a really screwed up joke.

Michael and Jesus are pals now. A joke's a joke. We can offend everyone while we're at it. So Michael, what do you miss?

He's showing me sweat.. he misses the work of singing to create the sweat... the sensation of dancing.

Who was there to greet you when you crossed over?

I don't recognize this person – his dad is still alive, correct?

Yes. (He was at this moment) His grandfather? A spirit guide?

I can't tell. He had a lot of people show up for him, but he showed me energies I don't understand.

Okay. Well you were taking that weird drug that makes you feel you're in nowhere-ville. When did you realize you'd crossed over? Right away? Or did it take awhile?

"Took awhile." He said he saw them (spirits) when he was here ... He's saying he was very clairvoyant. That's what he's telling me.

I have a friend in Chicago, Shayne who told me she had a dream...

...about dancing with him. He showed me. I see something about his feet being on hers, or hers on his... there was something about the dance she didn't get... it was something to do with crossing up feet.

I think that's correct, it's been so long I doubt she remembers. But I remember her telling me she had this dream she was dancing with you, and I thought I'd ask. How do people access you?

"Through the heart. Through writing... when you're writing about somebody, people writing about him – his unique code (or frequency) is embedded in a way that draws him in."

Anything you want to say to your loved ones that miss you so terribly?

"Sorry. Tell them that drugs is not the answer." (Jennifer laughs) Then Robin jumped up and said "Yeah! That's right!"

By the way Michael have you met Luana?

He said, "She's a gate keeper." He showed me her with a clipboard and a rope, "like a bouncer at a hot club saying "No. You can't come in." She's the gate keeper."

So drugs are not the answer?

Drugs are not the answer for someone who wants to get this life right, and not have to do it over 500 thousand more times.

Okay, thanks everyone; we'll see you on the flipside.

****

There's no point in rehashing *how* any of this could be accurate or true. All I can offer is these stories are consistent; when I "interviewed" Jesus via a dozen people in *"Hacking the Afterlife"* – even though none had ever met, they all told the same basic stories that were contrary to what the common dogma or beliefs have been about the fellow. (That he survived the Crucifixion, as is reported in the Qur'an, that he spent a lot of time in India prior to his troubles in Jerusalem, and afterwards. That the Crucifixion was something he knew was going to happen, but planned for it in such a way that his friends were able to save his life, and spirit him out of the country. That he spent the rest of his days with his family in Kashmir. Again, not just one story, but multiple accounts of the same story.)

If they had told me contrary stories or stories that line up with the Bible; I'd be happy to report that. But that's not what those stories lined up with. *Am I claiming we just had a conversation with Jesus and Buddha?* I'm claiming we asked questions and got answers, and if they line up with anything else in the research, then they're worth examining.

I wanted to share an insight Scott De Tamble gave me the other day. He's done hundreds of between life hypnosis sessions, interviewed or spoken to countless "avatars" "guides" or "counselors" who appear to be in the afterlife.

They often *appear* dressed in some kind of robe, sometimes wearing a hat, or some costume that says, "I am someone of great wisdom." Scott pointed out that he'll ask them to "reveal how they really look" to the person doing the hypnosis session and he said "They show them these blobs of light. They don a costume that gives them a certain amount of authority – monk's robes, wizard hat, clerical garb; but underneath, they're still *just blobs of light.*"

We are *all just blobs of light* – we tend to think of things in terms of hierarchy – but that's not what is described. One day Scott was doing a deep hypnosis session, this woman said her guide "looked like friar Tuck wearing a tunic with a cowl over his head." Scott asked, "Why are you wearing this outfit?" The woman laugh; "He just said, "Because my clown outfit is at the cleaners."

Rich, Luana and Dave Patlak in clown outfits

CHAPTER TEN:

AMELIA, A TRIP TO A LIBRARY AND A CLASSROOM ON THE FLIPSIDE

"Field Trips"

The famed aviatrix. Photo: Wikimedia

Another day, another pitch to a studio about making the real Amelia Earhart story. I've been at this for thirty years, and if Amelia didn't keep showing up and encouraging me to tell her story, I would have given up a long time ago. But how do you turn down someone patting you on the back, telling you to "give it another shot?"

*****

Rich: Hi Class.

Jennifer: Amelia is here.

Rich: Let me ask you, there was a recent documentary on the History Channel about you, which includes a photo of you and Fred Noonan on a dock in Jaluit. Was this you and Fred standing on a dock in Jaluit harbor in 1937?

> (Note: Referring to History Channel's, "Amelia Earhart." I was asked by the producer to contribute my extensive research – I spent a day with him, going over everything I had learned and we filmed a "sizzle reel" to help him sell the idea to History Channel. Ultimately when the show was made, his offer was too small for me to turn over my thirty years of research.
>
> I wished them the best of luck, but I passed on doing the show. In the show, one of the investigators, a former federal investigator Les Kinney, found a photograph buried in the Naval Intelligence archives of Amelia and her navigator Fred Noonan on the docks of Jaluit, not far from where she came down in Mili atoll.
>
> What's amazing about the photograph (which I've helped verify and put that research on EarhartOnSaipan.com) is that it also shows her plane being towed by a Japanese ship.)

Jennifer: She shows me – "No, but yes." **Yes, that's accurate, but something about the time being wrong.**

Rich: Well, my research shows you landed in Mili atoll in July of 1937. And the Japanese arrested you right after. I'd guess they took you to Jaluit in a few days, at the most a week.

"Yes."

The photo itself - is it of you and Fred?

"Yes. The mechanic." (Referring to the report from a French sailor who was in Jaluit at the time, who claimed he saw "Earhart and her mechanic there" as reported at EarhartOnSaipan.com)

Fred was her navigator.

"He worked on the plane too."

That Frenchman said something interesting; he said that you and Fred were taken by seaplane to Saipan?

"Like two days later, yeah. It was both though; the plane went on the boat, and she went on the (sea)plane." I'm seeing both.

Yes, eyewitnesses report the boat took her plane. And the seaplane took her and Fred. I have a couple of eyewitnesses on film who saw them arrive at the docks in Saipan.[45]

She's saying for you to ask the naval intelligence about that picture. Ah. **I feel like they're going to find... something**

---

[45] No point in rehashing her story here. I published what I learned in *"Hacking the Afterlife"* and use the website EarhartOnSaipan.com for photos and other details of corroboration. I have US Marines on film claiming they found her plane and briefcase on Saipan, and dozens of other islanders who claim they saw her on Saipan when she was incarcerated by the Japanese before and during the War.

with Fred, but not Amelia. She says it's not going to be organic... almost like someone will "plant" it.

They'll find something they planted?

She's looking at my watch... I believe she had a watch on at some point, they took it away from her when she landed... someone from Japan has it... [46] **Would they do that? I'm getting something small, like a fingernail. But it will be Fred's.**

I was warned by Earhart expert Elgen Long that he suspected something like that might happen. But on one hand; who cares? What am I gonna do other than say...

"That they planted it."

Okay. Odd argument; "It wasn't me, it was Amelia on the Flipside and she said it was planted." Is it a fingernail?

She's showing me teeth. She's making fun of Fred, hold on. It has to do with dental.

So that's why you're showing this to Jennifer?

"Yeah." [47] **She wants you to tell her story from her girlfriend's point of view, by the way**.

That's a great idea. Tell it "Citizen Kane" style – different people who had these differing versions of who she was, America's sweetheart, a spy for FDR, a tomboy, a lover...

---

[46] https://www.afar.com/magazine/armchair-aviators-you-can-own-amelia-earharts-watch

[47] Elgen Long wrote "The Mystery Solved." He's retired, but is often called to comment on the "latest find."

She says, **"I want my girlfriend's point of view and what it was like for her to be with me."**

Okay. I'd better remember to give you credit for that... telling your story from multiple points of view. Including the people in Saipan who took care of her.

Jennifer: **She just showed me what it's like in your head, putting all the pieces together, the mice that are going in your head.** You are the best interviewer. You bring out so many answers.

Rich: I love that I'm having a story meeting with Amelia about her life story. Like a Citizen Kane version of her life, including people who had an axe to grind, who opposed her... everyone telling different stories about who the enigma was.

She's showing me she loved animals, loved dogs. She's also showing me wanting to be a boy so much... that was a huge part of her. She showed me pictures of her young; wearing bloomers and hating them, wanting to wear boys' clothes.

She created the concept of the equal rights amendment – still not passed in all these years... being the devil's advocate is the best way to do this story.

"And her being in love with a woman."

It's funny; she's the one story that when I write about it, I get angry mail. People don't seem to care about me saying there is an afterlife, they don't give a hoot about me talking to Jesus, but when I mention Amelia they go crazy.

She's happy now. Why can't everyone be happy?

Right. She said that to us. "I'm here... stop looking for me."
That was my favorite quote from "Hacking the Afterlife."
She's right.

"Your job is to prove there is an afterlife with this story."

Gee, thanks. All of my research came directly from people on
*the flipside. In her case, her story was told to me **by her on***
***the other side.** If I dig up her body and her plane, it will*
prove that beyond a shadow of doubt. But not that I found her
bones... They'll stop talking about how she died and talk
about how she lived.

It's great stuff.

Okay, Jennifer, we were talking about a recurring dream you
had – where you'd see little girl in your dreams. My question
to you is, when you see this little girl, do you remember a
lifetime with her?

(She's) a little dirty girl with unruly hair I've never seen
before. She has spiral curls. She's wearing overalls. Fluffy
pant leggings, a big shirt over her fluffy pants. Her shoes
that tie up crisscross.

How tall is she?

Looks tiny.

What color eyes?

Bluish green. She's five.

What's this little girl's first name?

Diana.

What's her last name? What year is this?

241

Rutherford or something like that. 1807 came to mind.[48]

Hi Diana. How do you like to be called?

"Dee."

Dee, are you someone Jennifer knows, someone she knew in a previous lifetime or someone she was?

"Someone I was."

Is 1807 the correct date? Where are we?

1807 or 08. She's five. Near Manchester. (England)

Do us a favor and introduce us to your parents. Are these folks anyone Jennifer knows?

My dad. (Jennifer's dad, who had recently passed over.)

Look who showed up on your birthday (today) to remind you that you didn't need to call him! Let's go to a happy moment like having dinner with your family.

Looks like it was crazy, a ton of people having a big dinner.

Is this your home?

I'm fighting with my brother whom I don't like. Feels like a very large home, there are several families.

---

[48] Ancestry records show that the Rutherford family of Manchester were Scots, as in Scotland. There were a number of barristers in their family dating back to the early 19th century (Thomas, John, etc, all "Esquires") The Rutherford clan had a castle Edgerston, 6 miles south of Jedburg, Scotland.

What's the event?

It's our birthday. My dad and I shared the same birthday (in that lifetime).

Let's take a walk outside. What the name of the street? What does it look like outside?

Brynwick... or Brunswick. It's a big home by a lake. It's like north England... Where is Manchester?

North of London... about halfway up the peninsula. What does your dad do for a living? What's his name?

Rutherford. He wears a wig. He's like an attorney or a judge. In London. [49]

> (Note: Jennifer is not "under hypnosis." I'm just asking her questions about a recurring dream she had. She has an ability to see or interpret whatever pops into her head, so I try to direct the questions to see what, if anything we can find.)

Go to his office.

He's holding me... I'm sick. I have leukemia, that's how I die. At six.

What did Diana learn in that lifetime? What was her reason for choosing this short journey?

---

[49] Footnote: Brunswick Greens is a street listed in the London Post in the 1800's. https://newspaperarchive.com/london-morning-post-apr-17-1829-p-1/ There were a number of barristers "Rutherford Esquire" in London in the early 1800's.
http://reed.dur.ac.uk/xtf/view?docId=ark/32150_s12f75r800m.xml

To show my dad (Jim) what *family* was.

This was a teaching lesson to give your father?

Yes.

Let's skip ahead to your guide... what's your guide's name again?

Mary.

Mary, what did Jennifer learn from this short lifetime as Diana?

That it was ok to be myself, because everyone else was quiet or behaved in a certain way, and I was able to make everyone else laugh because of how I behaved. Now, she's showing me Princess Diana.

Can we bring Princess Diana forth? What's she up to?

"Yes." She looks beautiful.

Appears about what age?

28.

Is it okay to ask her some questions?

"Yeah."

So how do you occupy your time now?

"Playing with her kids. And grandkids."

Can they see you?

"The littlest one can."

How do you perceive them? How's your perception work?

It's like a bubble – it's so weird to see it. Like when we asked my dad, Jim, about how he is seeing us; he showed me this giant bubble. He showed me how you just have to focus your energy on going through it.

Do you hear all the sound outside the bubble?

"No."

Diana, was your death in Paris an exit point, and if so, why did you take that particular exit point?

She's saying, "That it would have unraveled... if she had lived. It would have unraveled their establishment. The Royal family."

Were members of the royal family involved with your demise, or a government agency, or was it an accident?

The part she blames her family for is having all the reporters around.

But the accident in the tunnel?

An accident. "No," she doesn't assign any blame. She says, "It was one person because of the phone calls that were made that..." (Listens) She blames how much the paparazzi chased the family because they tried to hide things, which made it worse. The next accident would taken her and her children.

So there was no conspiracy to have you killed?

"No." She says "I'm sure there were those who wished my death, but no. Not that."

It's not that all that important, because you still exist, you're not gone, you're just on the other side. Are you planning to come back soon?

She says, **"No. It's like a one hundred year break."** She's really beautiful... a beautiful person.

Mary, thanks for showing us that. Why did you show that lifetime to Jennifer?

It feels like I was shown a lifetime I had of a little girl who died young from having cancer and that lifetime was for my dad, for his purpose... **and then this time around my dad dying of cancer was for me to learn my own lessons for my purpose.**

Okay. Thank you for sharing that.

My dad is showing me a beautiful palace... it's like a temple.

A temple?

It's like a place with records. They treat it like it's a sacred place. I've seen this before.

Records? You mean like a library? What is this place? Are we looking at pillars?

He showed me the form of books.

> (Note: In many of the deep hypnosis sessions I've filmed and transcribed, people report going to an "Akashic library." I prefer to just call it *a library* because every account I've ever heard or filmed is different, as is this one.)

Before we go inside this building. How tall is it?

Three football fields high. White.

Can you touch the wall? What's the wall feel like? Soft or rough?

Soft. **He shows me books – and then he showed me what it really is – they aren't books, or books that contain records; they're colors. They are a frequency... and you access the energy or the frequency from those colors.**

Can you stand in front of the books?

I'm seeing that the books are these frequencies. The frequency is your soul – he's showing me the eye of the soul... which you access through the heart. It's our frequency... it's like the scan of an eye that they use for security when you're going in... They scan the eye of your soul to send you where your frequency is, where your history is. Where all of your lifetimes exist. What he showed me was... hold on, I got too excited. My dad and discussed this when he was here.

So you're on your way into this repository with him? Describe it.

You just know where to go without thinking about it. And you're led to the frequency; it's the same matching colors of who you are as a soul...

You scan the energy of your eye and that takes you to where your energy is?

No. When you enter this place somehow it scans your soul and then puts it up on a screen. I can see your heart's center... it's the color green.

What's the screen like?

It's a hologram, it's takes you into your own private room like a huge screen, it's in your mind.

It's like Albert Brooks film "Defending Your Life."

> (Note: Michael Newton mentions "Defending Your Life" in my interview with him for Flipside. It was a film starring Albert and Meryl Streep where he dies and goes back home to meet his guides who are about to sentence him to return to the planet, but he falls in love with Meryl Streep and wants to be with her instead. His depiction of the "past life review" is hilarious – and also, according to the reports, right on the money. I tracked down Albert via email and pointed this out to him – his secretary told me that he loved hearing about it, but also didn't believe it.)

Jennifer: **He's showing me this vast hall of records; my dad is able to show this to me through our connection. He shows me that the "books" are light – but they're dense with information. He showed me like trying to lift up a book but it was too heavy... over there it's all just light.**

Rich: How does your dad appear in this vision? What age do you see him as?

About the age of 33. He showed me a portrait of Jesus to give me an answer to "How old are you?" I used to call my dad by the nickname "The baby Jesus" as he could do no wrong.

So let's scan your book, or the hologram of this book, can we? What does he want to show you on this scan?

He showed me at the age of five. What a burden I was.

Why were you a burden? Were you an annoying five year old?

He's laughing. "Very funny." **He says it's because they knew I was different.**

Okay, even at five? How do you look in this memory?

I'm wearing a little plaid dress on my birthday...it's July 1ˢᵗ, 1976.

You're in a plaid dress, but something happened this day that was important to your dad because he wants to show it to you... roll the memory forward, what happens on this fateful day? What did you do that made him want you to see this?

He says he always knew I was "unique" is what he called it – That's when he knew something was special about me...

I get that. But what did you do on this day that made him want to remind you?

I don't know.

Your dad knows. Jim, can you show it to her please?

He says, "You said something about my father...." (Jennifer listens.) **He shows me that I was saying something to him about his dad, about how how his father was hurting physically. How he was ill, but that nobody knew...**

What did you say in your little five year old voice that made him realize you were connected to his father?

249

(A pause. Listens) Oh my goodness. **I told him that I thought we should move to California from Arizona to be with him and we ended up doing that. I said, "Daddy we need to move to California because grandpa's hurting."**

> (Note: Jennifer was not aware of this memory. She is not "under hypnosis." We are chatting over lunch. And we are at the moment in some etheric building accessing a memory that her father *wanted* her to see. When people report seeing their "library" they often just observe what it is. In this case, I asked her father to *"show her the memory"* he wanted her to recall. **Not his; hers.** And when she saw it, she remembered why it was *important to her father*.)

*I understand; he's showing you the moment **when you changed his life** – he's showing you that moment from your own "Akashic records."*

I didn't know that.

Focus on this moment for a second; it's not coming from you it's coming from him. It's the moment when he realized you were special and he understood what you were saying on some spiritual level about his father and that's how the journey changed for him. Okay, Jim, can you take her to another point that you want to show her?

(Jennifer pauses) **Graduating from seminary.**

Him or you?

Me.

What are you wearing?

A white graduation dress.

Let's ask him; why is this an important moment?

He was so happy that I made it – he was afraid for me, afraid something was going to happen to me in my life that would have prevented this day. He showed me the memory of that lifetime we had before when when I was sick and died at the age of six (earlier chapter); he was always afraid something wrong would happen to me.

But it did not.

I made it past a certain point. (The age which he feared she wouldn't make it again) and then I did it – I went to that seminary every morning at 6 am.

Anything else you want to share with your daughter on her birthday, Jim?

He draws a heart. He says, "to never give up." When he died (recently) I didn't open up for days in my work. I just felt closed, I felt like a band aid was being ripped off every day, even though I knew I should get back to work. He says my work is healing me, but that I don't know that it's healing.

Healing for Jennifer or her clients?

For other people... and me...

Let me ask, "How is this information for your records shared?" Are we looking at a time line?

He says, "Through the heart."

I understand that's the mechanism for transmission, but I want to ask a question about the physics of "searching for memories." So each time frame is recorded somehow back here in the record books like a hologram, so we can skip ahead or backwards?

He said (the process) **it's timeless. We're living in a timeless zone. Instead of a twilight... past, present, future shows up to me at the same time when I do my work.**

My question is how are you presenting this information to her? What's the physical way that you're doing it?

He's showing my energy field and his. And he merges the information with mine.

How do you do that?

Through the frequency. That's the thing that draws him in and allows him to share the information that's in our souls.

Okay, I have a philosophical question for you. Could I share my energy with a stranger? Or could I access their energy and experience their life? Could I do that consciously on the planet or do I have to be over there where you are?

He showed me how they pick up things from other people, based on fear or calmness... "You have to be open to it. So if you're open to it, yes."

But let's say I wanted to manipulate someone... not in the "Inception" movie kind of way... but to influence someone and their behavior. Like a leader in government.

"That's where the power of prayer comes in."

252

Well, they've done a number of scientific studies showing prayer is ineffective over here in terms of changing something outside of it.

"But prayer is what we use to talk to them."

I see. You mean like prayer is a form of a channeling or a focusing an intent? But focusing, we magnify it?

"Prayer is used to raise your vibration first..." Obviously it doesn't always work because I asked for a miracle to save my dad's life and it didn't happen... But he's agreeing with you.

The answer to how to make prayer work has been a question throughout human history. I understand that there is a myriad of factors involved – the kind of lessons or lifetime people sign up for, or experiences that occur now and pay off in lessons lifetimes from now. I was just asking about the transmission process.

"Prayer is like mediation, whatever you put into is is what you get out of it."

And then there are people who have used it for selfish ends... black magic comes to mind. Not that it works, just that history is replete with examples of people claiming it works.

"By doing something like that, it will take something from you – because you have to lower yourself to get that kind of vibration, as opposed to elevating your spirit."

The other theoretical, this conversation people have where they claim they were inhabited by some kind of entity that travels along with them. There are these tales of people being possessed, etc. My argument is that isn't possible because of free will – a person can only travel with you if you allow them to do so.

He says **"No, it's like schizophrenia; it's all in your mind. No one travels with you. However, it's real to the person experiencing it, so for them it is real."**

In their mind?

"There's no point in telling them it's different. For them it's their reality."

From what I've learned in this research, there's a "free will" law back home; where you can't interfere in another's path. Law is perhaps too formal; it refers to an agreement?

He's saying whatever your purpose is – "You have your own rules or laws." For example, there are rules that govern a country, but let's say one soul group is learning how to handle a crisis, they're going to use a different set of rules so that they can allow different experiences in to help them learn.

Let me ask you this, Jim. Are you involved in any classroom work or teaching in a classroom setting? Something you're learning or teaching?

He just rolled his eyes. He says, **"The learning is infinite, so much to learn not from just this planet or realm, but from so many galaxies."**

But what classes is he taking or teaching?

He's not teaching... he says it'll be another 300 years before he'll be teaching. Right now, he's taking a class, learning astronomy; "The Movements of the Cosmos."

Can I ask you a question about your class? Could you show Jennifer what your classroom looks like?

That's interesting; he just put on this huge space suit – I asked, "Why do you need a space suit to protect you on the way to your class?" and he said, "It protects you as you are going through the cosmos."

Is your class in deep space?

He showed me a star... and the speed of light... you go like a million years in the future the get there.

Okay, so can we go there with you, can we be there in the classroom? Are we inside or outside, and how many people are there in it?

We're outside. There are many, many in this class. They're all lights. He shows me like a stadium.

What does the teacher look like? Is the teacher male, female or something else?

The teacher... is something from their star system where the class is. So they look a lot different. My dad is like "Don't get scared (when you see this teacher.)" (Jennifer observes). **It's like they have different features, small ears... big eyes.**

Is it disrespectful for me to interrupt this class in this fashion?

> (Note: As I reported in "Flipside" during my first deep hypnosis session, I went into a classroom where the teacher seemed to know me and introduced me to the class. (I did not recognize her from this life, but she seemed to know me.) The class seemed

entertained by our exchange. But when I went to visit Luana's class during the same session, it was as if I was interrupting them. Everyone stopped when I entered and spoke. I continued speaking, like a tour guide, telling the hypnotherapist "this is a class in the healing light of the universe."

In my mind's eye, one of the students turned and scoffed. "You don't know what you're talking about" he said. I thought this was an odd exchange – he was openly hostile to me, and everyone in class was staring at me. Luana was in the back of the class looking at me as if to say "What the hell are you doing here? Is this a talk show?" I then continued to speak to the hypnotherapist – and explained that I was simplifying things, as "people don't always sign up to be cured, and people who use this healing light don't sign up to heal everyone. It's layered" which seemed to mollify the cranky student.

Then two years later, with another hypnotherapist, I went back to the same classroom I had been in before – only this time, it was after class was over, and I found myself standing before the teacher, and Luana was apologizing to him on my behalf for interrupting earlier. It felt like a few minutes had passed, but two years had passed on Earth between sessions. So I've been into classes before, and I try to ask the same questions I'd ask if I was the one "seeing" what Jennifer was seeing.)

Jennifer: **My dad says he's going to take me to a different time frame.** (To not interrupt his class). **We're jumping to the beginning of class. Wow. Time is so weird! I asked him**

256

"When did the class start?" and he said, **"Five hundred years ago."**

Five hundred days ago?

"Five hundred years ago."

I've heard that like 80 years here is like 20 minutes over there. A friend did a between life session, told me her 25 year lifetime on Earth felt like "a ten minute cigarette break" back home.

My dad is so sweet, he said **"I can't wait to introduce you to the teacher. They'll be fascinated that you're here."** I can see her; she has lots of arms...

Is there a name we can associate with her?

It's hard to... I get the letter "G." It's not like she has a name, but it's like a vibration.

How many arms? What are they used for?

Eight. It's like she's multi-tasking with them... but she can change into anything. Just now, she's appearing as a human to me... and looks like me. I mean she looks like me as that little girl with curly blond unruly hair but older. I think she tapped into my subconscious and used that image to project this to me, to make it easier for me.

> (Note: Eight arms? First time I've heard this visual; however in Tibetan art, it's a common visual. I always assumed people were using "multiple arms" in Tibetan Buddhist (or Indian) artwork as a metaphor – but hearing this makes me wonder if someone who was deeply in a "mind traveling meditation" might

have seen or been describing someone like this; a "multi-armed individual." In Tibetan artwork, each arm usually holds an object which does represent metaphor – i.e., a bell for enlightenment, a lightning bolt for the shock of wisdom, the drum for the beat of the dharma, etc.)

May I ask this teacher a question? What's the class about and what do you teach Ms. G?

"It's about... it's about how to travel time and space without having too many bumps in the road." She says my dad is "Doing well in the class, already."

Cool. A class in "How to negotiate time and space without the speed bumps."

"It's also a class in helping to plan your next avatar."

May I ask; are you teaching everyone at the same time or individually? Is your class like a general lecture or are your lessons one on one?

"It's like tapping into whatever frequency or speed you're in and they tap into your level..." (depending on your educational level.) **They give you the same information when you're there, you experience it as you are. If you're new to the class, the lessons are on your level of being new – (Jennifer laughs). They showed me like "old tapes" of all the information you're able to tap into based on your frequency and your awareness. No one feels bad or left behind for where they are in class.**

Have you ever had anyone from Earth show up in your class in the past like we're doing? Coming all the way from Earth to check out your class or talking to you?

I was just shown Lisa Williams (a medium from the UK).

Who's that?

My mentor. And Luana...

What was Lisa doing here? Attending class?

She's like a body guard. For me, for my spirit.

An advanced scout?

Luana says, "Make sure she gets back safely." (Jennifer aside) This is the best trip ever!

Can I ask Miss G, is this unusual for you to experience people from our realm to hang out with you? Do people do it unconsciously perhaps, when they're asleep?

"They do it but they're not consciously aware of it – people coming and going all the time."

It might be in a dream perhaps and remember it that way.

My dad just did air quotes... He will report that they have had a "unique" experience, like me.

Before we leave you, Miss G, can we ask you about information that can help people back on our planet?

Funny, Morton just showed up – the people that we've talked in our class are showing up... it's a frequency. And the people that we know or that we've talked to are learning from our frequency here.

Well, can we charge admission for this class? For piggybacking on the ride with us?

259

Jennifer laughs.

My question is, how can we help people on the planet to access you Miss G, or is that important for us to do so?

"It will take light years."

*Well; not so much. Here **we are.***

Hold on. It's so wild. **I'm seeing myself in the future, looking down on myself from the past talking about this. My dad's like "I told you..."** (it was going to be odd). Oh my goodness. Miss G. Like *God.* She's not god, but she carries that frequency.

The source frequency?

Of avatars, holy ones, Buddha, Jesus...

Jesus told in our interview that his energy was "closer to source;" why people reacted around him the way they did.

"Just talk to us," she says. **"That's all you have to do. And you hit the gateway."**

Can I ask you directly Miss G, what's a 1, 2, 3 best method of communicating with you on a conscious level?

"Close your eyes. That's the one. The 2 is to focus on the heart and have it go through your crown chakra.... (Jennifer listens) **That's it. There are only two. Because that's going to be your focus, and once you've done that, you talk; you're already there."**

So I should "open my heart and shoot my heart to the galaxies." Luana knows where this location is, now Jennifer knows it... but the reason we're doing this work is to prove that people still exist once they die.

She says I am being a conduit for that – skeptics included.

What an unusual conversation! Thanks Miss G and your dad Jim, who's in this class and doing well. How cool is that?

What would the world be like if you knew your frequency is untouchable? Nothing bad can happen, "evil spirits" can't touch you... No one can touch you but who you let in.

That's important to hear. Let's pretend someone is really drunk, high, loaded... does that make them more susceptible or even then is it a stretch?

"It makes you susceptible in your mind... they can't do anything anyway because of the rules."

Sacrosanct. Indestructible?

"And there's no hierarchy." My dad high fived you. He says, **"Thank you for asking the right questions."**

*****

Again, are we claiming to talk to Amelia Earhart, Princess Di and all these other folks? I can only offer I ask the same basic questions to people who show up in our classroom. I try to point out if they're accurate or inaccurate. If they don't match up, feel foreign, or disconcerting, that's worth examining as well. We just won't know unless we ask. *"Ask and you shall receive."*[50]

---

[50] Matthew: 7; 7-8. "Ask, and it shall be given you; seek, and ye shall find; knock, and it shall be opened unto you: 8 For every one

CHAPTER ELEVEN

"GHOST STORIES"

Ghost Hunting with Garry, Gilda, John, Anthony, Kate and Robin

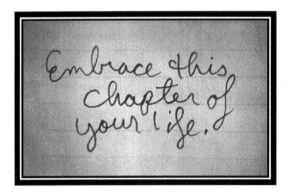

A Zen koan that Garry Shandling wrote to himself.

As noted, the film director Phillip Noyce once introduced me as *"This is Richard. He thinks he can talk to the dead."* I had to correct him; "I don't think I talk to the dead. I talk to people who think they can talk to the dead."

I must acknowledge that indeed it is a possibility this is all some form of random imaginary two-step. That my random questions to Jennifer elicit some kind of random response that comes from some etheric imaginary place, within me, within

---

that asketh receiveth; and he that seeketh findeth; and to him that knocketh it shall be opened."

her, or perhaps in the imaginations from people no longer on the planet.

But as I've noted, there are numerous times when an answer comes forth that is *new information* and later turns out to be forensically true. That does not mean *all* the answers are true, and as noted, there are a number of reasons why things are inaccurate.

For example, in this chapter, there's a brief conversation with Gilda Radner. I asked her some specific questions about her relationship with Alan Zweibel, the former writer of SNL who wrote a book about the two of them.

He called the book *"Bunny Bunny"* and it came from a superstitious concept that Gilda had that you had to say "Bunny Bunny" on the first of the month in order to bring good luck. I asked Gilda what the term meant (because I didn't know about his book) and she said, "It was about luck."

So that was accurate.

I asked if she had any message for Alan and she said (as heard by Jennifer) *"Tell him to stop eating fried foods!"*

Alan let me know he doesn't **ever eat fried foods.**

However, as I've noted before – she could be commenting on that – it could be something she said to him decades ago and he forgot. It could be that she's observed that he doesn't eat fried foods and was making a joke of it. It could be that was a comment that she made to her husband Gene Wilder at some point in his life... Either way, the only way to find out why she made that comment ... *is to ask her.*

But my point is – there's no possible way for anyone doing mediumship work to translate 100% of what someone is trying to say 100% of the time. First, they don't use language for the most part – but images. Second, as noted before they may have many reasons to answer a question inaccurately, including *"Jerking your chain."* (After all, Garry Shandling said that he was *golfing* on the flipside, and in his course there were only two holes; but the holes were *just very far apart.* That could be a joke... or not. Only one way to know!)

Or these incongruities could be to convince the person who doesn't "believe in this sort of thing" that they were *right all along*, and they should *return the book for a refund*.

And by all means, I highly recommend that! **If this book offends you in any way, shape or form, please, I beg you, get your money back.** As Jennifer has learned, and I've repeated often; "it's not her job to prove there is an afterlife;" it's her job is to report what she sees or senses as accurately as she can.

I film these sessions so I don't miss a word, and then transcribe them later. I edit them when they're repetitive, or when I say something ridiculous or we fly into a tangent. I'm just trying to show that questions can be asked to people no longer on the planet, answers can be gotten – but it's up to us to figure out *what they mean, what the person meant*, or what *new information they can impart to us*.

And by showing that a "conversation" can be had, it allows a person to open up to that possibility. Again, I apologize to any family member or friend who feels offended by this form of examination. All I can do is say that it "feels" like we're talking to them, that there are many "indications" as if we're talking to them, and what they have to say about the afterlife coincides with the decade of filmed interviews I've done with people under deep hypnosis or who've had near death experiences and believed they'd gone home.

I get emails often from people who "had a dream" or some other psychic event, and I suggest that they revisit it with a pencil and paper and ask questions directly to those involved. I get pretty amazing replies from people who claim to have learned "new information" from someone in their dream, vision, or out of consciousness experience.

New information is the key. If you've read anything in these pages that you haven't heard before, or that strikes a chord to remind you of something that happened to you, or puts you in a mindset to make your own communications with anyone you choose to and to learn the mysteries of the universe from them – and to pass them along to the planet, then by all means.

That's why this book exists. To inspire others to do the same. Perhaps better. More succinct. More scientists and less celebrities. *Whatever.* I challenge everyone to find their own classroom that they can converse with. And at the end of this book there will be a workbook to help people to do just that.

But meanwhile, back to our class.

****

Jennifer: Hello class. Someone's coming through.

Rich: Who came through?

Bill Paxton. Then my dad showed up and interrupted him.

265

Bill, what did you want to say?

Something about the fires in Ojai. I mean we all know about them. Um... says something, he's always so clever, he says something about "They're moving on."

Who?

They still live there, so I'm trying to understand.

Are they moving away from Ojai?

"No." (Jennifer listens) He's telling me like, "he's found somebody for her (his wife)." He says, "He's way better than he is. So he can help her... move on."

Bill, I don't even want to touch that topic. If you can help them, that's great. But I don't want to write about you finding someone to replace you. It's hard enough for us to wrap our minds around talking to you in the first place! By the way, as I edit this I assume y'all are contributing, making corrections.

Bill just put *Wite-Out* on your computer's screen.

Exactly. Any edits you want me to make Billy?

Isn't that interesting? Editing from the other side. My dad says, "Why not?"

Your dad Jim came earlier, before we began. Jennifer was telling me about being somewhere and hearing this song over and over... and then she looked up the words and thought about you. So was that you Jim, did you put that song in Jennifer's head?

"Yes." I asked him how he did it, and he showed me Prince.

266

Did Prince show you that technique? Putting the frequencies in her mind?

"Yeah," he did. "It was just subtle enough."

So who's in class today? Luana? Who's here?

Morton's here. So funny.

I have a question for him...

And someone is coming through as well, someone we interviewed before, Stephen Hawking. First he shows me himself, and then he gets up and looks very handsome.

I was reporting about an interview he did - with Erik Medhus's mom and Stephen.

He says, "Thank you."

Who does? Erik or Stephen?

"Both." Erik says, "By telling her (his mom) about ours, you made her feel verified."

She did tell me that. (ding!) I pointed out that the interview she did with Stephen was close with ours, how we'd talked to Stephen and some of the same things were said.

You're so good at asking these questions.

We were talking about how the class is going to help us write the foreword to this book.

My introduction is that I sent you a Facebook message.

I talk about that too... Whatever you want to talk about – up to you.

You've helped me gain tools. You ask questions I've never asked... Like what just happened with the song that ran through my head, *"You Sang to Me"* and you asked not only who was responsible, but how they were able to get it into my head. I would have never asked that question... You've given me the gift of asking questions to spirit. When I asked my dad, "How'd you do that?" Prince showed up.

And we know what he does. Helps people to manipulate frequency of music.

Robin Williams jumped up, and I need to ask why Luana just stepped in front of him and said *she* was going to write the foreword to the book. She thinks it's important for a collaboration from both sides – I think they want (to dictate) **their own foreword.**

Great, you'll be the conduit for them... Okay, so we wanted to invite someone here today, someone who has appeared in a couple of other sessions. Someone who helped pull one of our subjects on stage.

Jimi Hendrix?

That's who I had in mind. (ding!) Can we call him forward?

Did he die young?

He's part of that 27 club, Jim Morrison was as well. Hey, he showed up last week, can Jim and Jimi come forward? Who wants to talk first? Oh by the way, the image you saw of John Lennon a few weeks ago? Was he young, middle aged, older?

I saw him when he had long hair and glasses. He is looking out a window, light is coming through.

268

Okay, I was just curious because John, you put that image in her head, you found the file in her memory and then you dinged it and that's why you came to mind. Is that correct?

"Ding, ding, ding." Jennifer taps her nose.

So Mr. Hendrix – you've helped a few of our classmates into the flipside. Can we ask you about this journey? Who greeted you when you crossed over?

Feels like his grandmother.[51]

From Seattle I'd guess?

"Yes. She was there."

What was the feeling when you crossed over? Was this an exit point for you? Was it an accident or an overdose?

"It's what it felt like yeah. An accident."

I think had taken some sleeping pills, didn't realize he'd thrown up; asphyxiated.

"Yeah." (Jennifer, aside) Odd, that's the second time I've heard that in my work today.

Were you startled by that sudden exit?

"Pissed off. He wasn't even high," he said.

Who greeted you besides your grandmother?

"A little girl."

---

[51] His maternal grandmother was Clarice Jeter (Lawson) who died March 15, 1967 at 75 from TB. Buried in Seattle.

Who was that? Someone you knew or lost?

"Feels like she was his little girl."

From a miscarriage or...?

Felt like a girl who drowned.

> (Note: I can ask questions about this, get a rough
> outline for an answer, and then do the forensic
> research into how he might have known this little girl.
> Jimi had a couple of children "out of wedlock" but in
> these stories of life journeys, nothing happens by
> accident. However, when we return "home" we are
> outside of time, we may run into loved ones we knew
> from a previous lifetime, from our soul group, even
> people who normally don't incarnate – could be
> anyone. All I can do is ask questions and try to figure
> out who that person might be. In this case, I have no
> idea.)

Someone he knew as a kid, someone from your soul group?

"Yeah," he says. Like "his little girl."

He had a little girl who drowned at five we're not aware of?

"Yes, she was five when she drowned."

No one knows about it?

"No, they don't."

*Jimi, you met my sister in law, my brother's wife Jeanne
backstage in Sweden in the 60's. She has pictures of you.*

He said, "She smelled good."

So Jimi, why are you the guy pulling people on stage? Is that part of your gig?

He said, "It helps him."

How?

Hold on. (Jennifer aside) Show me again? (Listens) **"So they don't get sad." It's like that car ride... that Harry Dean Stanton talked about.** (A way of helping them have a "soft landing" on the flipside.)

A distraction so they aren't focused on the fact they're no longer on the planet. So you pulled John on stage to play "Blue Suede Shoes." I found you recorded it in 1969, and John a year later. So why that song? Because John knew it?

"No." He says "They were making fun of Elvis..." That's what they're saying.

When John recorded it he says on the recording, "I chose a song that everybody in the band knows." Is that why you used that song or were you just teasing Elvis?

"It did two things... homage to Elvis and picking a song John knew." When he pulled John Lennon onto the stage, I wanted to ask what song they played.

We did; we asked him what song it was and instead of giving you a title, he showed you a pair of blue shoes.

I don't remember.

He showed you a pair of blue suede shoes. It's an old Carl Perkins song Elvis made into a hit, and both of these fellows recorded it. Okay fellows let's turn to the guy from the Doors.

271

Yes, he's sitting on the couch.

Jim, why did you check out at 27?

"Second death event," he said; "There was another one at (age) 19."

At the age of 19. Who greeted you when you crossed over?

"His sister. Felt like."

Sister from this life or a previous life?

I think it was a sister from a previous life... that's interesting... (to me) why would you ask that question?

> (Note. I didn't know, but it turns out Jim Morrison has a sister born in 1947, Anne Robin who lives in Albuquerque. I felt he didn't mean his sister from this life, hence why I asked the question "from a previous lifetime." Again, his sister is alive, but for some reason, that's the impression he gave Jennifer. Could have been her "higher self" that was there to greet him, as two thirds of our conscious energy is reportedly "always back home.")

Because it just popped into my head. I know your dad was very controlling and a military guy.

"He beat the shit out of him," he said. He showed me somebody whacking his ass.

Now are you guys reconciled and you understand why you chose him as your father?

"Yes."

As a poet you talked about really unusual things. Why did you choose such interesting topics for your songs?

He showed me LSD.

The band was named after Aldous Huxley's book "The Doors of Perception." It's how the band was named, they were reading Aldous Huxley – LSD is a door of perception... but why were you so addicted to alcohol? What was that about? What pain were you carrying that you had to dull so much?

"He felt alone."

Why?

"I don't know."

Did you have a mental affliction or something? Were you bi-polar? Or just hated fame?

He was just depressed; "He couldn't get himself out of it."

So why did you choose this lifetime to be so famous and so depressed?

"Just to try to figure it out – tried to balance (it) and it didn't work."

I was in court with "The Doors;" all band members except you. My wife was working for one of their attorneys as they fought over who could use the name "The Doors." They were all these old grey haired dudes. By the way, her attorney gets a signed postcard from someone posing as you every year on the day of your death; signs your name. Who's doing that?

"It's somebody..." feels like a company.

I don't think the attorney ever told anybody.

273

Feels like someone he knew, someone who is part of a company that's doing it.

I have a friend whose photo appears in my book "Flipside," - a photo of you in the Per Lachaise cemetery – this woman was taking a photo of her friend, but you appeared in the background standing behind here, clear as a bell. So how'd you manifest like that?

What cemetery is he in?

Per Lachaise. In Paris. Edith Piaf is buried there... so how do you manifest in a photo? Are you just hanging around? People come from all over the world to leave poems for you, are you there sometimes?

He showed me a bunch of people playing guitars. "They make that energy happen."

I also took a pic of your tombstone, there was a weird light coming out of it... like an upside down pyramid.

"Like a prism ... there's a vortex there. It's easier to access him because of it."

But who creates the vortex? The people coming to visit or is it you? My guess is that when people deposit emotions at your tombstone that creates the vortex.

"Yes."

I walked into Anne Frank's house in Amsterdam. I wandered into this one room, there was an overwhelming sadness in it. I think it's people depositing their emotions there. It also happened at the Vietnam memorial. I was walking with a friend and started crying, and I thought why am I crying? I

274

realized I was in front of the wall – but in front of just this one panel. I went back a year later and filmed the whole wall, and only in front of this one panel did I feel it. Are people depositing their sadness there and that's what I'm feeling?

"Not only are you feeing that, but you're also feeling the sadness from the other side... at that moment."

How can we bottle that in terms of positive energy? Or can we?

"You can separate it, away from you." He's showing me a suitcase... like the metaphor you used. (Put your emotions into a suitcase while you examine a memory). It works, I use it all the time...

Thanks for talking to us, Jim. Come back soon and make some more music.

He said, "He's *done*. He's helping people here."

Who are you helping?

I just got the chills.

You're giving Jennifer chills about who you are helping here?

He's helping like musicians in punk bands... it's like he's helping them with the energy of being in a punk band.

Helping those kinds of musicians to play?

"No. To not fucking die."

> (Note: It's not the kind of sentence I normally hear from Jennifer. This answer is contrary to what most would think people would say; not that he's *helping*

275

artists be better musicians, but helping them to **not kill themselves** via drugs or drink. Novel concept.)

Okay. Well now we're going to talk to the headliner today. Garry Shandling. Jennifer, did you watch the documentary about him on HBO?

I haven't seen it. I've been on vacation.

Last time we talked to Garry, when I asked what he was up to, he said "Golfing." I asked, "How many holes do you play, 36?" and he said "Two. They're just very far apart." Like one is in California, and the other in Tibet. Very funny. Garry, who greeted you when you crossed over? And this time tell me the truth. If you say it's the same person you said before, great, but if it's not, I want to know why.

It wasn't that person.

> (Note: As reported previously, he said it was "his sister.")

Why did you deliberately tell us not the right person?

He said, "He was trying to see how funny he could be."

Like if I really knew him I would have gotten the joke?

He's showing me it was a family member... Someone who had a heart attack before him. I don't know anything about Garry. But this feels like a brother.

Feels like his brother?

Yes, he's showing me his brother greeting him as he died, saying "Dude, that sucks."

276

Garry had the heart attack... and his brother was there to greet him saying "Dude, that sucks"?

"Yes."

Describe what he looked like to you.

Young. About 15. His brother is saying he had been sick. Was it cancer?

He was sick but not cancer. Cystic fibrosis.

He showed me his skin was white.

The separation from his brother was stressful to Garry, but once you crossed over...

He was healthy (when he saw him). **He knew he wasn't sick. He saw his brother healthy and kind.**

I know you two were close.

"He just didn't make it..." Something about attending his funeral. "He didn't make it."

That's correct. (ding!) Garry was not allowed to go to his brother's Barry's funeral. One of his parents had a difficulty... over the brother's death.

Because Garry wasn't at his funeral. That's what he said. That's what he meant by "He didn't make it."

Why didn't you make your brother's funeral? What happened?

He was mad at one of his family members, he couldn't go.

That family member – his mom - prevented him from going. It's counterintuitive to even say it aloud... but that's what happened. Let's skip down.

The first thing his brother said to him when he crossed over was "It wasn't your fault." And then he said, "Fuck you."

So Garry, you chose this lifetime and chose these parents, knowing it would be difficult, but that it would inspire you to become who you were?

"Yes. 100 times more than if everything had gone right."

Okay, just want to confirm that.

Robin Williams is saying "Me too!"

What about seeing your mother when you crossed over. Were you mad at her?

He said, "No. Love. He learned a lot. She was in so much pain."

From what?

"Spiritual, mental, physical... all of it."

This is all accurate based on the documentary by Judd Apatow. I want to ask about a couple of questions about someone you knew; Brad Grey.

(Jennifer aside) I don't know who that is.

Garry, would you tell Jennifer who that is?

Were they friends when they were young? Best friends felt like they were together.

278

Yes, (ding!) he was his manager and a close friend for years, but then something happened.

A divorce. From a female?

Brad's around, he can pipe in.

What's his last name?

Grey.

"They split up, it was over financial... money. He's saying it was very stupid. It was big and that's what made it so stupid."

It was a huge battle.

Nine years?

Could be. They wound up in court Garry had to testify...

"How Brad mismanaged him."

Correct. Garry won big sum of money.... but lost because it took a toll on his life.

He said, "It killed him."

Well you're not dead now! Are you Garry?

He said, "Try using that joke on the other side."

So listen, Garry you helped a lot of writers, you helped make careers, can you help me?

"I already am."

You're a terrific writer, you helped Judd Apatow's career. He said you helped him. Did you help him write his script for "This is 40?"

He said, "A third of it."

In your tribute, so many, Jim Carrey, Kevin Nealon, Bob Saget talked about your gifts to other comedians, are you aware of that?

"Yes."

Oh, let me ask, have you seen Johnny Carson?

He just showed me angel wings trying to look for him. Kind of funny. What he said is that he hasn't seen him, "but I call on him."

What does that mean? Because he's on the flipside, you can call on him frequency wise?

"Yep, it's like dialing up people with cell phones... they should get rotary phones over here."

What's Johnny doing on the Flipside?

"Playing golf."

Funny. The documentary is called the Zen Diaries of Garry Shandling; what's your view of Buddhism now? In the film you talked lot about detachment.

"It didn't work," he said. He's laughing... He said he held that "hot stone."[52]

Luana can help here, she was a Buddhist, we've talked about this before Garry, how detachment is great if it means letting go of anger, fear, stress, all the emotions you don't want to have... but you can stay connected to love, unconditional love. It doesn't mean to detach yourself from love or the positive emotions, because that's why we're on the planet.

"Some people don't want to do all that."

Well, one example is that you were connected to the actress Linda Doucette who appears in the documentary; you were together a long time, she's very emotional in that documentary.

"She should be."

Wait a minute, you dumped her and fired her. What did you do that for? Because your mom did it to you?

He just squinted his eyes and glared at you.

I'm just cajoling you Garry. Why'd you fire her?

He couldn't... (do what she wanted) **He sabotaged it.**

Is it because you had a fear of having cystic fibrosis in your genes and that your child might die like your brother Barry. Is that correct? (I'm guessing this detail.)

"Yes. And she wanted to have it anyway."

---

[52] I've never heard of the "Hot Stone" with reference to Zen, but apparently it's a form of massage that I wasn't aware of: http://www.zenwellnessclinic.ca/

Thanks for talking to us. You're welcome to our class if you can put up with us. Okay, let's bounce around to another comedian, someone who I was a big fan of who I met on stage.

I saw River Phoenix though I know it's not him.

Well, this fellow died across the street from where River died in front of the Viper Room. A friend of Robin's.

John Belushi.

*Correct. **(ding!)** I asked him to appear today. Robin, we've never talked to John before, although for some reason, sometimes when I'm in my kitchen he pops in. Robin will you help us with this? Can you bring John forward?*

Hold on. (He shows up in your kitchen because) **"He's helping his family."**

Well, his brother Jim lives down the block. So that's what John's doing?

Another person just came through, who died of cancer? The actress on Saturday Night Live?

*Gilda. Wow, this morning I asked her to come along too. **(ding!)** Hi Gilda, I met you on the set of the Charles Grodin film "Movers and Shakers."*

She rolled her eyes when you said that...

John, do you remember when I said hello to you during a taping of Saturday Night Live? I mean you've met a billion people, but I said hello on behalf of a mutual friend from Second City.

He showed me his eyes, they were so glassy. He was high when you said hello.

> (Note: Not surprised he did not remember me shouting out *"Joe Forsberg says hello!"* (Director of Second City where I took comedy improv classes) John stopped, shaded his eyes and looked out at me. "You know Joe?" *"Yeah, I took her class."* He said "Cool. Tell her I said hi." If Jennifer had said "Yes of course he remembers you" it might have been what I wanted to hear, but the reality is, *highly unlikely*.)

So John you're helping your family...your wife Judy, do you ever reach out to Danny?

"All the time. Through his stuffed animals."

Does Dan acknowledge him?

"Yes." You're talking about Dan Ackroyd right? He's the one who created "Ghostbusters?" Dan's father has helped John come through to him.

My brother knows Bill Murray, they went to high school together. So Gilda you appeared with our professor Luana in a movie – Luana this is Gilda, you were both in the Hal Ashby film "The Last Detail." Gilda's first movie. Have you talked to each other since Gilda's crossed over?

They heard you this morning but have spoken before.

So Gilda what's up? Why does your pal Alan Zweibel post "Bunny, Bunny" on his Facebook page? Is that a reference to you?

She showed me buck teeth. (Rabbits) **"It's good luck."**

(Note: "Bunny, Bunny" is a play that Alan wrote about his relationship with Gilda. I wasn't aware of this until I searched for the words together and his name.)

Anything you want to say to Alan?

"Tell him to stop eating fried food!" (Jennifer winces as if Gilda is shouting this idea.)

How about you, John?

He's showing me all they used drugs, they all had their different drugs back then, and they talk about it, it's funny... You have mutual friends. He showed me a grid and how connected everyone is... He misses having coffee.

When I was in college, Bill Murray let me use his tickets to the dress rehearsal because of my brother. I got to see the first performance of the Blues Brothers, was a huge fan. John, you made a hilarious short film about being an old man dancing on the graves of all your fellow "Not Ready for Prime Time Players."

"Hahaha," he says.

How is he over there, Gilda?

"He's even better!" Her voice is so strong. "Kindness." All of sudden my heart got warm. "He loves himself now... he didn't love himself before."

Thank you. I was telling you about my friend Paul Tracey, who made an appearance at a friend of our's AA meeting this morning. It was a good place for her to run into Paul; he was in AA and rehab a few times.

284

I asked if they had AA meetings up there, they said "No. They have *mixology meetings*."

So Paul, what's going on? You told our friend to tell me "Tell Richard it was my time." Is that correct?

"Yes."

Was it one of your exit points?

"He says he had a trillion..." like a cat with nine lives... "it was one of those."

Paul spoke to me after he passed when I was walking in Tibet. I was having a hard time and I heard him say "You think this is hard? Try walking in my shoes." Paul had his hip replaced after a football injury in high school.

"It was hard to breathe. Like Everest base camp."

Not far from there. But was I was walking, I heard Paul say, "You were responsible for the happiest day of my life." I had forgotten about the day we got lost in the woods in Ohio; he did not. After he died, his mom sent me some of his ashes, and I found the ball from his titanium hip in the container. As our friend Dave Patlak said; "the thing he hated most in life he willed to you." I planted it inside a giant stupa in Tibet. So Paul's hip is holding up a stupa on Mt. Kailash.

He's a good advisor (to you) of some sort.

He also mentioned something about seeing Luana "over there" and referred to her as "a kind of saint." What did you mean by that Paul?

Okay, I'm getting that she was dearly loved by all of her friends here... I'm trying to be careful to translate for her,

I don't want to get it wrong. (Jennifer listens) She showed me herself, even though she was abandoned as a child, that she didn't have a home, her home is where her heart is. So that frequency is love, I don't know if we mentioned that before, but in her case, she had to hold onto that frequency of home while she was here, because she had none. It's just what she told me with regard to her frequency... and it's that frequency that everyone wants to know about.

> (Note: This is correct. *(ding!)* Luana's parents split up when she was born, her mom put her into foster care until she was a teen, and then she ran away from home. She reconnected with her mother and father, but both died from cancer. Becoming a Buddhist "saved her life" as mentioned in the foreword.)

Paul, when you crossed over, did you run into Luana?

Right away. They went to an amusement park together. I saw a Ferris wheel.

Oh, that's funny. Probably a good way to land... Another process your describing which is funny...

Paul said he's thankful... "We're really thankful you're doing this work." He called us... "Tonto and the Lone Ranger." He says you and I are doing this detective work like those two, solving mysteries. "The difference is that everybody over there knows we can talk to them but over here (back on the planet) they don't think so."

*****

A follow up to this class a week later:

286

Rich: Tell me your Garry Shandling story. What happened?

Jennifer: The other day a client came in, and I told her that "Something important happened to you last Thursday." She said, "I wrote about it on my blog, but I started watching the documentary about Garry Shandling "Zen Diaries." And I thought, "Oh, this is really long and I when I turned it off, I suddenly heard Garry's voice, clearly saying to me "Aw c'mon, you don't like my film, c'mon!" He said, "Turn it back on." So I turned it back on... and I thought it was the best movie ever and just what I needed to hear. This woman is a writer and I was reflecting on our conversation with Garry; he said he was "helping writers with their work."

Indeed, it is precisely what he said. And you had a story that reminded you of our class with Luana?

Yes, this couple reached out to me because their young son had died in an accident. I would never charge them anything, I put them on the schedule... but before they arrived, their son came in. I generally don't acknowledge spirits if they're "early," but this boy said "My mom is going to want something very specific. So just tell her "Teddy Bear."

So the parents came in, the husband seemed a bit shy or skeptical. I told them their son had told me there's a specific question that they want answered; it's "Teddy Bear."

They were shocked and told me they had made two teddy bears out of his clothing for his twin sisters, and that the twins kiss the bears and say goodnight to him every night... and their son jokingly said, "Those old clothes are getting kind of disgusting mom, can't they just say; "Good night?"

I asked the mom, "He's showing me there a dream you had when he passed?" The mom said "The night he passed I had this dream, I was walking him to school, holding his hand and when we got to this white building, he turned to me and said "It's okay mom, I'll be fine. I'm going to school now, so I'll see you later." I explained how Luana has been helping us coordinate this classroom and she began to cry. It's a simple validation, that whole day was a verification for me.

He's "he's not gone, he's just not here." In his class.

Yes.

Rich: All right class. Who's here?

Jennifer: **Garry with two Rs. Robin is here, as always, my dad Jim, Morton is here, Prince. And Amelia showed up again.**

Robin you're always first in class, anything you want to say?

He says, **"To speak up."**

You want to speak up?

He says, **"You should speak up."** I'll share with you what I see; **he wants for you to speak up, and he showed me a book and your writing it. He's saying, "Not to hold back."**

Okay. We talked about you in the last book, "Hacking the Afterlife" - I had taken the chapter out and you came to one of our lunches and said "put me back in." You want to add something?

He said, "Next time."

288

Prince, anything you want to add? Jennifer's dad mentioned how you put a song in Jennifer's head. Anything you want to add or subtract?

He comes so close to me with his smile. I asked**, "Are you real? He said, "No. I'm *eternal.* "**

What does he think about his protege Janelle Monae?

He said he works with her daily.

She just did a song on The Voice...

Two weeks ago?

Yes, (ding!) the performance was Prince oriented; apparently he helped her with it?

"Yes."

It was super sexy, topless, shirtless... very Prince.

He said "She's exceeded everything and then some. *And* she can wear the shoes."

That's funny. Yes, she was wearing six inch heels. She danced well in them; in the end Prince could not.

"Right."

Anything you want us to pass along to her?

He says she's fine on her own; "To not get caught up."

When you show up to help her rehearse, how do you let her know? That she'll know what I'm talking about?

She gets chills on one side... he shows me like immersing his energy to the side of her face...

289

She'll know what that is?

"Yeah. She doesn't believe it though."

Most people don't. Can Gilda come forward? Or is she busy?

She can.

Gilda we talked to you last week with John and you mentioned how he's warm and sweet and wonderful back there. I asked you a question about the term "Bunny Bunny."

"Wishing."

You told us it was a good luck charm the way you pet a rabbit's foot? Did the term itself came from you?

She gave me the impression of bunny rabbits, and how they used to use them, as good luck, with the idea of pregnancy. "Rubbing a rabbit's foot for good luck. Using it like a good luck charm."

Your pal Alan he says he learned it from you; the first day of very month you'd say "Bunny Bunny" for good luck.

(Jennifer aside) I could have never understood that from what I was seeing.

So where did the concept come from?

"Her mom or someone else."

A superstition her mom had?

"Or her aunt. But it came from her family."

When you crossed over, who was there to greet you?

"John." She showed me Belushi.

Was that a surprise to you?

She showed me Chevy Chase as well, I know he's still on the planet, but it's like that car situation with Harry Dean... with the three of them doing something they used to do... **"She didn't want to go, she didn't want to die."**

I understand. You've got that cancer survivor's Gilda's Group? You keep on eye on them?

"Laughter is the *best* medicine. She tries to make them laugh." (Jennifer aside) Of course she does.

I asked if you had any advice for your friend Alan and you said, "Don't eat fried food." Why'd you say that?

It's like **"He'll get the reference** (eventually)" **He either said it to her at some point as a joke, or it was something he wrote. She's saying, "She said it so that only he would get the reference."**

I did reach out to him. He told me about the book he wrote about you. He says you had a platonic relationship.

"It was love without the rest."

There's someone named Gene that Luana and I met, related to you, who has crossed over.

She's like **"We split up in the afterlife."** She's laughing. (Points to her head) **Did he have Alzheimer's?**

Yes he did.

She's showing me "not anymore;" they're dancing.

Luana you know this fellow, don't you?

She says she did.

Rich: Put him into Jennifer's mind.

> (Note: Luana and I had dinner with Gene and Charles Grodin a few times. He was hilarious. I remember he wore the cleanest white fluffy sox I'd ever seen.

Jennifer: Did he direct movies? It feels like the 70's... he looks like a cowboy.

> (Note: Gene played a cowboy in "Blazing Saddles.")

Rich: Gene, do your remember Luana?

Jennifer: "Yes. When Luana was younger."

Who greeted you when you crossed over? If you don't mind me asking.

His mom. "There were a lot of people there."

How was that, crossing over?

He said, "He was already there because of the Alzheimer's." He said he didn't have an attachment anymore because he was already there.

> (Note: I've heard this before. Their conscious energy is muddled over here, so they reconnect with their conscious energy they've left behind.)

Who are you hanging out with now?

It feels like a "Brat pack" of people.

With?

He's showing me actors like James Dean...

292

Why did you choose this particular life you led?

It felt like control. "To control everything."

And were you in control?

"No." He's showing me a view of all the land... from above. With different lenses. Like he wanted to be a director?

Who do directors direct?

He's an actor. Okay, he showed me that in the beginning being with a bunch of actors. Was there something with NBC?

> (Note: He starred in *"Something Wilder"* on NBC in 1994 and appeared on the network in a number of other shows.)

Gene, you acted sometimes with an African American actor. Is he available?

Okay, now they're fooling with me. They showed me the guy that was in the junkyard.

> (Note: Red Foxx. At this point I did not know that Richard had written a number of those shows.)

He's funny but not that guy. Gene can your bring him forward? Once we bring him forward we can ask him questions. Luana, put him in a chair.

Not Richard Pryor.

Yes. (ding!) He starred with Gene in a number of films.

I kept getting "Sanford and Son." Did he write some of those shows?

I don't know. Is that true, Richard?

He says, "He wrote some of them."

> (Note: I was not aware of this, but Richard Pryor co-wrote two episodes of Sanford and Son, The Dowry (Season 2, episode #3), and Sanford and Son and Sister Makes Three (Season 2, episode #11) with longtime friend and fellow comedian Paul Mooney. One of those **"bell ringing verifications."**)[53]

Richard who was there to greet you when you crossed over?

A female that was there... I don't know who it was. A wife of his of some sort...

> (Note: Richard was married seven times, sometimes to the same women twice.)

Richard grew up in a small town in Illinois; his mom was a hooker, he grew up in a whore house.

"How funny was that?"

So why did you choose this lifetime Richard?

He says, "He wanted to *be somebody.*"

Difficult beginnings.

He just says, "He wanted to be somebody."

What about the drugs?

---

[53] https://www.imdb.com/title/tt0694144/

"Fun."

You were hilarious in your stand up talking about crack and lighting yourself on fire. When you look back on that lifetime what did you learn?

"What not to do!" He died in his 60's, 70's?

(Note: He was 65)

Let's go back to Gene. He was in some famous movies before he met you Richard. Maybe you can help Jennifer with his name.

Was he a pilot, flying in a movie?

Well, of a sorts. I'll give you a hint; "Chocolate."

Oh my god. Willy Wonka? Gene Wilder! I really had no idea. But he was an aviator in that film, he was showing me that sequence when he flies over the village, how he was trying to control everything and that sequence when he was flying out of the factory.

Yes, so we have Richard and Gene and Gilda and Robin and Garry... some of the funniest people ever, who saved and changed lives. You're all doctors. As we've heard, one guffaw can instantly change a person's disposition or health. You're all surgeons at what you do.

"It is the best medicine."

Laughter changes a disposition faster than anything – it can literally cure people of illness. You're all doctors; you've all healed people.

Gene said to me "That's what it felt like for me." He's showing me what dementia felt like.

Why did you choose this path, Gene? That included Alzheimer's?

He says, "He wanted to get out of his head." **He's showing me this brilliant guy, but that his mind, his intellect made him close down. It was the only way he could get out – by acting and writing.**

You helped Luana and my pal Charles Grodin start his career, his first job.

He showed me that. He showing me boxers – like Muhammed Ali and Sylvester Stallone. He says, "I taught Chuck how to fight."

Richard, anything you want to talk about?

He says **"Coffee. It's good to use instead of cocaine or crack."**

Instead of crack; try coffee?

"That's it."

I got a question for you – you're old friend Quincy Jones was talking about you and he said you and Brando had a night in bed together, was that accurate?

They're all laughing and pretending to smoke crack. "Yeah. It's true."

The joke was that you guys would get so high that "Brando would screw anything including a mailbox." We know that

Marlon's in our class sitting in the back. Have you guys been hanging out?

They've already been hanging out, he showed me their energies melding together; "It's different over there." He's giving me the chills to get my attention.

I could talk to you guys forever.

Gilda just brought up your friend (who has cancer). I was thanking her for coming... and she wanted to tell your friend "She's fine." She's telling me your friend with cancer needs to know she's okay. There's a huge bond Gilda has with her. (I passed it along.) David Bowie just walked by.

Okay, I will tell my friend that, thanks. What's up David?

He says, "His wife is writing..." I don't know, he's telling me she's writing... –

She is. She's writing on Instagram, "Iman daily." So you appreciate that? Or are you helping her?

"I'm facilitating." (Jennifer winces.) Did you hear that? it's a piercing noise, a frequency change...

Do we have an uninvited guest?

Nobody's uninvited. Somebody with a turban. Whenever that frequency goes pop I always ask. He's ahead of me instead of over here to the side. (Jennifer asks) Who are you? He says, "He's a guide." He's associated with your son.

297

Why have you taken the opportunity to say hello to us?
Something important you want to tell us? Were you in Tibet
when I made that wish to have a son?

(Note: In Flipside, I wrote how our son told us that he
was a "monk in Nepal." I later asked where he met
me and he said "Tibet. On the path." I asked him if
the path was named "Kangra?" and he said "Yes,
Kangra." I was filming Robert Thurman in Tibet, we
were on Mt. Kailash where Robert said, "If you make
a wish here, it will come true." I thought about
asking for a million bucks, but instead out of my
mouth came "I want a son." I wasn't connected to the
thought, figured it must be in the male genetic code
somehow, but the name of that path was Kangra.

Years later, my wife called me on the set of "Salt"
and asked, "Did you show him this book?" Our son
had gone to the library of the person whose place I
was subletting and taken a book from the shelf. He
opened it, pointed to a photograph of Mt. Kailash and
said, "This is where I found daddy." He was too
young to read. That and a number of other
verifications proved to us that until he was about 8, he
recalled a lifetime as a Tibetan monk.)

Jennifer: **"Yes." Richard, did you miss a step or
something? Fall on the mountain?**

*Yes, I did. (ding!) I slipped on a large rock coming down the
mountain and I fell a few feet. I landed flat from a pretty high
fall, and thought "Oh god, if I broke something we're days
from help." But nothing happened.*

He was there. He's showing me that happened. You've never told me that.

A bell of verification. So how did that work – were you and my son listening to me and said "Oh, let's go with that guy..." or was this already planned?

Remember when I was doing a between life session with Scott De Tamble, and recalled seeing myself at my wedding? How at the wedding, I was aware that I was being observed by myself, and then under hypnosis, I recalled being the person observing the wedding? It was my higher self visiting something that was going to occur in my lifetime.

I do remember that.

He showed me the same thing, a higher self version of your son being there at that spot, his "future self" looking in on it. Really cool.

I'm going to ask to speak to someone I knew who is a musician who appeared in a movie I directed. Jennifer may or may not be aware of the film but I invited him to class today.

I'm being shown Richard Pryor.

Same skin color.

Now I'm shown Stevie Wonder, wearing sunglasses, moving his back and forth; but it's not him. He's alive.

Let's bring this fellow in. Can you sit down with us?

I see who you're referring to, but I can't remember his name.

I know his name, Luana does too.

Did he sing "Lucille?"

No, that's Little Richard. He's still on this side.

I'm sorry, I don't know his first name.

Rhymes with Bayyyy.

Ray Charles! That's so funny. I'm sorry. But I still don't know anything about Ray.

That's a logical progression... From Richard to Stevie to Ray, who was in a film Luana and I co-wrote and I directed. I asked Ray to do a joke that I pitched him in the morning. He loved it, we put it in braille and by the afternoon shot it. He taped his script to his leg, that's why when you see Ray performing, he's runs his hands on his pant leg. So Ray, you have a lot of people who miss you. Who was there to greet you when you crossed over?

His grandmother.[54]

Do you remember meeting me?

(Makes a gesture for small) Teeny weeny bit.

Your manager Joe arranged for us to meet.

---

[54] Ray was the son of Bailey Robinson and Aretha (or Reatha) Williams. Ray's father and his wife Mary Jane Robinson adopted Aretha when she became pregnant by Bailey, she and Mary Jane both raised Ray. His "grandmother" was Mary Jane, his father's wife, and his "mama" was her adopted "daughter." Ray said both "bathed me in affection and cared for me as long as they were both alive. I called my mother Aretha "Mama" and Mary Jane "Mother."" ("Brother Ray" by Ray Charles. Decapo Press. 2004)

"Yes."

(Note: I spent a few days with Ray, and met him again at the New Orleans Jazz fest. Both times, his manger Joe did the talking for Ray, Ray could have been nicer. I remember thinking *"There's no way that he'll remember me."*)

So when you crossed over your grandmother was there? What was it like for you to see again? Or was that an issue?

It's like it wasn't, as he didn't know he wasn't seeing.

Why did you choose this life where you would be blind?

"To help others with the cause, more research."

You were close friends with Quincy Jones – we spoke about him and Richard Pryor earlier... anything you want to say to those guys?

He's already talking to them. He's saying, "This is cool."

Quincy remembers you growing up. Any thoughts about your old friend?

(Note: Ray and Quincy met in Seattle, Ray was 16. From his autobiography; **"When you're blind you become a soul reader. Everything a person says is a *soul note*. It comes straight outta their soul, so you read a person immediately.** Quincy had a loving style about him... He didn't have a single evil strand of hair on his head. He was smart, he liked to have fun, he wasn't afraid to touch you and laugh...

He's just a goddamned kid. I love him to pieces." Ray Charles.)[55]

Jennifer listens: "I know things about Quincy, things that will never leave our space." (Jennifer asks him:) Like whatever stays in Vegas? He says, "What he knows about Quincy will always stay "back home."

Rich: Can I ask you some questions then? Were you and Quincy best pals? Or closer than that?

He's saying that Quincy was the love of his life.

They were young boys when they met. But this is my question what's it like for you to be sighted now? Or are you saying if felt like you could see anyway?

He's funny. I'm asking if he thought Quincy was "more handsome than he thought," and he said, "He had a bigger nose than I thought he did."

> (Note: That's pretty funny. Not something I nor Jennifer could have conceived. Ray Charles being able to see his friend for the first time and saying, "His nose is bigger than I thought it was.")

Is there anything you want to say to your pal Quincy that I can put in the book?

He wrote out the word "Love" for me. But hold on... He says, "I wish I would have stayed with him for longer than we did."

---

[55] Ray Charles as quoted in "Q: The Autobiography of Quincy Jones" 3 Rivers Press, 2002)

It freaked people out over here when Quincy talked about Richard Pryor and Marlon Brando being in bed together. Was that accurate?

Jennifer puts her finger to her nose. "Correct."

What song should they put on about you to remember you?

It's a song that has the words... I'm hearing *something*... tonight."

The word "Tonight" is in the title?

Yes. *Something*... "tonight."

> (Note: There's only one I could find in Ray's repertoire; "I Wish You Were Here Tonight" – by Jim Sullins. (Also recorded by "The Band" in 1986.) The lyrics fit; **"My love is all imagination, just a dream without you to make it real. And, baby, I got a dream burning inside. No one else around, it's just you and I loving in the fire, it made us so right, and I wish you were here tonight."**

Ray anything you want to say to wrap this up?

He just put the Pharrell Williams song in my head. "Happy."[56]

That's your recommendation? To sing that song?

"Tell them to not hold back. Love who you want to love, be with who you want to love. Doesn't matter if it's a boy or girl, fall in love with their energy."

---

[56] "Because I'm happy, clap along if you know what happiness is to you, because I'm happy, clap along if you feel like that's what you wanna do." Lyrics to "Happy" by Pharrell Williams.)

Thanks Ray. Robin, you showed up in an email. Someone reached out to me and quoted you about love.

> (Note: The email said, "I was thinking of making some art (with Robin's quote) "Love love" when Robin appeared. "No, you don't have to give me credit. The message is what matters, not who said it." He pantomimed taking a beautiful crystal gift box from me, then turning and giving it back. "It doesn't make sense to take something you already have, give it to someone else just so that they can give it back to you to prove that you have it." I heard his voice; "Make the artwork (*"Love love"*) for yourself. If someone sees it, you've put a drop of love into the world. It never hurts to put more love into the world. Don't be afraid to do that.")[57]

You said, "There's not point in giving something to somebody they already have." It was about love; something they already know and possess.

"Right."

Okay, Ray thanks so much for joining us, we appreciate it ... some of these people you already know.

"Yes."

I'm thinking of someone else, a film critic.

Roger Ebert?

*Correct. **(ding!)** We met in an airport in Dallas.*

---

[57] From an email by F. Galvan

"Yes."

*You're a chapter in the book "It's a Wonderful Afterlife."
What do you think about that?*

(Jennifer gives me two thumbs up, then laughs.)

*The funny thing, I was reflecting on inviting you to class
today, aware you'd already insulted the teacher whom you
gave such a lousy review to the movie we co-wrote together.*

He says, "He did not insult the person she is now."

Oh no? Take a look at her; hands on hips, tapping her pencil.

He's laughing.

*And we also have the African American actress who played
Nancy Allen's guardian angel here in class... you dissed
Danitra Vance as well!*

**Danitra says "Actually, she didn't do that well in the
film."**

Okay, I'm just teasing... I understood your criticism.

He's laughing.

*Here's what I think about your review Roger. The film was a
fantasy about the afterlife, way before I started doing this
research. I later learned you were an avowed skeptic of the
afterlife, adamant it didn't exist. So when "Limit Up" came
out with Ray Charles playing God and Danitra playing a
guardian angel, you were predisposed to dislike it, and
brought your prejudice into the review.*

"Correct."

So the "thumbs way down" had to do with the theology of the film rather than the film itself?

"Yes."

I recounted in your chapter how when you had a near death event, you "spoke" to your wife, telling her they shouldn't pull the plug because you were still alive. She heard you, and they revived you for another...?

He's showing me six years. *(That's correct.)* He totally changed after that.

I read your article reporting what happened and yet you still claimed not to "believe in an afterlife."

He's showing me *thumbs down* on that article. He says, "He was afraid."

Hey, how's Siskel doing?

Which was the short one and which was the tall one?

Roger was wide and Gene was thin; they were the Bickersons. I met Gene on line when he was the resident critic on Prodigy, an early online service. I called him to the carpet as well for giving us a "thumbs down" for "Limit Up." He replied, "I'm not supposed to be a cheerleader."

"You should bring it back out," he says.

Well, from your lips to God's ear Gene. I don't know who owns it.

He says, "Someone will figure it out."

I think it's pretty funny I am using my ability to speak to the flipside to whine about old reviews. To quote an old poem,

"Father he cried after the critic's chewing, forgive them for they know not what I am doing." Imaginary apology accepted. Roger you and my older brother were both on the school paper at the University of Illinois. Do you remember working with him?

(Makes a tiny finger gesture). He says, "A little bit."

I know you loved going to Cannes. That's where I last saw you, dining al fresco at the Hotel Du Cap.

He said, "He got called in from Cannes." Is the festival going on now? He said, "He got called back from being in Cannes to come here."

It is. So where do you go in Cannes when you're in spirit? Do you hang out with bar flies, the celebrities... people who are asleep or awake?

He goes where the essence is. He says, "He goes and sees what the actors are doing."

Does anyone see you?

"Yes." (Jennifer laughs) **He says, "Mostly animals." He shows me dogs barking at him.**

Any humans? People sleeping?

"They don't know how to."

Would you like them to?

"Yes!"

Why don't you help them?

307

He says, "That's what you're supposed to do." He's showing me inside of my head seeing you in front of me.

Okay, will try to do so. Say Roger, can we get a quote for this book from you?

Yes. "Take things literally. And expect things not to make sense at first, (but then) you will release your opinions... or opinion... once it festers in your heart. Or when you've experienced someone else going to the other side."

What about just a "thumbs up?"

He's showing me a long line of thumbs being up.

One hundred "Thumbs up?" Let's get this joke right. Ebert gives "Backstage Pass" a "one thumbs up for all?"

"For everyone above and below."

"One thumbs up! from Roger Ebert on the flipside."

He's laughing.

I don't know if you've met our teacher Luana before.

He knows her essence and who she is over there...

Funny, when you reviewed our film I called Luana because she had the review in hand and was going to read it to me over the phone, I said "Just read the good parts, edit out the negative stuff." She said "Okay... the review says... "Limit Up... (pause) is a film... (pause) directed by Richard Martini." She left out the negative parts.

Jennifer laughs.

Some of it was accurate, but some of it felt like, "How dare you?" It was a lighthearted comedy with Ray Charles as God! What more did you want?

He says, "You were ahead of your time."

*I'll be sure to put that on the DVD if it ever comes out. "**Ebert says ahead of its time.**" But I appreciate being able to talk to you guys... just having some fun. Anyone else?*

My dad comes in. Jim.

I was going to ask about how you put a song in your daughter's mind.

"He learned that from Prince," he said. I'm asking him, "What was it like for you to meet Prince?" (in class) **and he said, "It was amazing." He said, "These classes allow us to finally get to know each other."**

When Jennifer and I are not here, are you guys hanging out?

They showed me by their consciousness together... the group raises their vibration which makes it (the frequency) **more; higher, stronger... it's conducting, changing the frequencies... Stephen Hawking just appeared in his wheelchair, and I'm telling him "You don't have to use that anymore** (to identify himself)**" He says, "The vibrant part of the book is what they're saying, these words whether you believe in it** (the Flipside) **or not, the words still hold the vibration."**

He's saying the vibration of the words themselves will increase and amplify the frequency over here? Or that the frequency of the words themselves will help people to figure out how to communicate to people over there?

309

"It increases the frequency on your side." He showed me like a room opening up and growing bigger. **It's like** (people who read their words) **"Their minds open up, so people** (on the flipside) **can talk to them. The best thing about the frequency is that this book is going to hold a frequency which they can use to open** (people) **up – so they can talk to them."** That's funny. **They're calling it "ghost stories..."**

*Great idea. Talking to people who are no longer on the planet is like telling "ghost stories." **It's a great term, because then people can dismiss it easily and have no fear about them. People who need to hear them will understand what they're saying, and those who don't can dismiss them as "ghost stories."** We have a workbook at the end of this to help people figure it out on their own. All right. Is that it for now class? Other dead people have to come and talk to Jennifer.*

*****

A Message from Prince in a shop window in Vegas:

"Love God"

CHAPTER TWELVE:

WEDNESDAY PEOPLE

Luana Anders in "Dementia 13"

Funny, how the Pixar film "Incredibles 2" ends with an homage to Luana's film with Francis Coppola – except the 113th version of it. *"DementiA 113"* reads the marquee. It's a Pixar Easter Egg, I know, but *What are the odds?*

Some years ago, I gave a book talk in Virginia Beach, and spoke about suicide with regard to the research. What people were claiming was that when someone did themselves in, there was no punishment in the afterlife, it's a very forgiving place. There might be disappointment, the but the person who "did themselves in" suffered the most.

A number of things occur when someone does this self harm. First they think they're going to "end it all." Unfortunately, they haven't ended anything. They've just made it impossible to return to their body. They get to see and experience all the pain they caused, they get to see the damage they've done – but nothing has ended. They're not gone; just not here.

311

Further, when they get home, they have to deal with all the people who were depending on them to "finish the play." There may be people who signed up for a later role and now they won't get to play it because one of the actors decided to "quit early." It's one thing to realize how much chaos our actions can bring to our loved ones, but there are lots of people who are depending upon us to being around here to help them learn their lessons as well.

Quitting a show in the middle of its run is not very polite. It kind of ruins the entire show. Sure, when they get backstage there's no "spanking machine" to put them through – but there is disappointment; they are the ones who signed up for a lifetime they claimed they would be able to "handle."

I'd like to report that attorneys are the first people who greet them on the flipside, pointing to the fine print. *"Did you not bother to read the terms of service agreement?"* Or *"If you look carefully, it says here in your contract in return for quitting the show in the middle, you're going to suffer repeatedly for many lifetimes and won't be able to graduate or move forward until you make up for your sins."*

But that's not what's reported. We have loving, caring guides – and they even go out of their way to warn us before we choose a particular lifetime ***"You may not be able to handle this one, I know you say you can, but you might not be able to."***

And that doesn't dissuade us from doing so. We claim *"Yeah, that was the old me – the new me, I've got this covered. Sure, I've picked someone who is high strung, whose genetic disposition is prone to addiction, but this time around I'm going to overcome it. Besides, when we get to the third act, all of us are going to Italy!"*

And my point is this**; "If you had just waited until Wednesday! That was the day that plane tickets to Rome were going to arrive, you were going to win the lottery and everything that was depressing about your life was going to change. Oh man! If only you had waited until Wednesday!"**

After this particular book talk, a young woman approached me and said, *"I'm a Wednesday person."* I wondered what she meant. She explained, *"I was suicidal. Beside myself with pain and sorrow. I went online and looked up how to do it, and then I went down the hardware store to get the chemicals to do it. And while I was in line, I overheard these two young boys speaking.*

They were Africans who had escaped the war zone, but had lost their parents. And they had no idea what they were supposed to do, who they were supposed to turn to – and in that moment "I knew what my purpose on the planet was." She told me she spoke with the boys, took them in, and now runs an orphanage in Africa taking care of "lost boys" who lost their families in the war."

She had waited until Wednesday.

So in light of recent folks who have not been able to do so, I decided to see if it was a topic we could talk about with our class. The following is a reflection of that conversation.

*****

Rich: Hi class.

Jennifer: Kate Spade wants to come through.

Hi Kate, how are you?

"I didn't want to think about it."

Does Kate want to talk to us?

The class will help her.

Who wants us to talk to Kate? Someone in our class? Who popped that thought into Jennifer's mind?

Someone who knows David Spade, her brother in law. That's what it feels like. I know that sounds weird.

Doesn't sound weird at all. We appreciate you coming in Kate; just so you understand what we're doing allow me to introduce you to the class... We get together with our friend Luana who helps facilitate our communication with everyone in this room's loved ones.

"She's the gate keeper."

She helps people past the velvet rope into this classroom. It's a class in translation helping people on your side to talk to people over here... I'm sure there's a lot of stress or emotion involved. (This was one day after her passing.)

She's still trying to understand - not necessarily about her passing but with the people that were affected (by it).

Well Kate, you're welcome to join us.

I just got that Prince and David Bowie are in class.

Maybe she met them. A note about our class, Kate: we're here to talk about frequency adjustment, or help people adjust. If you want to talk about why or how you did yourself in, that's up to you.

I'm getting the impression it was about someone close to her.

I saw that folks said it was "out of the blue," but she was being treated for depression and anxiety with medicine for 5 years... As we've noted before, one of the pesky side effects to SSRI drugs appears to be checking yourself out in small amount of cases... but enough to make it a warning: "May cause ideation of suicide or violence."

Robin just repeated "Irony." But she says the medicine played a part, but it was also emotional issues.

From this perspective can you now see why chose this lifetime, or chose the difficulties that occur during your life? I'm sorry, I'm speaking on your behalf. Please.

(Jennifer gives me a glare.)

Okay, I'm sorry. You want to share with us why that was?

She says, "I don't want to think it was just because of the drugs, although that was the spring board or the combustion."

The spark or the engine?

"Yeah." (Long pause)

Do you feel this was this an exit point?

She said, "I just didn't feel that good." (Jennifer aside) I'm asking her, "Why did you choose that method?" It's so dramatic.

Well, yes, but also the clothing designer L'Wren Scott. Mick Jagger's girlfriend – did the same kind of exit strategy.

That's what she did?

Kate, please show Jennifer.

She says, "She doesn't remember." She does... but she doesn't want to talk about it.

Okay, I know this is hard to look at from this perspective. You've had many lifetimes. Luana back me up.

She's saying, "I don't believe everything happens for a reason, but this was...."

It was meant to be?

"Yes."

So who was the primary beneficiary of this decision?

Beneficiary? Hold on... this is the first time I've seen this. She's showing me that her dying has created a lesson over here on the flipside. Not reversed. Her having to speak to everyone who was affected and trying to help them over there. It was a lesson for her.

She is learning what the effect of suicide is on people back on the planet?

This is a lesson that was done... it created a lesson for her on the flipside. I've never heard that doing yourself in, somehow can help you "over there."

Well, from what I've heard it creates as soul lesson. I'm thinking of Erik Medhus' suicide – what's amazing is people think when they kill themselves, they're "ending it." But

316

unfortunately they haven't ended anything. You're just "outside of time." Erik, on the flipside, found a way to call his mom on her cellphone to tell her he was still alive, that he's okay. By seeing the after effects of what his death caused, he experienced all the anguish and pain that people felt cleaning up after shooting himself. "What was I thinking?" He learned a lesson in what the reverberations of suicide caused but not until he saw it from his perspective over there on the flipside.[58]

By seeing the collateral damage.

That's a difficult soul lesson. If you're going to sign up for difficult lessons, and people often do, that lesson – I'd suggest she's learned a tough lesson. Luana, can you tell us if that's true?

I'm like "Luana help us out here." She's like "It's okay. It's okay." What I'm getting is that Kate couldn't hold back when it came to work, or business or anything like that, so she wants to participate in our class right now... She wants to talk to her loved ones. Luana is brushing her off as if that would help her energetic field.

Well, we have a number of people in our class who have committed suicide, or come close to it through drugs and other methods. There's Robin, Prince overdosed...

Prince is saying "He died from high heels," (dancing which caused hip pain that caused the addiction to pain meds). But Robin showed up when you said that.

---

[58] "ChannelingErik.com" I recommend his book "My Life After Death" (written with Jamie Butler). I've interviewed Jamie and Erik, as well as worked with his mom, Dr. Elisa Medhus.

(Note: Prince made the point in *"Hacking the Afterlife"* he hurt his ankles jumping off pianos, eventually all of his dancing wore down his hips. He was in constant pain, and took medication to help that; none of that was "deliberate.")

We offer people who come to our class the chance to examine these kinds of things.

She showed me when you're *so* separate from source... you just "leave." Like when you're depressed down here, you can be so depressed or disconnected - you are so alone from missing source, from being connected to source... She showed me energy being low here and how it when it gets too low, it separates, and then "boom" you (feel you have to) leave.

Well, I guess my point is that our research in this field – talking to people who have done themselves in - somehow makes it easier for their relatives to realize "they're not gone." I'm trying to say that we need to find a way to help people stay here – to show them their guides are always accessible to them no matter how low or depressed they get. Luana, can you help me make that point for her?

Kate says, "She already feels that from all the pain that she's feeling from everybody."

So how do we convince people to not take that particular journey?

"You can't convince them," she says, "but she hears what you're asking." (Jennifer reacts). **She heard the pain... the screams from her loved ones. She hears the sadness. The sorrow.**

318

Let's focus on something else; what do you miss about not being on the planet?

"The sunshine... rainbows..." but it's like she misses the man-made stuff the most. I asked "But can't you recreate all that over there? She said "Yes, you can create it over here... but it's not the same." She loved color.

You knew how to use it in your art; you changed a lot of people's lives with your work.

They are trying to help heal people from over there (on the flipside) and the people over here don't know they can be helped.

You left a note behind?

"To make sure they knew it wasn't their fault." She's showing me again the whole energy thing, how that influenced why she left... along with the medications, she's telling me it was a bad mix, wrong medication – one medication influenced another, and it combusted, threw her over. She wrote the note because she wanted her daughter to know it wasn't her fault.

Kate, let's give you some time to decompress... there will be more to talk about later.

She has such a great voice. She's so happy to be with Luana.

Kate, can you reach out to your daughter?

She showed me you – you're going to reach out to her.

Me? Perhaps through this book, I guess.

She loved her daughter so much.

People often claim under deep hypnosis that the difficult relationships they've chosen to have in this life may have been related to other lifetimes they've had with the same person. Did you experience that energy before?

"In another place. Yeah."

Kate, we'd like to help anyone who gets into the same head space you were in.

She doesn't feel like it will help anyone now, but it can in the future. There's too much pain right now, but it can.

Perhaps Robin, can step in and help you a bit; he's the best person to talk to you about this experience, Kate. Laughter is great medicine, and Robin is our head of surgery in that regard. Okay, there's the class bell. Thanks everyone.

*****

In the week following the death of Kate Spade, another much beloved person checked himself off the planet; Anthony Bourdain. Again, we are not claiming that this is "the only version of Anthony that exists" or that this is "actually Kate Spade and Anthony speaking to us from the flipside." Jennifer, Luana and I all did not "know them personally." All we can do is ask questions and then report the answers.

It may be that they are "presenting one side of themselves" to us, and another side of themselves to others. It may be that we are misinterpreting what they're saying, or what we think we are hearing. All we can do is ask the same questions and see if the answers line up with what other folks say, or carry any resonance as to their lives. It's possible folks on the flipside are tailoring their answers to our questions. To paraphrase

Anthony; *"Take this following interview with a dollop of salt."*

After he passed, I was in my kitchen when I felt him "around." I don't know why that is, but as I was about to cook something, I heard his distinctive voice saying things like *"That salt sucks, get fresh salt"* or *"Try the feta instead of mozzarella!"* I would laugh out loud and think **"Really? You've got nothing better to do?"**

The day before this interview I was making an Indian dish. At "his *insistence*" I added vanilla yogurt to the mix, something I've never done before, but literally "took his advice." It was much tastier than the 100's of times I've made it before. So – one can argue my subconscious somehow "wanted the yogurt" - but if you've gotten this far in the book, you know I'm not about to argue with folks on the flipside.

The morning of this interview, I asked for Anthony to come forward as well as two other "members of the class" – Robin and Kate. All had one thing in common.

When I arrived at our usual place, Jennifer was aware that Anthony had been on my mind. I had texted her "Anthony's been showing up" and she had replied "I can't wait to meet him."

Rich: Hi class. Okay, it's pretty loud here in the Fishbar restaurant today. An apt setting for the interview we're about to conduct. So class, we've done something a bit different today, asking someone we don't know to show up.

Jennifer: He's here.

Who?

Anthony Bourdain. I feel like someone in our class knew him when he was younger.

First, let's say hello to everyone in class – are we still waiting for them to assemble?

They're all here. They showed me lights; like on a map all flickering at the same time, which means they're all here.

Hi class. So the book is kind of finished.

He wants to be the last chapter.

Who does?

Anthony.

Okay, you're talking to the writer, so we can try and work that out. We did speak to someone else I invited today...

Oh yeah. Kate Spade. She's here.

(I did not tell that to Jennifer) I thought "Let's have a group of people that are unified by a single event." I was thinking about our class.

Robin showed up.

Yes, he was the third person I was suggesting; Robin... this is Anthony.

They all just went like this (a hanging gesture) making fun of themselves hanging.

That's weird and funny. It's exactly what I suggested this morning. Like "What do these three folks have in common?"

322

So they all just did that at the same time; trying to be funny.

So, we'll call them, what? "The guys who are just hanging around?"

> (Note: Not trying to make fun of, or be irreverent about anyone's path or journey. As noted in "Flipside," when I was staying at the home of Phillip Noyce and Jan Sharp in Sydney, I awoke to a painter hanging from a noose over a rafter. I jumped awake and the "ghost" looked at me, and said in an Aussie accent "Oh, sorry mate, it's just something I feel the need to do." Then he climbed down a ladder and pulled the rope with him – all of which then disappeared. I asked Jan "Who's your ghost?" I described him and she said "Wow. That matches the description of the guy who painted our home. But he didn't hang himself here, he did so in his own house." I said "Well, obviously, he liked hanging around yours too.")

Rich: I invited one other person we've not talked to ... I thought this person might have some insight. (I was thinking of L'Wren Scott, the designer who did herself in, the same way Kate Spade had done, but years earlier.)

Jennifer: Is this person related to John Lennon?

I did ask for John to answer a question today but for another reason, which we'll get to later. First, I wanted to introduce everyone to our newest class attendee; Anthony.

They just gave him a "First prize" award.

Luana, can you let Jennifer know what he looks like to you? About what age does he appear?

He's about 55. He's showing me cufflinks and a white shirt... and jeans and a jacket, like a sports coat.

So Anthony, are you familiar with what we're doing?

Is there a funeral for him today?

Could be.

> (Note: There was; his body was cremated on this day but neither I nor Jennifer could know that, as it hadn't yet been reported.)[59]

So are you familiar with what we're doing here?

He's been filled in... through your mind, he's showing me the top of your head. (Jennifer aside) I'm asking him **"How'd you find Rich?" He said, "He was surfing the ethers."**

He's quoting the book!

He says "A lot was coming in from your experience... from what you're doing..."

From our class?

Yeah, from the connection to the class. Then he said, "The groups of people (here) have the same intent..."

Who do you know here in our class?

---

[59] https://people.com/food/anthony-bourdain-death-cremated-france/

I saw David Bowie. Anthony's dad is over here – he's showing me a brother as well over here, he had a brother or someone he considered a brother who killed himself with a gun?[60]

I don't know. Anthony who greeted you when you crossed over?

(Jennifer laughs) **He showed me all the animals that he ate.**

Ha! Is that true?

No... he's kidding. It was his... (Jennifer asks him "*Your* daughter?"

A daughter from this lifetime or a previous lifetime?

Both.[61]

How old was she when she crossed over?

(Jennifer listens) She appears now as 21.. but I think she was a miscarriage from a previous relationship at 4 months.

I see; so she is someone that Anthony knew both from this lifetime and from a previous lifetime?

He got someone pregnant 21 years ago, and she had a miscarriage or termination or pregnancy...

---

[60] That's accurate. His father Pierre died of a heart attack at age 57. Anthony's close friend Bernard Loiseau shot himself in 2003, which Anthony was interviewed about. http://www.newsweek.com/last-word-anthony-bourdain-132517

[61] Anthony has a daughter 11, Ariane with ex Ottavia Busia

What is this child's name, what do you call her by?

"Bella." (Jennifer aside) Bella Bourdain.

> (Note: We heard something similar in a previous
> interview, where a musician said he was greeted by a
> 5 year old daughter no one knew about, or Harry
> Dean Stanton who said he was greeted by a baby no
> one knew about (but that people in his hospital room
> claimed he said aloud before he passed; "Hand me the
> baby" when none was visible in his room.)

*I'd like to ask Anthony some specific questions about your
path and journey.*

"Bring it."

> (Note: An unusually Anthony way of saying "go
> ahead, and doesn't appear in any of our other
> interviews. Just saying.)

What do you miss about being on the planet if anything?

He went like this ... (as if wafting smell to her nose) **"The
smells. But he doesn't miss the food."**

> (Note: At this moment, our lunch is served, so we
> have to pause the interview until after lunch.)

*Rich: Okay, we're back from lunch. As we were dining, I had
the impression he was continuing to talk in my ear. Like he
was annoyed for being interrupted.*

Jennifer: **By food! He's saying, "You frickin' cut me off
because your food was delivered!" That's so funny.**

326

So there's a group of people who have that thing in common. Who wants to talk first?

Robin Williams wants to speak first.

So Robin, can you tell us about this particular path that you took?

"*They* weren't supposed to follow."

Is that accurate, did they follow you?

(Jennifer laughs.) He says "No! Don't be silly."

Let me ask you, Robin, had you researched the topic of how to do yourself in prior to doing it?

"Yes." And he's showing me different options; pills, syringes, everything.

So why that method that you chose?

"It was a split second decision. Ultimately, it's not something they can think about or know about, it's easier to do it that way."

Let's ask everyone that same question. Let's ask Kate same question; was that a split second decision or did she plan it?

She says, "She planned it 2 minutes before."

So not a deep planning thing?

"No."

And you chose a scarf or a tie, why did you choose that method?

She said, "She chose something that had meaning." She said that "But in terms of making that final decision, it's been something on a person's mind for a long time." She's telling me she was taken off something... they changed her medication, a drug of some sort.

She mentioned that earlier. "It was a wrong mix."

I don't remember.

> (Note: She said a week earlier: "She's telling me it was a bad mix, wrong medication – one medication influenced another, and it combusted, threw her over.")

Are you familiar with a designer...

That *was* Kate the designer.

Yes, But I'm asking about a designer; who did herself in, in the same fashion; we know her through a mutual friend.

She showed me a picture of Tom Ford.

That would be correct (ding!) L'Wren Scott and Tom were close friends. She was a close friend of Mick Jagger's; she checked herself out like Kate, and I was wondering if there was any influence between the two.

"No."

Okay, let's go to our 3rd fellow we've invited... now that he's had a chance to see what we're doing. He's kind of our star here today.

He's got his "First place" award.

328

You did mention what he's wearing; white shirt, cufflinks, in sport coat and jeans.

But he doesn't have tattoos (over there.)

Right, you don't have tattoos over there. You said you were greeted by your daughter from a previous relationship who preceded you on the flipside by 21 years?

"Bella." She's 21, she showed me, almost like, she was aborted as a baby because of drugs. There was this girlfriend of his, and now she's with her dad. (Jennifer gets tears in her eyes.)

So what's happening with Jennifer that she's feeling emotional about this moment?

I feel bad.

Who put that in Jennifer's consciousness?

He said, **"You should feel bad about cutting short our interview to eat."** He's joking. (Jennifer observes**) It's because I felt bad learning about his daughter Bella being aborted because of drugs...**

But now that you are there Anthony, are you aware or becoming aware of your previous lifetimes?

He's learning about them. He said **"It's like having a whole big book, it's like having the whole book of your life handed to you; because it's in the book doesn't mean he's seen it yet, or that he knows everything... It's a big book."**

He hasn't had a chance to go through the book yet. Listen, if I may, you were a great interviewer – who would you like to ask questions to in our class?

First he showed me his friend who shot himself.

Okay, that would be a good idea, but it would be hard for me to follow up on any of his answers. Is there anyone from our class?

He'd like to interview John Lennon.

That's kind of who I thought you'd suggest, since you were such a fan of music and musicians. But before we begin, let's ask Anthony, were you taking any medication, drugs or chemicals prior to your departure?

He says, "He wanted them."

But did you take drugs like Prozac are antidepressants earlier in your life?

I don't feel like he did.

Okay, so what precipitated this dark moment of the soul? How long did it take you to plan your demise?

He said, "I didn't plan it."

Was it like Kate said? Two minutes before?

"Yeah."

(Trying to be light) So should we ban bathrobes from all hotels?

He's laughing. He said, "I'd look really ugly then."

I'm sorry that was my attempt at a joke.

He says he got that and appreciated that joke. (After a pause) Okay, he's going to interview John.

Is that okay with you John? Do you mind? I had an email exchange with one of your sons yesterday; did you precipitate that or influence that?

He says "Yeah." (Jennifer aside: Did you really have...?)

I did. But my question is; is what I sent him going to help or hurt him?

He said "Both. It is going to hurt him emotionally but it was the right thing to do."

> (Note: I sent his son (who appeared in my film) the chapter in the book where his mom and dad speak about him. I'm sure he's had a billion people wanting to trade off of his heritage, but if someone claimed to speak to my dad on the flipside, I'd want to know what he said, even if I felt it inaccurate. As we'll hear later, Jennifer tells me it was appreciated.)

I just wanted to hear your blessing.

He said, "You have it." He gives it.

So Anthony the mic is yours... Our camera is on. Can you turn to John and ask him something we can share?

(Jennifer laughs.) He's asking him "How did you do all those drugs on not die from them?"

What does John say?

He says, "He just decided he did not want to die that way."

Very good.

Anthony asked him; "Are you concerned about your sons?" He says "Yes, I'm always concerned about them." (Jennifer listens) He says, "I'm always concerned about my boys, but I don't need to be."

Why is that?

He says, "Because it all works out."

No matter what we say or what we do, "It all works out" or as I like to put it "all roads lead to home."

Anthony said, "Some roads lead quicker than others." He just showed me a person getting mowed down by a car... "boom."

Well, once you got over to the flipside, when did you realize "I'm still here, I haven't ended anything?"

He said, "He was pissed." He says, "He was pissed he left his girlfriend...

Asia Argento.

He says, "He was so stupid." But he says, "She knew about his pain and torment."

What would you like to say to her? Let's mix it up and have you say it in Italian.

"Belissima..." (Jennifer listens) and something... I'm sorry... it sounds like soup.

"Mi dispiace?"

Yeah, that's it. I'm sorry, I don't speak Italian.

It means "Beautiful; I'm sorry."

332

He just said "Je t'aime."

French for "I love you." Well, he was in France when he passed. He probably speaks French better than Italian. Is that true Anthony? La lingua d'amore?

I'm getting that he spoke Greek?

Did you speak Greek? Or is that something you knew from before?

He said, "I speak *all* languages."

Anthony what message do you want to impart to your CNN colleagues?

Tell them "They'll get over it." He's kidding. He's always making jokes. He said, "My contract was not long enough." I asked him, "You mean it was up?" and he said, "No it was not long enough."

Was this an exit point for you? I'm sure the class can help you understand this concept; but had you decided you'd done enough, or needed to plan for your next lifetime?

"Yeah." He says he put that question in your head.

Sometimes folks say they were "in a hurry to get back home because they needed to work on their next lifetime."

He said "Yeah, and that he's going to do it with his daughter that is over there with him."

So you're saying "This was a good exit point, you'd done what you needed to do?

He says, "I had the best life."

333

Any messages for friends or folks who loved your show?

He said "He's not in hell. Please tell my friends I'm *not* in hell.. or purgatory." Then he showed me like a Buddhist scroll... What's it called... The book about the dead?

The Tibetan Book of the Dead?

"Yeah."

What about it?

(Jennifer shrugs) I don't know.

Hold onto that for a second. Anthony, what are you telling us? People should read that? To become familiar with the bardo?

Was he a Buddhist? He's saying, "So many things in that philosophy that explain life." He's saying, "The book of the dead has lessons on life." [62]

I'm familiar with the book... and the guy who wrote the book; one particular monk.

He's saying, "Thousands of monks did."[63]

*Actually thousands have written **about** the book –contributed to understanding this book - but only one monk experienced it. His name is Padmasambhava. Tibetan Buddhists considered*

---

[62] Note: his best friend Eric Ripert was a Buddhist. The best translation of the Tibetan Book of the Dead is by Robert Thurman. https://bobthurman.com/the-tibetan-book-of-the-dead/

[63] I've had this discussion with Robert Thurman, who did a translation of the book; thousands of monks did contribute to essays on the original text, but the original was written by one person who experienced it; Padmasambhava. https://bobthurman.com/the-tibetan-book-of-the-dead/

him an enlightened Buddha as well, but he wasn't a monk, he had a girlfriend, wrote about tantric sex; he was an unusual cat – maybe one day we'll have a conversation with him, but the book was his experience making the journey into the afterlife, perhaps through meditation or a near death event, but contrary to what we've been doing.

He claimed once we get to the bardo, the between lives realm, there's no consciousness per se. Between lives, consciousness is like a wisp of smoke ("Clear light.") But obviously not so; because here we are having a conversation with a "wisp of smoke." However there are many things in the book that were accurate about crossing over, I understand that... is this something you're aware of now, Anthony?

He said "It's something I knew when I was there (alive)... but he didn't believe in the smoke thing (either). Besides smoking a lot, he didn't believe in the whole smoke thing... or snorting..."

I'm sorry, what?

He's making a joke about snorting instead of smoking. **He's showing me the scroll – (how) the words in the book are important, you (should) go through it and highlight the stuff that is important to remember, taking in the underlying threads of the book that are about wisdom – and he's saying, "but some of it is smoke."**

Our friend Robert Thurman wrote an excellent translation of the book which I recommend. I noticed when my mom was crossing over, the notices handed out by the hospice care nurses – "signs of impending death" were identical to what I'd read in the book about the dissolution of the senses. So

335

back to you Anthony; you told us you miss the smells back here, what else do you miss?

He says he misses his girlfriend. "Being with her," he said.

What would you like to tell her?

That he *will* **see her again**.

This might be unusual, but it is in our research. I knew Harvey Weinstein, he always generous to me and Rebecca Broussard; tickets to the AmfAR benefit in Cannes. I had no idea what a creep he was behind closed doors. But he had his own purpose as well, correct?

He says, "He's glad Harvey isn't up there because of what he'd do to him."

Okay, but as we discuss in this class; we all choose our lifetimes to learn or teach lessons in love or the loss of love.

"Yes." He saying, "That's true." What happened with Harvey and his girlfriend eventually led her to Anthony.

From that perspective not only did it result in a good thing, but the stones in her path resulted in the diamond of your relationship.

"Yes."

Anything else you want to tell your friends, fans or family?

"Tell them to love themselves. To not give in... to the madness that our minds create."

What would you recommend people do to avoid that kind of madness?

"HAVE THEM STUDY MINDFULNESS."

> (Note: I did not hit the caps key. After I typed it, I went back later and thought, "Hmm. That's odd." Or maybe not so much.)

Very good, so... Anthony to continue that thought. By mindfulness do you mean meditation?

"Yes." He said, "That makes you get more grounded."

Is that something that you did, did you practice meditation?

He said, **"No. If I did, I would still be alive."**

Very funny. Okay this is a bit weird – this is something I repeat often, the research that shows how meditation can supplant SSRI drugs. The drugs stops serotonin release, which causes people to "stop feeling pain" - but meditation can help regulate serotonin in a better way for the brain, for the emotions; is that what you're talking about ?

"Yes."

I'm sure people are tired of me going on about it; but Richard Davidson's epic study of meditation, which they now call "mindfulness" to avoid any connection to yoga or religion- but that it can cure or alleviate depression. Is that what you're saying? [64]

---

[64] RichardDavidson.org explains the science behind his epic study. He used the Tibetan form of meditation called "Tonglen" – but he proved a single session of meditation can change the shape of the amygdala, further that it "cures or alleviates symptoms of depression." With zero, no side effects. Should be prescribed.

He's saying, "That's part of the thing that connects the both of you."

Let's talk about something else; you were a guy of great taste.

"Very well put," he says.

How would you recommend people acquire your sense of taste?

He's showing me a blindfold. He's saying, **"By blindfolding yourself first, then whatever occurs after that, you don't have any prejudgment for it."**

You're referring to a "blind taste test" but also to the metaphor of "not judging things?" When you blindfold yourself you experience people and things from a different level?

"Yes. (Because) When you look at something you judge it." (Jennifer aside:) It's kind of like my work as a medium, the less I know about someone, the better the information is that comes through.

So the idea of putting on a blindfold is a....

"Metaphor."

For us to blindfold our "judgment mode" when we meet a new person?

"Yes." He's saying, **"To not care about where they're from, or anything about their past... people can change."**

Not to worry if someone says, "they're an asshole."

"Well, some people who were assholes remain assholes... but if you blindfold yourself, you learn from them what they present to you. In my case, I was nice to everyone."

Why was that?

"Because I felt like *I was* them." He shared with me a quote that I remember reading that he said awhile ago – something about "My life is so great, I'm just waiting for them to catch up and take away my car."[65]

I should ask this; "So why'd you give up the car bro?"

(Jennifer laughs) He said, "He wanted a new one."

You decided it was time for a different dish, you were done with this meal and wanted a different dessert?

He's showing me "tons of ice cream everywhere."

You were sick of the ice cream? So now you're having and ice cream headache?

He says, "Starting with you." He laughs. He says that last Saturday you had a dream about him?

I did yeah. (ding!) Since he died, I've had these odd moments of hearing his voice, sense of humor; funny, charming and like just a great voice to have around in your mind, which I appreciate. Who wouldn't? Okay anyone else in class, Robin? We had Kate and Anthony.

---

[65] "I should've died in my 20s. I became successful in my 40s. I became a dad in my 50s. I feel like I've stolen a car –a really nice car– and I keep looking in the rearview mirror for flashing lights. But there's been nothing yet." Anthony Bourdain quote
https://www.biography.com/news/anthony-bourdain-biography-facts

"They want us to learn from them. What not to do. That we have control over it."

*And if someone does die we'll track you down and interview you over there – because **you can't hide from us.***

Funny; we are the ultimate ghost hunters.

So anybody else in class?

They're showing me a picture of you in my mind's eye. They want to talk to you. John Lennon is coming through. Hold on. He says that he approves whatever it was that you did with his son... He said, "Tell him that I do."

I sent his son a copy of the chapter of the book where we interview John, as well as a PDF of the book – for context. I know how odd this is for someone you know to claim they're "talking to your father" on the flipside. And in his case, one of the most famous fathers in the planet. But if I didn't share it with him, or I just let him hear about it from someone else – I felt I had to share it with him.

Jennifer: It's like we were talking about earlier. Some topics people don't want to talk about – often involved with cancer, or suicide. *"Hey, let's talk about suicide..."* Not many folks want to do that.

Rich: The reason we're doing it is it's hard to keep people here. To remind them they had courage to come here in the first place, to choose a life and be incarnated. "Hey, you had the courage to come here – you promised to sign up for some shit. You took the role! And you promised to stick around to the third act." Same could be said to our friend Anthony; "Dude, you signed up to come here, and you got off stage before the third act bro."

He laughed and said, "Bigger better deal."

Yeah, but what does that say to your fans? "I don't have to stick around because it's hard?"

He said "Mindfulness."

Okay... but you see what I'm saying.... I'm just reminding you....

He's protesting comically; "It's abuse!" And he's showing me a picture of you! (Jennifer laughs.) He's kidding. He said, **"He came to you, don't forget that."**

> (Note: Yes, it does sound like I'm badgering the witness. I'm grateful he reminded me I didn't ask for him to show up initially. When I was writing for "Epicurean Rendezvous," chef Jean Michel (Citrus) told me "Every great chef has the taste of his mother's cooking in his mouth." Anthony had great taste.)

Robin Williams just came through and said "Birthday." Is it his?

It's yours. Coming up in a couple of weeks. What's the class going to be doing for you?

I want to hear the whole class sing "Happy Birthday."

Does anyone in our class not like our class?

(Jennifer laughs) **Luana.** She says **"It's exhausting. You're exhausting!"** No, she's saying **"You are very prepared, she says, and you're very open to passing along information."** She says **"It's helping people learn on the other side. We're helping people learn how to tap in over here."**

They say they're learning how to communicate to us. How to get us to open ourselves up to their conversations?

"Like seeing the symbol 11: 11 – (they are) signs to get you to open up to them."

Are you guys slowing down your frequency to communicate with us? Or is that not the right syntax?

"No. They're getting better transistors – by learning about our frequencies and how our thoughts work. They're making it quicker... quickening us."

*In a deep hypnosis session, a spirit guide was asked about "about a shift in consciousness" and he said, **"Over here, we call it "the quickening."** In essence you're not slowing down but you're causing us to speed up?*

"Yes. And some people can't handle it and they escape."

Is it getting people to think or experience things faster?

"No. To be more aware."

Is there a physical way we can help us tune in or become more aware?

They showed me the ocean, the forests, something out in nature – "That's your patch, that's the place to find vibrancy to tap in."

It's something I've been talking with with virtual reality scientists about, creating VR to help people not check off the planet... or help them with brain trauma or PTSD, depression using the work of Richard Davidson. It just feels like this is something that might help people.

A lot of people. Anthony is giving me the chills.. so follow that where ever it takes you.

How do you guys like the book?

"They love it."

It's long.

"It's needed," they said.

Anthony, any final thoughts?

"Tell everyone; life should not be taken for granted. It should be revered, lived and loved. And that it's much more difficult expressing love from over there (where he is) **than when it's right in front of you."**

Kate, do you concur?

"1000 per cent."

Robin?

"It's stupid; people are still going to leave the planet that way... but hopefully we can help talk them out of it."

And one's enough?

"Just one."

*****

For those who are suffering from depression, please seek help from a medical professional. But if you've gotten this far in this book, you should by now realize one solution is to "open up your heart" to our guides and loved ones that are no longer on the planet, and ask for their help. They claim they are "always available" and can help. They may not respond in the way we want ("winning the lottery" "finding the ring" "seeking revenge") but will respond in the best way they can given our limitations. (Or a dream, as we'll see in the next chapter.)

We just need to be open to their reply. It may be getting medication, it may be putting a stray animal in our path to love, it may be shifting our awareness to a song, it may be something we least expect. A belly laugh in a film we completely forgot about. A phone call from a best friend we haven't talked to for years.

But stay open. There's a reason we sign up for this trip; try to allow that it's for *a good reason. That's why Jennifer and I created this book.*

*****

On Mother's Day, our daughter dreamed of an image on her wall; a block figure with no face but in shadow. I asked her to draw it. We asked Jennifer about it; she said "It's from her friend in middle school who died from an accident. He says the image is from a card he drew for his mother as a toddler. He wants you to reach out to his parents; it's his "mother's day gift." The parents searched and found the card on the right drawn by their son in preschool; it's captioned *"My mom and me." Drawing courtesy Olivia, Leslie & J-M Zuczeck.*

344

Afterword: "Let It Be"

Luana in Rockefeller Plaza

A couple of weeks went by and prior to our next session I asked for "everyone in class to show up." I had some follow up questions.

*****

Rich: Hi class.

Jennifer: They're all here.

I just came back from Las Vegas. Where were you guys when I needed you?

You did win. It came from your buddy. What's his name?

Billy?

He says, "You're welcome." I had to get that out of the way. He says he did give you a winning number.

Yes, Billy and I used to play roulette in Cannes together – and we always lost. While at the roulette table this past week, I insisted my friend Dave Patlak play a number, because I never can win if I play them. A number popped into my head and it won. So thanks dude.

It's what Billy told me; **"I gave the number to him."**

Why can't you guys make it easier to gamble and win?

It's the energy. (Jennifer aside: "Maybe we're on to something here.") **There's a lot of energy in a casino, everyone wanting to win. It's a pool of energy; if you let someone else bet for you, it frees the energy to go where it's supposed to. If you're trying to win, it pulls the energy tight.**

Well, when people "feel lucky" they're loose, not focused on the result. Dave and I noticed years ago, whenever we started counting how many chips we had, we'd lose them. As if the focus on the money shifted the paradigm.

If I was in a casino, I would be profiling. (Figuring out who was going to win or lose and bet accordingly.) **Luana is showing me a baby. "When you're a child, you're always a winner, but as you get older, you start losing, and that gets in your consciousness."** [66]

What we're talking about must feel mundane to our class.

Yes, while we're wondering how to win in Vegas, they're worrying about people starving in Africa.

---

[66] Turns out science agrees. The "quiet eye" research shows people are more successful when they are focused yet relaxed.
http://www.bbc.com/future/story/20180627-is-quiet-eye-the-secret-to-success-for-athletes

Anyone want to say hello?

Luana says she talked to you this morning.

That's correct. (Ding!) I was chatting about our class.

Anthony Bourdain says that you chose a meal on Tuesday night, and that you talked to him about it.

Yes, that's correct. (Ding!) I was in Vegas, choosing a burger and thought "I wonder which Anthony would choose?"

He held his nose. It smelled... the onions.

Yes, there were raw onions on the turkey burger. We talked to you a couple of weeks ago Anthony, what's up since then?

He says, **"He's been busy."** (Jennifer listens) **He's trying to understand *why* he did it.**

Let me ask you a couple of questions about that.

He just said, **"And that was a full segue into that."**

> (Note: I worked briefly in TV, helping produce the award winning Charles Grodin show at CNBC. I don't think Jennifer knows what a *"full segue"* is, but Anthony does.)

You were quite good at doing segues in your shows. The last time we spoke, you suggested an interview "with your brother;" was that a literal brother or a close friend of yours?

"A friend."

Was he also a chef?

He just showed me someone who looked like Wolfgang Puck.

347

Was it your friend Bernard who checked himself off the planet?

He's saying "Yes, that's who it was."

> (Note: Bernard Loiseau was the chef of La Cote D'or, who committed suicide. At the time of his death, news reports claimed it was because of rumors he was going to lose one of the prized Michelin stars from the Michelin guide for restaurants. Since Anthony referred to someone who had shot himself, I looked up who that could have been. In his younger days he did look like Wolfgang Puck or vice versa.)

He did look a bit like Wolfgang; less hair later perhaps. Since you've been home, have you been able to talk to him about that?

Yeah. They are sharing their experiences... (Jennifer laughs) **He says, "It's like an AA group up here." They're sharing experiences... "What it is that you learned? Why, you know, why your guardians didn't help you** (not commit suicide.)"

When Bernard died they said it was about the pressures of the Michelin stars, that he was worried about it.

Anthony said, "No. He drank too much."

> (Note: Jennifer doesn't know the news reports surrounding Loiseau's death. We tend to explain "the why" when people check themselves off the planet and it would have been easy for him to say "Yeah, that was it." But Anthony replied, "No. He drank too much." The only way *"to know"* is to ask.)

348

Okay. Well, there's a fun question; are there "Michelin stars" for you chefs back home?

He says "No." But he showed me the star that Tony Stockwell spoke to you about; he actually brought that in to show me.

> (Note: In an interview with British medium Tony Stockwell, we were speaking to his "guides" and I asked if any were "wearing ornamentation." Tony reported one of his guides was wearing a star, which I thought was a badge. He said "No, it's an actual star, and it represents a portal to allow transport to different realms." Not something Tony or I had ever heard of before.)

Ah, very cool. Those kinds of stars.

"They come from way above." (Jennifer aside: I asked, "Are the stars awarded for lifetimes or for food?") **He said, "For both; it's for everything. It's all encompassing... how you earn it is through** (actions of) **body, mind and spirit."**

Okay, I understand.

I don't.

> (Note: In the research, guides who appear on councils have "earned the position" through some accomplishment during a difficult lifetime. When asked, guides have said they "earned their seat on the council" of the person being interviewed for various accomplishments. Courage, compassion, patience, history are some that have been reported. Sometimes they "wear a symbol" of that achievement, as Michael Newton reported in "Destiny of Souls." In my

interviews, I've heard a number of descriptions of ornaments; a living tree, representing connectivity, or a bear representing courage.)

I think he's saying people earn those stars for all the things they did with regard to their acts of compassion and love when they were on the planet. Anthony, I forgot to ask you before, do you have any message for your daughter?

His first word was "Love." He says, **"Tell her that she needs to love herself first and to know that she's going to be taken care of."** (Jennifer aside: I asked him "Do you regret what you did?) He said **"No, it's not like that. He regrets how our interpretation of them is wrong."**

> (Note: I think he means how we consider suicide a sin, or an act of cowardice, or other pejoratives. We generally don't take into consideration what led to it, how planned or how sudden it was, or that they may have been in a hurry to "get back home" to get ready for another life - or just the fact that they don't actually die.)

How about something more specific for your daughter? She may run across this book later in life.

He says **"Tell her not to give up on singing, she loves to sing."**

Okay, that's pretty specific.

> (Note: Jennifer did not know that Anthony had a living daughter. In our previous interview with him, he spoke of a daughter on the flipside that he was with from a previous lifetime. In this case, this is one of those **"bell ringing moments of verification;"**

unbeknownst to me or Jennifer, his daughter is already an accomplished singer. She performed a few weeks after his death, and it was not something I knew, but discovered when I searched for it. **"Anthony Bourdain's 11-year-old daughter performed in a concert just days after her father died of an apparent suicide in France. Bourdain's ex-wife, Ottavia Busia, shared a photo on Instagram of their child, Ariane, appearing on stage at a music venue in New York." Jun 11, 2018.** An example of *"new information"* from the flipside.) [67]

It almost feels like she will sing something like opera... **"She has an amazing voice. She has an amazing voice but she doesn't know it yet."**

Anthony, your dad had heart attack when you were young, have you talked to him since arriving back there?

"At length." He's telling me he was "scarred from it." He said, "Interesting that it gave him a certain amount of freedom – he thought it allowed him to have freedom but he didn't look at it that way at first... (After his father's death) **that's when he realized that "nothing is permanent."**

Hey, this just popped into my head. I've got someone I'd like to talk to.

Is it John Lennon?

---

[67] https://www.cbsnews.com/news/anthony-bourdain-daughter-performs-concert-after-his-death-2018-06-11/

Well, I did suggest John show up today, but I was thinking of someone else at the moment. I'm asking for Hal, a friend of Luana's.

Why is she laughing?

> (Note: A week prior to this session, I attended a screening of "Hal," a documentary portrait of Hal Ashby, the director of "Shampoo," "The Last Detail" "Harold and Maude" "Being There." Luana did two films with him. He died in 1988 at 59.)

Probably because he's funny.

He's already here. She said she put it the thought in your head (to ask about him).

Hal, who was there to greet you when you crossed over?

Like an aunt. A motherly figure, someone who took care of him... not his mom... it's somebody that he knew well.

> (Note: Hal was raised in a Mormon family in Ogden, Utah. Parents divorced, his father committed suicide when he was 12, and he dropped out of high school to get married. He eventually got divorced and made his way to Hollywood, where he was an editor *("In the Heat of the Night")* and later a film director *("Shampoo" "Being There."))*

When did you realize you'd crossed over?

He says, **"At first, he thought it was a dream. When he got up** (out of bed) **he realized there was no weight." He showed me an image of himself standing up from his bed.**

Do you remember what you said to our mutual friend while you were in that bed?

He said, "He told her goodbye."

Indeed. But you said something specific and I made her repeat it the other night.

He showed me the heart and that frequency... and said that he'll "Never be away from her."

I know she feels very close to him to this day.

He showed me the heart part and then said, "There's no way for her to ever let me go."

That's right. She said that when she went to say goodbye to him, she told him she was sorry she had to go, and he said to her "Hold me in your heart and never let me go." Hal, put in Jennifer's mind what your career was.

A director.

That's correct. (Ding!) Could you put some of your films in her mind? Luana and you did two movies together.

Was one of those movies... it was one you have a lot of insight into?

Yes, come to think of it, I adapted one of them into my first film. Are you referring to that? Or the one with a hairdresser?

He's showing me Warren Beatty. Yes, that's why I was being shown the hair dresser... "Shampoo?"

> (Note: It wasn't until I was transcribing this question that I remembered my first film *"Three For the Road"* was an adaptation of Hal's film *"The Last*

353

Detail." I was working for the screenwriter Robert Towne when I "borrowed the gist" to write my first feature film (starring Charlie Sheen and Alan Ruck.) Hal directed both *"The Last Detail"* and *"Shampoo."*

Yes. Hal, did you know at the time you made "Shampoo" that Luana had been dating the hairdresser that screenwriter Robert Towne partially wrote about?

He said, "He does now."

Hal, can you give Jennifer your last name?

They're laughing; I asked if it was *"Gillespie."*

That's close... the last part is correct. I'll give you a hint.

He's showing me the Marlboro man...

There was a famous ad over Times square. Blew smoke rings. He would tap the cigarette; what does a cigarette make?

Ash... espie?

Hal Ashby. I helped you figure that out to demonstrate that you don't know Hal Ashby's name or work at all, and so this information is completely new to you.

I don't know anything about him, really.

Hal, let's go back to you, do you remember meeting me?

Yes, you were playing piano... at a party. He's showing me you playing the piano.

Wait a second. Now that you mention it, I think I did play the piano... at your house in the Malibu colony?

He's showing me that. "Yes."

*I forgot I did that. (**DING!** I texted his friend Cis; "Did Hal have a piano at his place in the colony?" **She replied; "YES. An old upright."** The thing I often do at a stranger's piano, sit down and play; have done it my whole life.)*

They don't show me things like that if they didn't happen.

Wow. I forgot until you said that. I remember we spoke briefly Hal, you offered me a puff of a joint – and it was the strongest pot I'd ever tried in my life. Jack Nicholson, Warren Beatty, Pauline Kael and Robert Towne were there – and that one puff got me so stoned I interrupted Robert in the middle of a story and said, "Can you hold that thought?" walked over and turned on the TV and sat on the couch. It was the only thing I could think of doing instead of fainting. Luana came over and said, "Are you okay?" I said, "I'm not okay."

He's agreeing with you. He's saying, "You are definitely not."

Very funny. So at what point did you talk to your dad?

It felt like he didn't have a good relationship with his dad; he didn't show up at first, something happened with his dad... were they fighting?

Could be. He was a kid when his dad died.

Did he commit suicide?

Yes. Can you tell Jennifer how that occurred?

He showed me he was in pain, he had glassy eyes, like really drunk... Did he shoot himself? I always ask not to see that. His eyes were glassy; he was out of it. Like on a three day bender.

355

He did. Have you forgiven your father for that?

He said, **"You don't have to forgive (over here)..."** Which is interesting. **The father reintroduced himself to his son, everyone else he knew came first to greet him, and then he started remembering things, hanging out with his friends.**

So what was it like for you to get to the flipside and see how many people you influenced with your work?

He was shown that he inspired millions. Was there something to do with *"Star Wars?"*

Well, Princess Leia was in his film "Shampoo." That was Carrie Fisher's first role.

That's why I was shown *"Star Wars."*

Is Carrie around? Anything you want to say Carrie?

"There's a bigger club up there." (Jennifer listens, smiles) I felt like she said, "Suck it!"

What about your mom, Debbie Reynolds?

"They're having the best time ever," she said. She showed me her and her mom shopping.

> (Note: As we've learned in these accounts, people "create" places, buildings, libraries, golf courses, even horse tracks on the Flipside. Sometimes it's a combination of a real environment or a manufactured construct.)

What was up with you guys checking out, like a day apart?

> (Note: Carrie and her mom died a few days apart.)

356

She showed me that they charted it.

Anything you want to say to Mark Hamill?

Mark who?

> (Note: Jennifer isn't teasing. If I had said *"Luke Skywalker"* she would have known who I was speaking of, but since she doesn't, it's allowed.)

Carrie knows who he is.

She said**, "Tell him not to become how I was when I left the planet."**

What, like angry?

"To say the least," she said. **"Bitter."**

Anything you want to say to our mutual friend Charles Grodin?

She showed me a lot of love for Charles. She said that some part of him is up there with them at the same time he's here; he's entertaining them with his wit.

How about for Paul?

Paul who?

Carrie knows who I'm talking about.

She said "Tell him to slow down..."

You mean like "Slow down, you move too fast, you got to make the morning last... just kicking down the cobble stones..." Tell him that?

What does that mean?

357

(Note: Jennifer is not aware that Paul Simon and Carrie Fisher dated for a long time. I've met them both through Charles Grodin, so I'm aware of their tempestuous relationship. Suffice to say, I was having fun with Paul Simon and Art Garfunkel's song; "The 59ᵗʰ Street Bridge Song." As noted, Luana dated Paul Simon years before he dated Carrie... as if *time* mattered.)

It's okay, she knows what I'm talking about – It's okay if the only people who get my jokes are on the flipside. Sorry class. I know you guys get my goofy jokes. Hal, any last words for our mutual friend Cis?

Cis who?

He knows who I'm talking about.

He said, "Tell her to never stop loving us."

And Carrie, anything you want me to say to Paul that he would know came from you?

She showed me throwing some dice.

You mean like "Give it a shot?" Will that mean something to Paul? Luana, can you help her with this?

She's showing me Las Vegas.

You mean he should play Vegas? Or go to Vegas?

She says, "He should remember how much fun he used to have."

Okay, that's good. John, we asked you to come forward today, my apologies for interrupting you.

358

He's saying very dryly; **"The VIP line is getting longer** (for this class.)"

Is there anything you want me to tell your family or friends?

He wants to say something to Paul McCartney. About the carpool karaoke thing.

> (Note: James Corden did a brilliant "Carpool Karaoke" with Paul, where they sang songs together and visited Penny Lane in Liverpool. Corden broke down in tears at one point, remembering the first time his grandfather played him the song.)[68]

With James Corden? (To Jennifer) Have you seen it?

Jennifer aside: "I heard about it, but haven't seen it.**" John is telling me he was there in the car with them. That he "helped Paul write a song;" there's a song Paul wrote recently and John said, "He's going to continue to do that, help him to write music."**

The karaoke bit was amazing; Paul went to the house he used to live in and walked through the rooms where he used to write and sing with John. He's helping Paul write?

He says, "It's a new song, but it's based on an old song." He's saying, "There's an old song that John recorded that never got released," but he wants it to come out. Then he showed me "Hey Jude."

That was written by Paul for John's son; he used Jude instead of Julian.

---

[68] If you only watch one "Carpool Karaoke" watch this one: https://www.youtube.com/watch?v=QjvzCTqkBDQ

Oh, I didn't know that. **Feels like it's a song that would be for Paul's kids, like "Hey Jude" was for John's son. He wants Paul to know that he was there with him in the car... Paul knows he was, because he had "the chills" while he was in the car.**

Paul told the story behind "Let it Be" – the song refers to his mother Mary McCartney.

I thought it was about Jesus's mother Mary.

Everyone did. "When I find myself in times of trouble, mother Mary comes to me" referred his mom. When he was stressed about money, he had this dream that his mom, who passed when he was a kid, came to him and told him everything was going to be okay. To just "let it be." He said it gave him such peace and comfort he remembered it when he woke up, said "Wait a second, what did she say?" John, do you know Mary?

They're hanging out.

Can she say something to Paul?

He said, "She talks to him all the time!" Hang on, "Hey Jude" keeps coming up – he's trying to tell me something. I didn't know that song was about his son Julian, by the way. (Jennifer listens) He's showing me you. Whatever it is that you said to his son got through to him.

In a good way, I hope?

Yes, in the same way that vision of his mother Mary did for Paul. John is saying "Thank you."

Well, when I think of all the decades I've sung or played their tunes, I often think, "This must be what it's like for people who saw Beethoven." I am grateful to be alive at a time when the Beatles were playing and I got to hear and play their music. So thank you, maestro.

No one would do this, what we're doing. Talking to the flipside.

Well, no one is ever going to believe it.

We're not here to make people believe.

Funny, I said to my skeptical friend last night, "Thank you for giving me something for the book – you're such a skeptic I realized I don't have to make everybody believe in this research. I just have to focus on the details we can verify, to help those who need to hear it. Not everyone signs up to know how the play ends; they're not meant to hear "Just let it be."

If we had everyone agreeing with us, we probably wouldn't like it anyway. Who would sign up for this job by the way – "Hey, let's talk to people no longer on the planet?"

*Well obviously **you** signed up for it. And thank you for doing so. That's it, thanks class. Thanks Luana, Paxton, everyone.*

I had no idea you gambled with Billy. He said to me, "Why didn't you have the connection (to the flipside) when you guys gambled together in Cannes? He lost his shirt!"

Very funny. He did, but then so did I. A nice book end. Thanks Billy. Thanks class. Catch you on the flipside.

*****

In the episode of "Carpool Karaoke" with James Corden, Paul said he wrote "Let it Be" when he was "having financial worries" and his mom came to him in a dream to let him know "everything was going to be fine, not to worry." He said he heard her say to him the words "just let it be."

James Corden wept as they sang it together, said "I remember my grandfather playing the song for me... I wish he was here to see this." Paul said matter of factly, "He is."[69]

Recently, in "One Strange Rock" astronaut Jerry Linenger said his father came to visit him several times while he was on the international space station. He said he could "see him out of the corner of his eye" and the impression he got was that his father stopped by to "tell him how proud of him he was."[70]

It's important to repeat this for those suffering from depression, loneliness; we are never, ever alone. We have guides and loved ones watching over us always. They're always accessible. They know what we are going through and sometimes they can "get through the clutter" to give you a direct message to save your life.

When I did the first of five between life sessions (in "Flipside: A Tourist's Guide On How To Navigate the Afterlife") I never thought I could be hypnotized, didn't "believe" other worldly events could be accessible or I would "get anywhere." But after 4 hours of hypnosis, I was experiencing a conversation with "spiritual beings" I'd known forever.

As the session was ending, I asked them "Is there a message I can bring back?" I heard **"Just let go."** Let go of anger, let go of fear, resentment, let go of everything holding you back from being who you are, from being who you want to be. **"Just let go" sounds a bit like "Let it be."**

---

[69] The best ever: https://youtu.be/QjvzCTqkBDQ
[70] "One Strange Rock" episode "Survival."

So thank you Mary McCartney for giving us your son *and* giving your son these lyrics: "When I find myself in times of trouble, Mother Mary comes to me *(from the flipside)* **speaking words of wisdom, let it be**. And in my hour of darkness, **she is standing right in front of me** *(clearly he saw her in this vision)* **speaking words of wisdom**, let it be. Whisper words of wisdom, let it be.

And when the broken-hearted people living in the world agree; there will be an answer, let it be. **For though they may be parted** *(on the flipside)* **there is still a chance that they will see; there will be an answer**, let it be. And when the night is cloudy, **there is still a light that shines on me** *(the healing light often reported during hypnosis, near death events or dreams)* shine until tomorrow, let it be. I wake up to the sound of music, Mother Mary comes to me, speaking words of wisdom, "Let it be, let it be, let it be, let it be, yeah, let it be.

There will be an answer; **"let it be."**[71]

Indeed.

*****

---

[71] Written by Paul McCartney and John Lennon.

WORKBOOK FOR TALKING TO THE AFTERLIFE:

YOUR OMNISCIENT UNIVERSE - "Y.O.U."

A workbook on how to communicate to the other side.

Photo: Nasa

As noted in these pages, what we're hearing is that people on the other side are trying to get through to their loved ones here. They know what's going on over on the other side and would love to have a way to speak to, communicate, help heal or encourage loved ones *back on the planet.*

So we're going to do our best to synthesize the process. As Jennifer has said, "it's not my job to convince anyone there is an afterlife or that I have the ability to speak to someone over there. My job is to report honestly what I see or hear."

Friends ask me if I "believe I am communicating with people no longer here" and I reply "I try to leave belief out of the equation. If the answers are consistent and the process to hear them can be reproduced, I'll let the data speak for itself." In terms of what we've heard, this workbook is to help people to focus on the process that is most effective for them.

MORTON'S METHOD

Michael Newton was a psychologist who spent his life helping people to access the "between lives realm." As noted, he apparently has come through a number of times to give us "noetic" advice. I asked him for a "one, two, three" method to communicate to loved ones.

1. Say their name.

I asked Michael if we needed to say their name "aloud or in our head." He said, "It doesn't matter." I prefer to say a person's name three times, aloud because it forces me to focus on them. Plus it sounds like some kind of old "spell" that people would talk about, so that's fun. *"Say my name thrice!"*

I asked if he liked my method of suggesting people take out a photograph and meditate on it. He said, *"Don't use the word meditation because people associate it with having to do some kind of exercise."* But take a look at a photograph, try to remember when it was taken, where it was taken, who was around when it was taken, what the photographer looked like, what time of day it was – everything that helps focus the mind on the person you're trying to reach.

2. Ask your questions.

I recommend asking questions you don't know the answer to, because then you have a better chance of considering if it's *new information.* People tend to ask the simple questions of "How are you?" or "Where are you?" I've done both, and the answers are often "I'm fine" and "I'm here next to you." Which are both technically accurate. It's a bit like calling someone on a cell phone and saying, "Where are you?" The answer might be "Where do you think I am, you called!" And "How are you?" might be answered with "How do you think I am? I'm talking to you, aren't I?"

I recommend five or ten questions that you might be curious about but have no idea what the answer might be. Like "Who greeted you when you crossed over?" "What do I look like from your perspective?" "If you could look in a mirror, what color of light would you see from your perspective?" "Can you zip anywhere at will? If so, where have you been?"

3. *When you hear the answer before you can form the question you'll know you have a connection.*

Which is pretty basic; when you start to ask a friend a question and they answer immediately then you know they have anticipated the question. Time works differently "over there," so don't be surprised if before you can get the first part of the question into your mind or out of your mouth, you've "heard" an answer.

I suggest writing down the first thing that comes to mind, whatever it is. Sometimes it's hard to not judge the answer, especially if it's counterintuitive, or something we didn't expect to hear.

Our first instinct is often to think "Well I must be making this up." Indeed, that's a possibility. But it's not entirely clear how you could know an answer prior to asking a question, especially if the answer is not something you expected.

For example, the night my father died, I felt him walk into the room where I was sleeping in the home he designed and built. I felt his presence, then literally felt his hand on my shoulder. I woke up saying "Dad!" He said, "I'm experiencing indescribable joy." It's not a term I'd ever heard him use.

He said, "I need you to write something down." At the time, I thought "I must be making this up, but if I'm not, maybe I should just have him say it, and I would remember it. I was afraid that turning on a light and searching for a pen and paper would disrupt whatever this experience was that I was having.

I said, "Just tell me, I'll remember." After a pause, he said it again "I need you to write something down." So I turned on the light, got the pen and paper and sat back, expecting that I wouldn't be able to hear him again.

His voice appeared inside my head, but as if it was about a foot to the left of my head. He said "I'm here with mama and papa, my sister and brother. Tell your mother I'm here with Pat, Harry (and four other people). Tell her I love her very much. It's beautiful over here." He also had specific messages to each of my brothers. Finally at the end of this five minute exchange, I asked "So why are you telling me and not my other brothers?" He said simply "Because you can hear me."

The next morning I mentioned this to my mom, who didn't seem phased by it. When I asked who the six people were that he mentioned, she said "Oh, those were our friends who died in World War II."

They were not people I knew, and the information could not have come from my subconscious. I had never heard their names before, and it was his way of proving to her (and me) that indeed, he was speaking to me from the flipside.

I've had many of these kinds of experiences since then, both on my own, with other mediums and/or with the help of Jennifer. She may something that I don't know – that is *new information* – and I'm able to learn later on what that person meant by it. They want to speak with you. It's up to you to try to listen to them.

Jennifer often speaks of how anyone can do the kind of work that she's doing. In a nutshell, here's her method for developing your own skills in this area:

JENNIFER'S METHOD

This method is discussed in a chapter in Part Two about guides telling us how to reach out to them. I asked for a "one, two, three" on how to do that, and a teacher gave us the recipe.

"Just talk to us," she said. "That's all you have to do. And you hit the gateway."

I asked; "We've heard this from others and some of those with us now – can I ask you directly, what's a 1, 2, 3 best method of communicating with you on a conscious level?"

She said; "Close your eyes. That's the one. The 2 is to focus on the heart and have it go through your crown chakra.... And that's it. There are only two. Because that's going to be your focus, and once you've done that you talk and you're already there."

LUANA'S METHOD

I'm only aware of this method from hearing it via my wife Sherry. As noted, Sherry met Luana only once when she was paralyzed from her illness in her bed in Mar Vista.

Sherry recently had a dream where Luana appeared before her. Sherry said in the dream "Luana! How can you be here? You died 20 years ago!" Sherry said Luana showed her a miniature Lego Star Wars fighter. "I took this to get here." Luana laughed, holding up the tiny Lego model. Sherry and our son had been looking at that same model, earlier in the day. Sherry asked, "But how is it that I can see you?"

Luana said "Think of 11:11. We meet at the decimals."

As mentioned previously, I interpret that to mean; "If you think of each 11 as a hallway – the way they look in architectural blueprints – then imagine your loved one is on one side, and you are on the other. In order to communicate, we both have to "lean in" or adjust our frequency. You adjust the frequency so you can "meet in the middle" but both sides need to desire that outcome.

How do you adjust your frequency? Quiet solitude sometimes works, playing a song that your loved one liked, looking at a photograph and remembering them are all methods of recalling their "frequency." If you have a video of them, or a recording of them – that too will have some reference points for you to access.

It might be a letter they wrote, or a poem they left – or even their favorite book, favorite pillow, favorite article of clothing. Somehow, we instinctively "know" their frequency when we are around these things, and it helps to "amplify the

369

signal." You send out your message, thought, or reminiscence in such a way to allow them to come forward and reveal whatever it is they want to show you.

Sometimes it takes a few hours, perhaps days or weeks for them to find the appropriate response. Sometimes its instantaneous. The idea is to "stay open to their reply." It doesn't mean we have to take every doorbell, phone call, song on the radio as "evidence they're trying to reach us" – but if there's a song on the radio and the thought pops into your head, "That's my loved ones favorite song; did you do that for me?" and you get a response – then the odds are that it is them.

There are some folks who fear that "demons" or "evil spirits" will show up instead. All I can say to that notion, is that in all the accounts I've examined, worked with, or been privy too – none include anything of the sort. Your loved ones know that you're trying to reach them, they'll do their best to respond.

Recently, I was conversing with a woman on Quora who lives in Turkey. She was distraught because her husband died suddenly and had not reached out to her. She begged for some method to reach out to him. I suggested a number of modalities, and she wrote that she had "followed them to the letter but had gotten nothing." She was beside herself with grief. Finally I suggested that he *had* reached out to her – and that she was *just not revealing that he had.*

She replied that she forgot about a dream that she had just after he died. The dream was fleeting, and didn't end well – but for a few moments, he was there at the top of a hill, looking distraught.

I pointed out that dreams are an effective way for them to reach out to us, but they're also holograms – more information than we can imagine is included in them. If we can "freeze the dream" for a moment, we can access new information. I asked her to do so – freeze the memory of seeing her husband, go up and take his hands in hers, to tell him that you'd like to know what happened or why.

She wrote that she tried that and did get *a sensation* which included a feeling of "overwhelming love." She also got the message that he "would reach out to her in the future" but right now her "emotions were too distraught for him to do so." She felt she had reached out to him and he had responded.

I have no way of knowing how accurate that was. It could have been her subconscious, wishful thinking, or indeed, that he had "spoken to her." But her demeanor changed instantly – from the depths of despair to something closer to grief.

She had adjusted her frequency, to allow for a moment that maybe he did still exist, and that maybe she could "take hold of his hands in a dream." And by doing so that allowed her to change grief to nostalgia. If we both adjust our frequencies, or energy, we can meet at the "decimals between the two elevens."

TRY HYPNOTHERAPY

Deep hypnosis is an excellent tool to access loved ones on the flipside. I didn't believe I could be hypnotized, nor was I convinced people could "see anything" during that process. That changed with Paul Aurand, former President of the

371

Newton Institute, said I could film their conference in Chicago. Put me directly on the path to this sentence.

While I was filming others doing hypnosis sessions, he suggested I try one and film it. I thought, "Well this will be one way to prove it's not accurate. I'm not trying to find a past life, I don't truly believe I've had one, and I don't think I can be hypnotized. It's a perfect way for me to prove it false." **I came out of the session feeling as if the earth had shifted slightly on its axis. Everything I thought I knew had to be reexamined in the light of what I experienced.**

Not everyone is meant to see their previous lifetimes, or to experience the between lives realm. I've filmed 45 sessions, many with Scott De Tamble (*LightBetweenLives.com*) and in all of the sessions he was able to not only take someone into a previous lifetime, but to help them explore their own between lives adventures. I consider him a virtuoso in the field.

But the Newton Institute has a searchable database for people trained by Michael Newton at their website (NewtonInstitute.org). They're across the globe now, so there is someone nearby who has learned how to direct people into the flipside, and can be a tour guide for that adventure.

I highly recommend interviewing whomever you choose and explaining what it is you're looking to learn. I recommend practicing "speaking aloud" while doing a guided meditation. When you hear *"picture yourself on a boat on a river,"* not only picture it but speak aloud about what you are seeing sensing or experiencing on that river.

Doing so gets you in the habit of speaking aloud – the oddest thing about these sessions. It's like having someone next to your bed whispering "And now what are you seeing?" And you must reply – otherwise the therapist will never know what you saw, and you won't have a record of it.

And that's key as well – any form of hypnotherapy should be accompanied by a recorder – either the therapist's or your own. Some therapists take notes – others use cameras, some use tape recorders. The reason to do this is because often what you think happened did not – and by reviewing the tape, you can hear yourself speaking; while you're doing so more images come to mind. The next thing to do is write up a transcript. It's all about searching for the jewel.

People see their lost loved ones, and can embrace them. They can ask questions about why they had to leave, or what they are up to now. They often get a complicated, profound message about their path and journey – and almost always are only given as much as they need to hear so that they don't upset their own path or journey too much.

So aside from what Jennifer and I are doing – asking direct questions to people no longer on the planet to see what we can learn from them – I can recommend hypnotherapy as a tool to do the same. I've done five between life sessions – with different hypnotherapists. And each and every time I get to visit with my friend Luana.

She's not across the field, or on the other side of a room. She's standing next to me, holding my hand, laughing with me – scolding me – often telling me deep profound things that I had no idea that she would access to. And for some reason, when she and I talk over there, **it feels like I know exactly what she's talking about.**

Think about that for a moment.

She's telling me things about math, science, how energy or frequency works, things that I have no access to in my current role on stage. But backstage, where she is, she's showing me – demonstrating to me – helping me to understand the most profound ideas. And I know myself well enough, know what my limitations are in this body and mind, to realize that "over there" I feel as if I know what she's saying – and that **it doesn't really matter if I get it over here.** It is what is is. I'm only here to report what I've experienced.

So check into it. If you can't find a Newton trained hypnotherapist, find one who understands the idea that we choose our lifetimes, or that we come here to experience the journey, and when we get "back home" we share it with our loved ones. If they understand that concept, then you've got a pretty good chance of having them escort you around to see and interact with your loved ones.

THE HOLOGRAPHIC MEMORY

Perhaps you remember the book by Michael Talbot "The Holographic Universe." [72] It was in his research that he observed that everything in the universe is holographic in nature. An object exists in time and space, and therefore retains some memory of that time and space.

Photographs are holographic because they retain the magnetic energy of the moment they were taken. That means they

---

72

https://www.goodreads.com/book/show/319014.The_Holographic_Universe

retain the time and space of that event, and the people that are in it.

I've also found that memory is holographic. Any event that has ever happened to an individual is stored in their memory, and therefore accessible. The mind has no delete key. But more importantly, that memory holds all of the information from that moment in time.

For example, when interviewing people who've had a near death event, I've found they can access the event again in real time – either while under hypnosis, or not. The memory of the event still exists in their mind; if they can access any part of it, they can access all of it.

Jennifer and I both strongly believe that by accessing the flipside, we can help heal the planet. We can get people to see that they need to leave behind a clean campsite, if not for their children, but for their own return. We can get people to see that those who've gone before us are not some mysterious or frightening entity – but that we can ask them questions to help us on our path and journey.

As Harry Dean Stanton put it; **"You don't have to believe in an afterlife, or what religion tells you. However, you should believe in the possibility of an afterlife, so you won't waste any more time worrying about it."** If it's possible that there is an afterlife, then it is possible that everything you've seen in this book is true.

MEDIUMSHIP

Needless to say, one way to speak to your family and friends on the flipside is through a talented medium. I was fortunate to find Jennifer, as I know that she's worked with law enforcement agencies nationwide in helping with missing person cases, I've met an FBI agent who asked for her help, and I know that she's effective in the kinds of work they've asked her to do.[73] But before pulling over at the next "Psychic" shop or sign on the roadway, do the research on who it is you're going to be asking questions to.

Many people seek out mediums for help with their love life and in the search for predictions of the future; as noted, neither one of these objectives were part of my research. In this case, asking for assistance in speaking to loved ones no longer on the planet was the reason I've sought their help.

In the acknowledgment portion of the book Jennifer discusses some of the organizations she works with that may offer guidance in finding someone of her caliber. I recommend finding someone whose abilities you trust because you know someone who has worked with them in the past and find their work effective. In my case, I was just fortunate to find someone who lived nearby who happens to be very good at what she does.

Finally, a word about truth.

One of our sessions addressed prevarication from the flipside. In an interview, Jennifer asked, "How do I know you are you really telling me this accurately?" The person replied, "We can't lie from over here." He went on to describe how anyone can mistranslate from either side, or not impart their message

---

[73] Other mediums I've worked with, interviewed or recommend; James Van Praagh, Tony Stockwell, Jamie Butler, Pattie Canova, Kimberly Babcock. Gary Schwartz PhD has done extensive studies in mediumship at the University of Arizona.

properly – but the act of lying isn't possible "because of the frequencies involved."

Jennifer: "When I started this work, I was worried about how accurate this information was – I've given thousands over readings, I'm at over 3000 right now. What I've learned is that they may not know everything or can make a mistake presenting it, or I may make a mistake in my interpretation. But they are always truthful."

Rich: So why can't you prevaricate over there?

Jennifer: "Over here anyone can do that, but over there, the frequencies don't match up if you aren't truthful, so you can't communicate. It's different if you're unaware that what you're saying is untrue – but if you're consciously trying to say something you know to be *not true*, over there everyone can see that the frequencies don't match up. It shouts out that you're lying."

Rich: So everyone would know you were being untruthful?

Jennifer: Everyone.

*****

Some will find these accounts of speaking to "the dead" or "dead celebrities" offensive. Some may find them to be manipulative. The person is "no longer here to defend their previous point of view, and by our claiming they still exist, it flies in the face of what they spent their lives claiming."

Well, this book isn't for you. I'm sorry if that's how you feel about it, but in nearly every interview we've done with people they've *insisted* we pass this information along. Either privately to their loved ones – and we both do that as best we can – but also they've insisted we "aim for the fences" with this work. It's not enough to offer that it's a possibility that life goes on, but to shout it to everyone in listening distance.

No one has said; *"Gee, I don't think you should write this book. It's too controversial."* The best maxim I've heard doing this research came from a film director on the flipside who said, **"No one comes over here wishing they held back more in their lifetime."** So in that vein, neither will we.

In Jennifer's case, I know she's helping families who've lost loved ones, I know she's helped people heal or to find out what really happened to their loved ones. And she does that work pro bono – she's helped countless law enforcement agencies, and has a network of mediums who do the same for no charge.

I had one woman come up to me during a book talk and say, **"I just wanted to look you in the eye and say, "Thank you for saving my life."** I know that there's no film project I would ever work on where someone would give me that kind of *review*. And in this research to understanding *"why we're on the planet"* I see clearly that the reason I'm on it, is to pass this information along.

Recently, I pointed out to a close friend that the loss of her husband wasn't a loss, as he was still available to her. She said **"I don't want to hear all that about being able to contact him. I'm holding onto my pain, as it's all I have of him."** Not up to me to take that from her.

As I'm fond of saying, **these reports are not belief, theory or opinion** – just reporting verbatim what we're hearing from people on the flipside. Jennifer is the conduit and sparkplug for this information, and my ability to remember details about the architecture of the afterlife, allows us to put these reports into a story line.

We're demonstrating that anyone can do the same kind of investigation. If you get no answers, try a different method. If you get some answers, then it bears further investigation. If you toss a jewel into a pond, it sends out waves; there's no knowing where they might end up. But only you can judge whether its effective for your path and journey.

I like to say, some people are in their caterpillar stage, some have gone through their chrysalis stage, and are now in their butterfly stage. We are here to focus on those butterflies.

Enjoy your flight.

Our professor Luana and puppy

✷✷✷✷✷

ACKNOWLEDGEMENTS

ABOUT JENNIFER SHAFFER

With husband Fred

Jennifer M. Shaffer is a World-Renowned Evidential Intuitive Medium who is setting the standard for what she refers to as "The New Normal." Founding Member of JS Intuitive Investigations Academy and JS Investigation Alliances

Social Activism Award Winner, Best American Psychics Psychic of the Year. Guest on Monica the Medium, Dr. Drew on HLN, Below the Deck and Ricki Lake. Investigation Cases Profiled on Dr. Phil and 20/20. As Seen on Bravo, CBS, HLN on CNN, Fox and Free Form on ABC Television

Author, Speaker and Intuitive Spiritual Teacher, Vice President and Law Enforcement Case Expert for Beneficial Intelligence Syndicate. Impartial Witness Case Expert Through BIS for Law Enforcement, FBI Officials and The Intuitive Investigation Alliances and Academy. Advisory Board Member for FOHVAMP Families of Homicide Victims and Missing Persons.

Jennifer has been seen on CBS Television, HLN on CNN, FOX, Free Form on ABC and she just had an appearance on BRAVO. Her heart is with her JS Investigation Alliances where there is a collaboration of Intuitives that donate their time to families and law enforcement for unresolved homicides and missing person cases.

Jennifer's JS Intuitive Investigations Academy will serve as a platform and safe place for individuals to learn about investigations. She will be mentoring those who want to learn about their own abilities while working on investigations. Jennifer was recently asked to serve as an Advisory Board Member for FOHVAMP, an organization that helps Families of Homicide Victims and Missing Persons. Evidential Intuitive Medium Jennifer Shaffer Sees, Hears, and Feels those Spirits who have Crossed Over.

Jennifer is a "Translator of Spirit." She is a Clairvoyant Medium, Medical Intuitive, Intuitive Investigator and Profiler. Her investigation cases have recently been featured on "20/20" and "Dr. Phil," and she has also been a reoccurring guest on the "Ricki Lake" show. Jennifer is clairvoyant, clairaudient and clairsentient which means being blessed with sight, hearing and feeling from the spiritual world that both enlightens and brings comfort. Jennifer receives guidance that gives you confirmation of past events, informs you of the future, brings clarity to issues, and messages from your departed loved ones. Spirit wants to help by giving powerful insights from the other side.

She can be reached at JenniferShaffer.com

A THOUSAND THANKS

First and foremost, thanks to Jennifer. I bow to your skills as a medium, a medical intuitive, as someone who helps people heal. We've had many laughs during our sessions; there's nothing quite like hearing something profound and being able to laugh about it.

A shout out to Scott De Tamble, lightbetweenlives.com, to Michael Newton, thank you for your work and your research. Thanks to George Noory, his Coast to Coast and "Beyond Belief" crew at Gaia.com.

But most of all, a special thanks to Luana whom I met *40 years ago*! To think she would have such a profound influence on me in life and after is really wild. I appreciate her relentless patience, her ability to herd cats – the members of our class. Thanks to all those in attendance; Robin, David, Prince, Michael, Julian, John, Jim, Jimi, another Jim, George, Tom, Rance, Billy, Harry Dean, Cis, Randal, Harry, Robert, Edward, Craig, Sydney, Howard, Roger, Gene, Ray, Anthony, Kate, Uncle C, Rig, Paul T, Craig O, Billy M, Mom, Dad.

Thanks to those who've generously donated towards the research: Mary Fesler, Chris Rawls, Julie Harmeyer, Tash Govender, Diana Takata, Don Thompson, Alex Broskey, Savarna Wiley, Robert Thurman, Carin Levee, Chris Monaghan, John Wylie, Daniel Kearney, Maureen Johanson, Bill Dale, Eric Harrington, Lisa Yesse, Tamara Guion-Yagy, Lynette Hilton, John and Lucy Tibayan, Jon Burhham.

One of our last photos together

Dedicated to my wife Sherry, daughter Olivia and son RJ – I love you! *Thanks for choosing me.*

Richard Martini is a journalist, author and award-winning filmmaker. Boston University, USC Film School, Master of Professional Writing. He's written and/or directed 8 theatrical features including "You Can't Hurry Love," "Limit Up," and "Cannes Man." He wrote for Variety, Premiere and Inc.com, documentaries include "White City/Windy City – Sister Cities" "Journey Into Tibet with Robert Thurman" and "Tibetan Refugee." His books; "Flipside: A Tourist's Guide on How to Navigate the Afterlife" "It's a Wonderful Afterlife Volume 1 and 2" and "Hacking the Afterlife" are available at all online outlets. The documentary film "Flipside: A Journey Into the Afterlife" is available through Gaia TV or online. For further info: RichMartini.com

Clips and book talks can be found on www.YouTube.com/user/MartiniProds

Stay Tuned for **Part 3**

"Backstage Pass to the Flipside: Talking to the Afterlife with Jennifer Shaffer PART ONE" interviews:
*****

1 - "A Class in Translation" The genesis of the classroom model for chatting with the flipside.
2 - "Open yourself up to the possibility" Atheist and actor Harry Dean Stanton proves he's on the flipside.
3 - "The Concierge of Connectedness" Part 2 of Harry Dean's interview after his memorial service.
4 - "He's Over Your Shoulder" Michael Newton makes an appearance during a session.
5 – "Faster, Smarter, More Efficient" Michael gives noetic science advice on how to communicate with the flipside.
6 – "Harvard to Oxford and Back" Julian Baird PhD – Atheist and freethinker Julian Baird reports on his crossing over.
7 - "Backstage Pass" Tom Petty makes an appearance in our class, comes up with the name for the book.
8 – "The Cowboy Buddha" – Actor Rance Howard reports who was there to greet him on the flipside.
9 - "Irony" – Robin Williams continues to give us advice on his journey into the flipside.
10 - "It's Fun. I Can Fly" Bill Paxton proves that he's aware of where he is on the flipside.
11 - "I Love Him" Part 2 of "talking to my old friend Billy."
12 – "Surfing the Ethers" Prince makes an appearance to give afterlife advice.
13 – "Don't lose the attachment" Prince part 2 on his journey.
14 - "It's My Party" Famed film director speaks to an old friend on the other side.
15 – "Existential Happiness" – a group chat with members of the class, including Amelia Earhart.
*****

"Backstage Pass to the Flipside: Talking to the Afterlife with Jennifer Shaffer PART ONE" is available online.

33656300R00215

Made in the USA
San Bernardino, CA
25 April 2019